LITTLE-KNOWN
SOUTHWEST

17973

LITTLE-KNOWN
SOUTHWEST

outdoor destinations beyond the parks

BARBARA & DON LAINE

THE
MOUNTAINEERS
BOOKS

Published by
The Mountaineers Books
1001 SW Klickitat Way, Suite 201
Seattle, WA 98134

© 2001 by Barbara and Don Laine

Published simultaneously in Great Britain by Cordee, 3a DeMontfort Street, Leicester, England, LE1 7HD

Manufactured in the United States of America

Project Editor: Kathleen Cubley
Editor: Uma Kukathas
Cover and Book Design: Ani Rucki
Layout: Alice C. Merrill
Mapmaker: Barbara Laine

All photographs by Don Laine unless otherwise noted.

Cover photographs: Top: *Hovenweep Castle looks as though it would be more at home in medieval Europe than at its actual location in Hovenweep National Monument in southeast Utah.* Bottom: *Prickly pear cactus in bloom along the Sandal Trail at Navajo National Monument*

Frontispiece: *Colorful butterflies enjoy the nectar of the wild blossoms at Bandelier National Monument.*

Library of Congress Cataloging-in-Publication Data
Laine, Don.
    Little-known Southwest : outdoor destinations beyond the parks / Don
and Barbara Laine.— 1st ed.
      p. cm.
    Includes bibliographical references and index.
    ISBN 0-89886-759-2 (alk. paper)
    1. Southwest, New—Guidebooks. 2. Outdoor recreation—Southwest,
New—Guidebooks. 3. National monuments—Southwest, New—Guidebooks. 4.
Historic sites—Southwest, New—Guidebooks. 5. National parks and
reserves—Southwest, New—Guidebooks. 6. Recreation areas—Southwest,
New—Guidebooks. I. Laine, Barbara. II. Title.
F785.3 .L35   2001
917.904'33—dc21
                                      00-011544
                                       CIP

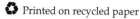 Printed on recycled paper

CONTENTS

COLORADO

NATIONAL PARKS

NATIONAL MONUMENTS
AND OTHER LESSER-KNOWN FEDERAL LANDS

NEW MEXICO

NATIONAL PARK

NATIONAL MONUMENTS
AND OTHER LESSER-KNOWN FEDERAL LANDS

UTAH

NATIONAL PARKS AND RECREATION AREAS

NATIONAL MONUMENTS
AND OTHER LESSER-KNOWN FEDERAL LANDS

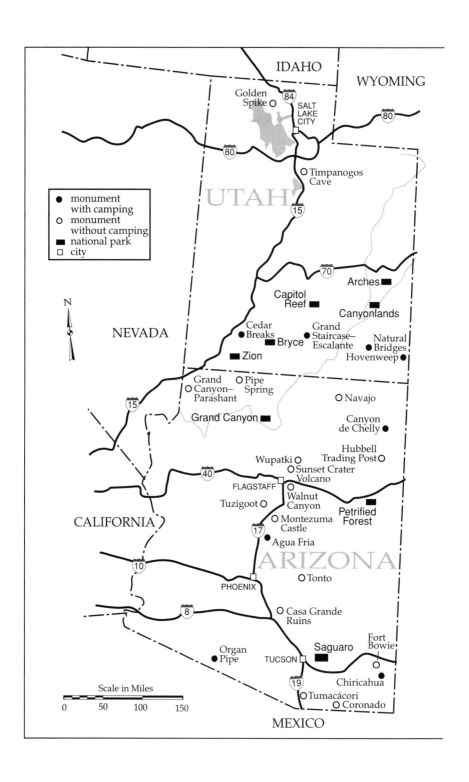

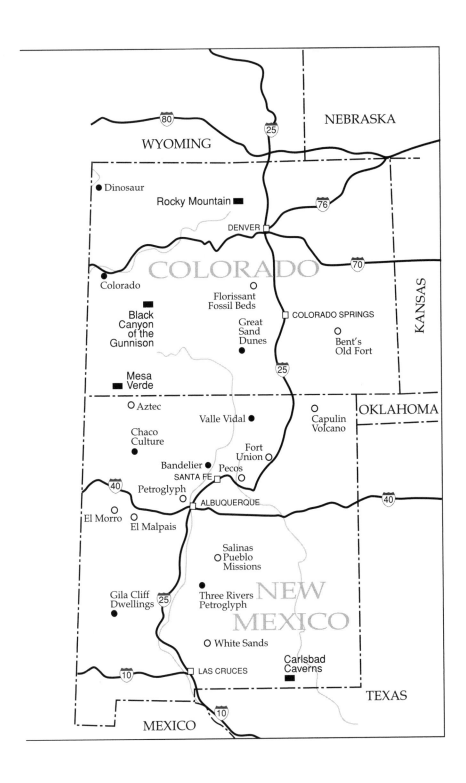

ACKNOWLEDGMENTS

One of the great pleasures in researching and writing this book was meeting and working with so many fine and dedicated people. The ones who really made this book possible—who make the Southwest's federal lands such wonderful places to visit—are the employees and volunteers. Each superintendent, ranger, and volunteer we spoke with—and there were many—was helpful and knowledgeable. In addition, it was obvious that they love these national monuments and other sites, were proud of them, and were anxious to share their enthusiasm. Our sincere thanks and admiration go to these deeply committed workers.

Thanks also go to the staff at The Mountaineers Books: Ani Rucki and Alice Merrill for their advice and support, and to our editor, Uma Kukathas. Special thanks to our project editor, Kathleen Cubley, who guided us through the myriad hidden shoals of the publishing business.

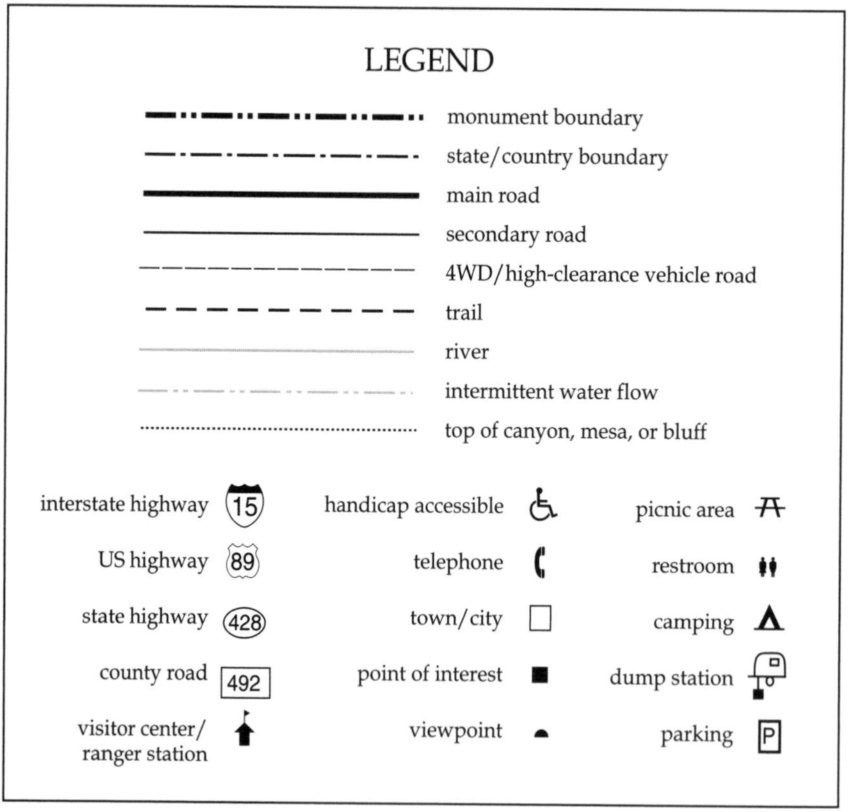
LEGEND
monument boundary
state/country boundary
main road
secondary road
4WD/high-clearance vehicle road
trail
river
intermittent water flow
top of canyon, mesa, or bluff
interstate highway
15
US highway
89
state highway
428
county road
492
visitor center/ ranger station
handicap accessible
telephone
town/city
point of interest
viewpoint
picnic area
restroom
camping
dump station
parking
P

INTRODUCTION

The Four Corners states—Arizona, Colorado, New Mexico, and Utah—are wonderful places to be outdoors, to explore and experience a rugged landscape of deserts, canyons, mountains, and forests. This is a land of variety and extremes, a harsh and sometimes unforgiving environment where rattlesnakes, bears, and mountain lions have lived for centuries. But it's also a land of incredible beauty—often stark, occasionally lush—where delicate wildflowers spread a blanket of purples, yellows, blues, and reds on rocky hillsides; snowcapped peaks stand out against a deep blue sky; and rushing rivers awaken the desert with life-giving moisture. This is the heart of the American West, with its rich history that includes gunfights and cattle drives, Spanish conquistadors, and ancestors of today's American Indians.

One of the striking aspects of the American Southwest, and particularly the Four Corners states, is the amount of public land—federal land—that is available for outdoor recreation. There are national forests, wildlife refuges, historic sites, and dozens of national monuments. In addition, there are the well-known and often overcrowded national parks.

This book is a destination guide to the most exciting federal recreation and historic sites in this region. While the national parks, such as the Grand Canyon, Rocky Mountain, Zion, and Carlsbad Caverns, will certainly be discussed, the main emphasis is on the lesser-known federal lands, including national monuments, national historic sites, and other recreation areas. These are the places that often offer many of the same outdoor recreation opportunities as their more-famous national park neighbors, but get little publicity and far fewer visitors. In short, these are the relatively unknown and uncrowded gems of the National Park Service and related public lands agencies.

Among the dozens of federally managed lands discussed in the following pages, choices abound for a wide variety of outdoor and occasionally indoor adventures. There is hiking along the rim of the spectacularly colored natural amphitheater of Cedar Breaks National Monument or over the gleaming white quartz crystals at White Sands National Monument. You can go kayaking at Flaming Gorge National Recreation Area and whitewater rafting through Dinosaur National Monument. You can explore the desert at Coronado National Memorial and see some of nature's strangest plants at Organ Pipe Cactus National Monument. Or you can hike down inside an extinct volcanic crater at Capulin Volcano National Monument.

Those interested in the early peoples of this region can explore the homes

11

A ranger gives a quick geology lesson to a group of visitors at El Malpais National Monument.

and see the fascinating and perplexing designs created by prehistoric American Indians at Chaco Culture and Pecos National Historical Parks; Petroglyph, Walnut Canyon, and Gila Cliff Dwellings National Monuments; and Three Rivers Petroglyph Site. But these are just a handful of the opportunities that await the visitor at these relatively unknown gems.

ACTIVITIES AND FACILITIES

The main activities at the federally managed lands discussed in this book are hiking, wildlife viewing, bird-watching, exploring archeological sites, and enjoying the incredible scenic beauty of these areas. But there are also opportunities for fishing, swimming, scuba diving, boating, mountain biking, horseback riding, cross-country skiing, snowshoeing, and rock climbing. Programs offered include guided hikes and walks, nature and history talks, and slide and video shows. Visitor centers often have displays on local plants, animals, history, and recreational possibilities, and a number of these sites have top-notch museums. There are also concessionaire-operated marinas, stores, lodges, and restaurants at some of the larger facilities.

Hikers will find a wide variety of trails, ranging from short walks to a scenic viewpoint to strenuous backpacking trips of a week or more. In addition, some of these destinations offer backcountry hiking opportunities with no trails at all for those skilled at map reading. Desert hikers are strongly advised

A desert cottontail rests a few feet off the Macaw Trail at Petroglyph National Monument.

to wear sturdy hiking boots for protection from sharp rocks and cactus spines, and to carry plenty of drinking water.

Throughout these four states there is an abundance of wildlife viewing possibilities, with hundreds of species of birds—some quite rare—and other animals ranging from tiny lizards and pocket mice to bears, mountain lions, and elk. The best time to see mammals is usually early or late in the day. Those who want to see snakes and lizards will have the best luck in the middle of the day, when these cold-blooded creatures venture out to soak up the warmth of the sun. Birds are seen at most any time.

Although facilities vary considerably among the federal lands discussed here, most have strategically located toilets, parking areas, and pay stations with park information. What are called developed campsites usually have picnic tables and a grill or fire pit. They occasionally include shelters. A few national monuments have RV hookups, but most do not, and showers are rare. Undeveloped sites may have only a picnic table or fire pit, and primitive sites usually are little more than flat areas where one can pitch a tent or park an RV. Restrooms are generally well-maintained and clean, and even the newer vault toilets, which are basically outhouses, are relatively odor-free. There are almost always disabled-accessible toilets.

FEES, HOURS, AND REGULATIONS

Day-use and camping fees (where applicable) are collected at most of the areas discussed in this book, with national parks being by far the most expensive (often $10 to $20 per vehicle for up to one week). National monuments operated by the National Park Service are next highest in cost. Then come the national historic sites. The least expensive or free are sites operated by the Bureau of Land Management and U.S. Forest Service. In most cases, there are no extra charges for ranger-guided hikes, talks, and other activities. Exceptions include guided cave tours.

The federal government offers several passes that offer discounts or free admission to a number of federal recreation and historic sites, including most of the properties discussed in this book. Persons covered by the passes are the pass holder and any accompanying passengers in a personal vehicle. For those traveling by some other means, such as by bike or on foot, the pass admits free the pass holder, spouse, children, and parents. The passes are good for one year from date of purchase and cover entry fees but not what are called user fees for such activities as cave tours, camping, boat launching, and certain forms of transportation.

Two passes are available to the general public. While they are not usually worth the purchase price to those visiting two or three facilities, travelers who plan to visit six or more, especially the higher-priced national parks, can usually save money by buying one of the passes. The National Parks Pass is valid for entrance fees at all sites operated by the National Park Service. The slightly more expensive Golden Eagle Passport is similar except that in addition to National Park Service properties it provides free entry to all other federal government fee areas, such as those operated by the U.S. Forest Service, Bureau of Land Management, and U.S. Fish and Wildlife Service.

It is strongly recommended that those who qualify for two special passes take advantage of them. One is the Golden Age Passport, a lifetime pass similar to the Golden Eagle that is available to those 62 years or older. In addition to covering site entry, the pass also provides a 50-percent discount on user fees for all park services and facilities, such as camping and cave tours, but not what are called "special recreation fees" or fees charged by concessionaires. The second is the Golden Access Passport, which provides the same benefits as the Golden Age Passport and is available to those who are blind or permanently disabled, regardless of age.

Camping costs vary according to the facilities provided and the popularity of the park, monument, or site, and can range from free or $4 to $5 per night for a primitive site to $10 to $20 per site for more developed campgrounds at national parks such as Rocky Mountain or Zion. Campsite reservations are not available at most of the smaller properties discussed here, but can (and should) be obtained for the more popular national parks. Campground reservations are also available for many national forests in the Four Corners states. See the Appendix for contact information.

Backcountry camping usually requires a permit, with fees ranging from nothing to $10 and up.

Regulations vary, depending on the agency administering the particular site. The National Park Service is generally more restrictive than are the U.S. Forest Service and Bureau of Land Management. Most regulations are based on common courtesy and common sense, such as quiet hours in campgrounds, usually from 10:00 P.M. until 6:00 or 7:00 A.M. During these hours, loud music, the use of generators, and making noise that disturbs other campers are prohibited.

One of the major differences among federal agencies' regulations, and even among different sites under the same agency, is the way in which pets are regulated. Most National Park Service properties, and especially the larger national parks, are not pet friendly, and those planning to visit them should consider leaving their pets at home. With some exceptions, dogs are prohibited on all hiking trails and in the backcountry and must always be leashed. This means that if you take your pet into these parks and monuments they can be with you in the campgrounds and inside your vehicle, and you can walk them in parking areas, but that's about it.

Lands administered by the Bureau of Land Management and U.S. Forest Service are less restrictive, and you will usually find that dogs are permitted on trails, although they must be leashed.

Boating regulations differ by state, but in general, boaters must have personal flotation devices and must not operate boats while under the influence of alcohol or drugs.

OUTDOOR ETHICS

The general rule of thumb for those spending time in these federal lands is the same as for those visiting public lands anywhere: Use planning, knowledge, and most of all common sense to have as little impact on the land as possible. The ideal situation is that every visitor sees no evidence that anyone had been there before. However, even here in the relatively empty Southwest, that's a bit too much to hope for.

The message here at Cedar Breaks National Monument, as well as at other public lands, is to leave everything as we find it.

Our goal should be to minimize human impact by staying on trails, properly disposing of all trash, and being especially careful to avoid polluting lakes, streams, and rivers. A number of these sites contain American Indian ruins and artifacts, or relics from Spanish colonial times or the pioneer and Wild West days of the 1800s. These irreplaceable artifacts and prehistoric and historic sites should be observed, appreciated, and photographed, but never disturbed. Even when we simply touch ancient rock art we risk damaging it because of the natural oils in our skin.

CLIMATE, HEALTH, AND SAFETY

One look at a national weather map and it becomes clear that the Four Corners states are lands of extremes. At the same time that winter snows close roads in Colorado and northern Utah, vacationers are basking in the warm sun of southern Arizona or playing golf in shirt sleeves in southwest Utah and southern New Mexico. During summer, when temperatures soar to well over 100 degrees in the desert areas, the mountains of all four states remain pleasantly cool and can even be downright cold. This wide range of temperatures is caused primarily by differences in elevation. Together these four states have elevations ranging from a low of 70 feet above sea level near Yuma, Arizona, to a high of 14,433 feet at the top of Colorado's Mount Elbert.

What this means for visitors is that those planning to explore different sections of this region will be carrying a great variety of clothing, so let's hear it for a duffle bag stuffed with Bermuda shorts, sandals, and a down parka! Preparation and planning are the keys, plus choosing the right season for the particular sites you plan to visit.

Elevation can also slow you down and even cause health problems, because the higher you go, the less oxygen there is. Visitors from lower elevations who have heart or respiratory problems should consult their physicians before planning trips to the mountains, perhaps anywhere above 5,000 feet. Those in generally good health need not take any special precautions, but can ease the transition to high elevations by changing altitude gradually.

New Mexico has the highest skin cancer rate in the nation, and the three other Southwest states are not far behind, so those planning to be outdoors are strongly advised to wear broad-brimmed hats, wear sunglasses that block ultraviolet rays, and use a good-quality sunscreen. If traveling in the mountains in winter, make sure your vehicle has snow tires or chains, and carry extra blankets and emergency food and water—just in case.

Area health officials warn outdoor enthusiasts to take precautions against Hantavirus pulmonary syndrome, a rare but often fatal respiratory disease. It was first recognized in 1993, and a large percentage of the country's almost 250 confirmed cases have been reported in the Four Corners states. About half have resulted in death. The disease is usually spread by the urine, droppings, and

Yuccas are found throughout the Southwest, and are especially beautiful when in bloom, which usually occurs in late spring or early summer.

saliva of deer mice and other rodents, and health officials recommend that campers avoid areas with signs of rodent droppings. Symptoms of Hantavirus appear anywhere from three days to six weeks after exposure. Symptoms are similar to flu—fever, muscle aches, nausea, vomiting, coughing, and diarrhea—and can lead to breathing difficulties and shock.

Another hazard is the rattlesnake, the most common poisonous reptile of the Southwest. Snakes are cold-blooded, and often lie in the sun. Wise hikers always watch where they're stepping, and check carefully before putting their hands into spaces between rocks. Snakes enjoy the heat that rocks absorb, and take immediate offense when a human invades their space. On the other hand, snakes aren't usually aggressive and will avoid people whenever possible.

One of the great joys of going into wild areas is the possibility of seeing wildlife, but the last thing you want is a confrontation. Mountain lions, which are nocturnal, rarely bother people, although there have been a few reported cases in recent years. Black bears, however, are another story. Although generally shy, bears have learned that wherever there are humans there is food. In especially dry years when their usual food supplies

RATTLESNAKES

RATTLESNAKES MAY BE FOUND IN THIS AREA. THEY ARE IMPORTANT MEMBERS OF THE NATURAL COMMUNITY. THEY WILL NOT ATTACK, BUT IF DISTURBED OR CORNERED, THEY WILL DEFEND THEMSELVES. GIVE THEM DISTANCE AND RESPECT.

Federal agencies and employees, such as the rangers at Petroglyph National Monument, like to remind us that public lands are not amusement parks, and present both hazards and responsibilities.

are low, bears head to public lands, often visiting campgrounds at night. For this reason, those camping or hiking in bear country need to check with park rangers about any current bear problems. If hiking at dawn or dusk, when bear encounters are more likely, make noise by talking or singing. Although this goes against the usual ethic of being quiet on the trail so as to not disturb other hikers, it will prevent surprising a bear, or worse, finding yourself between a mother bear and her cub. Campers should store food away from tents and other sleeping areas and dispose of garbage properly and promptly.

Safety is an important concern in all outdoor activities. For even the shortest wilderness excursion, we recommend that you bring along the following Ten Essentials:

1. extra food and water
2. extra clothing, in case of accidents or weather changes
3. a first-aid kit, with tweezers to remove cactus spines
4. matches in a waterproof container
5. sunglasses and sunscreen, especially in snowy or desert climates
6. a knife
7. fire starter, such as chemical fuel
8. a flashlight, with extra batteries
9. a compass
10. a map of your immediate area

Photographers try to find the right angle for a shot of the historic Ring Ranch, one of many pioneer structures in the Valle Vidal Unit of the Carson National Forest.

You may also want to bring along water purification tablets or a water filter, raingear, and insect repellant. In addition, it is always a good idea to leave information about your trip (where you will be and for how long) with a reliable person, such as a ranger or family member, so help can be sent if you do not make it home on time.

A NOTE ABOUT SAFETY

Safety is an important concern in all outdoor activities. No guidebook can alert you to every hazard or anticipate the limitations of every reader. Therefore, the descriptions of roads, trails, routes, and natural features in this book are not representations that a particular place or excursion will be safe for your party. When you follow any of the routes described in this book, you assume responsibility for your own safety. Under normal conditions, such excursions require the usual attention to traffic, road and trail conditions, weather, terrain, the capabilities of your party, and other factors. Keeping informed on current conditions and exercising common sense are the keys to a safe, enjoyable outing.

The Mountaineers Books

HOW TO USE THIS BOOK

The purpose of this book is to help those visiting the public lands of Arizona, Colorado, New Mexico, and Utah to maximize their enjoyment while minimizing frustrations and disappointments. The sites are arranged by state, and brief descriptions of the major national parks and recreation areas are provided in each state introduction. Detailed descriptions of the lesser-known national monuments and other federal sites that are the focus of this book are then presented in alphabetical order. Please keep in mind that some of the sites cross state lines, and these are generally discussed under the state in which the headquarters or main visitor center is located. There are also maps showing the locations of the sites in each state, an overall map of the entire Four Corners region, and maps for many individual sites.

After reading the introduction (please do—it contains important information about costs, regulations, and safety as well as an overview of why we wanted to research and write this book in the first place), glance over the state sections, and then zero in on those sites you find to be of most interest.

Each site description begins with a list of vital statistics that provides a thumbnail sketch of what each monument or federal property offers. Following that is a bit of the site's background or history, its reason for being, and a discussion of its facilities and activities—essentially, why you would want to go there. Because these four states have extremes of elevation and climate, quite a bit of space is devoted to weather and what to expect during different seasons at a particular location. Those unfamiliar with the climate extremes found in the Southwest would be wise to look carefully at this part of the description before planning their trips.

Finally, the appendix provides a comprehensive list of addresses and phone numbers for additional information.

Right: *Saguaro, organ pipe, and teddy bear cholla cacti along the Desert View Trail at Organ Pipe Cactus National Monument*

ARIZONA

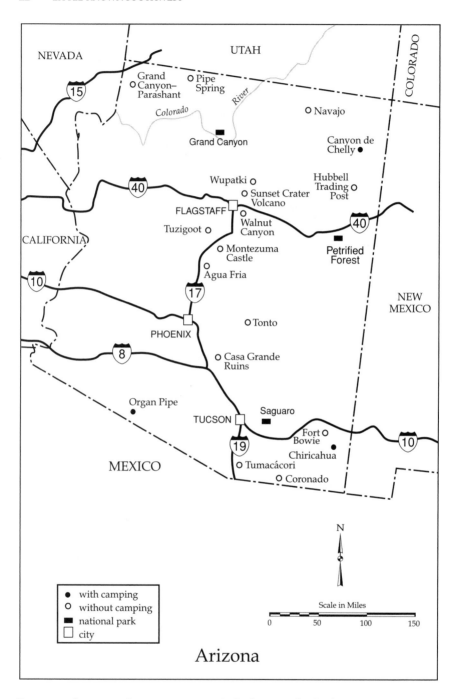

Arizona

For most of us, two pictures come to mind when we think of Arizona. One is the towering saguaro cactus, which dominates the Sonoran Desert, and the other is the truly grand Grand Canyon, a place of fascination for geologists and one of supreme beauty and almost unlimited recreation opportunities for the rest of us.

In many ways, Arizona—all 114,000 square miles of it—is truly the nation's playground, for in addition to Grand Canyon National Park, which attracts about 5 million visitors annually, Arizona is a paradise for boaters, campers, hikers, and bird-watchers. The same Colorado River that carved the Grand Canyon has been tamed to produce Lake Mead, a huge reservoir along the Arizona–Nevada border, plus several other water playgrounds including Lake Powell, which begins in Arizona and covers a big chunk of southern Utah.

The southern Arizona desert, known for its delightfully warm winters, has become one of America's prime destinations for snowbirds, those retirees from practically everywhere else in the United States and Canada who head to the Tucson and Phoenix areas at the first hint of a snowflake back home. The scorching summers are the price paid for beautiful winters. However, this same delightful winter climate also attracts birds of the feathered variety, more than 400 species, that makes southeastern Arizona the most popular bird-watching spot in North America.

In addition to deserts, lakes, and spectacular Grand Canyon, the state has mountains, forests, and an abundance of prehistoric and historic sites, from the abandoned villages of early American Indian peoples to the genuine Wild West of Wyatt Earp and Doc Holliday.

Arizona has three national parks—Grand Canyon, Petrified Forest, and Saguaro—plus about twenty national monuments and historic sites. Several of these lesser-known sites, such as Chiricahua and Organ Pipe Cactus National Monuments, are delightful destinations for hikers and other lovers of the great outdoors. Others, including Walnut Canyon, Canyon de Chelly, and Tonto, were set aside to protect significant archeological or historic sites, but also offer hiking, bird-watching, and similar outdoor experiences. Finally, sites such as Montezuma Castle National Monument and Tumacácori National Historical Park offer fascinating journeys back in time. Although these sites may not be your prime destinations, they will certainly add to the enjoyment of your trip.

ARIZONA'S NATIONAL PARKS AND RECREATION AREAS

Rocks, water, and cactus comprise the landscape of Arizona's national parks and recreation areas, where visitors can discover year-round opportunities for hiking, boating, and exploring.

View of the Grand Canyon from the North Rim

GRAND CANYON NATIONAL PARK

The Grand Canyon, the best known of the United States' many scenic wonders, has become a symbol of America, and particularly of the American West. The park contains 277 miles of the Colorado River and the incredible canyon that the river has carved over millions of years. However, in many ways the Grand Canyon is more than its river or even its canyon. Its allure is its vastness and the spectacular vistas experienced from the canyon's rims.

There are numerous ways to see the Grand Canyon—by car, on foot, riding a mule, and on a raft are among the most popular—and you can experience the park either by looking down from the rim or getting down into the canyon, on its trails or river. Both methods are worthwhile, although for those who have the time and inclination, getting down into the canyon adds the rewards of exploration to the joy of seeing this awe-inspiring work of nature.

The Grand Canyon was carved by the erosional power of water over the course of 6 million years. The South Rim, where most visitors go, has an elevation 1,000 feet lower than the North Rim's 8,000 feet, and the Colorado River is 5,000 feet below the South Rim. The distance from rim to rim averages 10 miles across.

On the South Rim, you can get excellent views of the canyon from a number of overlooks along the 26-mile (one-way) Desert View Drive. Nine-mile (one-way) Hermit Road also provides access to some splendid overlooks, via a free shuttle bus that operates from mid-March through mid-October, and by private automobile at other times. The South Rim is open year-round.

The North Rim, which can easily be seen from the South Rim, is more than 200 miles away by car or 21 miles by foot on a very strenuous hike. There are a number of overlooks along the North Rim's 23-mile (one-way) Cape Royal Drive. The North Rim is generally open from mid-May through mid-October, depending on weather, although it may be open for day-use only later in the fall if weather permits. During winter the North Rim is closed due to deep snow.

There are hiking trails along the rim and into the canyon. Hiking into the canyon at least a little way is an excellent way to experience the park, but hikers need to keep in mind that it's a lot harder coming back up the steep canyon walls than it was going down. Mule rides are offered from both rims by park concessionaires, and guided raft trips down the Colorado River through the canyon are also available.

The park has several visitor centers, campgrounds on each rim, and offers a variety of ranger programs. It is also an excellent location for seeing wildlife, such as elk, mule deer, desert cottontails, several types of squirrels, golden eagles, red-tailed hawks, great horned owls, violet-green swallows, and white-throated swifts.

As one of America's most popular vacation destinations, the Grand Canyon is often crowded, especially along the South Rim in summer. Reservations for lodging, camping, and mule and raft trips should be made well in advance, and those with flexible schedules would likely be happiest visiting in the comparatively quieter off-seasons.

PETRIFIED FOREST NATIONAL PARK

A fascinating display of delightfully colored petrified wood, as well as a painted desert, ancient fossils, and archeological sites are the attractions at Petrified Forest National Park. Conveniently located for a quick stop for travelers along Interstate 40, the park has a scenic drive, walking and hiking trails, and visitor centers/museums.

Conditions in this arid land were considerably different 225 million years ago, when tall conifers dominated a tropical forest. As trees died, they were swept into the shallow waters of a floodplain, where they were buried by silt, mud, and ash from nearby volcanos. Decay was delayed by a lack of oxygen, and silica from the volcanic ash replaced the wood's cells, eventually leaving quartz crystals in their place. Iron, manganese, and other minerals streaked the quartz with shades of reds, greens, yellows, blues, and purples. The same sediments that buried the trees preserved other plants and animals as well, leaving a superb collection of fossils.

The park also offers wondrous views of the Painted Desert, with its badlands in shades of red, orange, maroon, tan, and gray. There is also evidence that people have lived here for thousands of years. Among them were the Ancestral Puebloans, the predecessors of the modern Pueblo tribes, who occupied this area from the 1100s through the 1300s and made tools and even houses from the petrified wood.

The park's seemingly barren landscape is in fact home to a rich diversity of plant and animal life. This includes wildflowers, such as Indian paintbrush and globemallow, plus juniper and other trees. Wildlife includes pronghorns, desert cottontails, black-tailed jackrabbits, porcupines, coyotes, collared lizards, and a variety of birds, the most prominent being the common raven.

The park's 28-mile scenic drive leads to pullouts and short trails, which offer close-up views of the petrified wood. One short trail takes hikers to the Agate House, a prehistoric pueblo made of petrified wood, while a nearby path loops among some of the longest and most spectacular petrified trees in the area. From an overlook you can see Newspaper Rock, with dozens of petroglyphs including an image of the famous humpbacked flute player, Kokopelli. A bit further along the road is a short trail to the remains of a 100-room pueblo occupied in the 1100s and again in the 1300s by the Ancestral Puebloans. There are also overlooks of the Painted Desert.

A variety of guided hikes and talks are presented throughout the park, with the greatest number offered during the summer. The park has no campgrounds, but camping is available nearby.

SAGUARO NATIONAL PARK

This park is dedicated to the symbol of the American Southwest, the giant saguaro cactus, and also protects an impressive area of Sonoran Desert. The park is divided into two sections. The Tucson Mountain District (also called Saguaro West), which is west of the city of Tucson, is primarily Sonoran Desert; the Rincon Mountain District (also called Saguaro East), on the east side of Tucson, includes Sonoran Desert plus foothills and mountain terrain. Each section has a scenic drive (with road guides available), a visitor center, trails that wander among the saguaros and other desert plants, plus good wildlife viewing and bird-watching opportunities. When the weather cooperates, there are also spectacular shows of wildflowers and cactus blooms.

The most prominent cactus in North America, and arguably a plant with a great deal of personality in its appearance, saguaros stand tall, their arms stretching to the sky or pointing the way. Though saguaros can reach heights of 50 feet and weigh 8 tons, they are slow growing. It usually takes them 15 years to reach 1 foot tall, and about 100 years to reach a height of 25 feet. Their maximum lifespan is about 200 years. At about 30 years old, saguaros begin to flower and produce fruit, but their branches, or "arms," don't appear until they reach 75.

The Sonoran Desert is among the hottest and driest parts of North America, but it also has an amazing variety of life, more than any other of the continent's deserts. Although the saguaro towers above the landscape, and so is the most prominent feature here, the desert is home to dozens of other cacti, grasses, shrubs, flowers, and trees. The best wildflower displays are

Saguaro National Park's namesake saguaro cactus

usually from mid-March through mid-April, although cacti bloom a bit later. Wildlife also abounds here. One particularly interesting desert inhabitant is the javelina (also called the collared peccary), which has a mouth so tough it eats prickly pear cactus pads, spines and all.

Both sections of the park contain impressive rock art believed to have been created by the Hohokam people, who lived here from about A.D. 700 to A.D. 1500. Visitors can also see historic sites from miners and settlers who arrived in the Arizona Territory in the late 1800s, including several lime kilns and the remains of a mine and a 1920s adobe house.

GLEN CANYON NATIONAL RECREATION AREA

Lake Powell is among the largest manmade lakes in the United States and is the centerpiece of this national recreation area. Glen Canyon combines some

*Rainbow Bridge in Glen Canyon
National Recreation Area*

of the West's most spectacular red rock canyon country with practically unlimited opportunities for boating, water-skiing, and fishing, as well as camping and backcountry hiking. Covering more than 160,000 surface acres, the lake is 186 miles long (most of which is in Utah) and has dozens of side canyons, which give it almost 2,000 miles of shoreline.

The lake was named for Major John Wesley Powell, a one-armed Civil War veteran who led a group of nine explorers on a scientific expedition down the Green and Colorado Rivers in 1869. In 1963 Glen Canyon Dam was completed and the lake was created. The dam stores the water for agriculture and recreation, and uses eight generators to produce more than 1 million kilowatts of electricity each day. The project was controversial from the start, and some environmentalists, including those with the Sierra Club, have in recent years proposed that the lake be drained and the dam torn down.

The recreation area is best explored by boat. It offers absolutely stunning scenery, most impressive being the erosion-sculpted rock formations that line its shores and form its canyons. Among its most impressive sights is Rainbow Bridge, which is protected within the recreation area in Rainbow Bridge National Monument. The bridge is considered sacred by American Indians, and, at 278 feet wide and 290 feet tall, is the world's largest known natural stone bridge.

Although water sports are the main activities here, most of this recreation area is solid ground, and there is plenty for hikers and other land-based recreationists to do. However, there are only a few marked trails, and changing water levels create a constantly shifting shoreline.

There are also prehistoric and historic attractions here, including Defiance House, an archaeological site occupied by Ancestral Puebloans (also called Anasazi) in the thirteenth century that includes ruins of several impressive stone rooms, a kiva (a circular chamber traditionally used for religious rites by South-western tribes), and a rock art panel. Also worth a look are an 1870s stone fort, a trading post, and the dam itself.

The recreation area has several visitor centers, four marinas accessible by road or water and one by water only, three full-service RV parks, and several less-developed campgrounds. Those without the foresight to bring a boat can rent practically anything from a small fishing boat to a fully equipped houseboat, or take one of the many boat tours offered.

LAKE MEAD NATIONAL RECREATION AREA

At twice the size of Rhode Island, huge Lake Mead National Recreation Area covers 1.5 million acres and offers myriad recreation possibilities on its two lakes and vast areas of desert and mountain land. Lakes Mead and Mohave attract a wide variety of water-sports enthusiasts, and the recreation area also has scenic drives, hiking trails, and campgrounds.

Lake Mead National Recreation Area was the United States' first national recreation area. Its namesake lake came into existence in 1935 with the completion of Boulder Dam (now called Hoover Dam), a concrete wall 726 feet tall that tamed the wild and often violent Colorado River. Almost 20 years later, Davis Dam was built downstream to create Lake Mohave. Together they form the core of Lake Mead National Recreation Area.

As expected of a giant water park, summer is the busiest season here. Water temperatures often reach the 80s during this time. The lakes provide opportunities for canoeing, kayaking, sail boating, power boating, water-skiing, swimming, snorkeling, scuba diving, and sunbathing. These are also wonderful fishing lakes, where anglers catch largemouth bass, striped bass, rainbow trout, channel catfish, crappie, and bluegill. Scattered throughout the recreation area are marinas with boat ramps and rentals, boat tours, motels, campgrounds for RVs and tents, picnic areas, and swimming beaches. There are no lifeguards.

For those who prefer their sightseeing high and dry, there are several scenic drives offering spectacular views of the deep blue lake set against a backdrop of rugged desert mountains.

Although there are few maintained hiking trails, the recreation area provides ample opportunities for hiking. One short desert hike leads to an area of colorful sandstone formations, while another takes hikers into a picturesque canyon where prehistoric American Indian petroglyphs can be seen. For extended backcountry travel, topographic maps and good map-reading skills are necessary. Long hikes are discouraged from June through September, when temperatures often climb to over 100 degrees.

Wildlife thrives here, especially away from the more developed areas, and visitors should be on the lookout for mule deer, desert bighorn sheep, bobcats, coyotes, kit foxes, ringtails, jackrabbits, desert tortoises, and numerous birds, such as peregrine falcons, white pelicans, cormorants, egrets, and other waterfowl.

ARIZONA'S
NATIONAL MONUMENTS AND OTHER LESSER-KNOWN FEDERAL LANDS

The relatively unknown national monuments, historic sites, and other federal lands that dot Arizona make excellent side trips for those visiting the Grand Canyon and other big-name attractions, or in some cases, as destinations for several days of camping and exploring. Many of these sites contain prehistoric American Indian ruins, and most have wonderful scenery and at least a few hiking trails.

AGUA FRIA NATIONAL MONUMENT

HOURS/SEASONS: Overnight; year-round
BEST TIME TO VISIT: Late fall through early spring
AREA: 71,100 acres
ELEVATION: 2,150 to 4,600 feet
FACILITIES: None
ATTRACTIONS: Archeological sites, historic sites, hiking, primitive camping, four-wheeling (high-clearance vehicles)
NEARBY: Tonto National Forest
ACCESS: From I-17 exit 259, east on Bloody Basin Road (Forest Road 269) to Forest Road 14, then south

Agua Fria National Monument is one of two new national monuments created by presidential proclamation in January 2000. The site is rugged and undeveloped, and at this writing is suitable for exploration primarily by those with high-clearance four-wheel-drive vehicles and who are in good condition for strenuous hiking. Map-reading skills are also needed for those who want to get into the backcountry.

Some 600 years ago the mesas along the Agua Fria River just 40 miles north of the city of Phoenix comprised a bustling metropolis. Perry Mesa, along the east edge of the Agua Fria, contained seven major settlements, or what we might

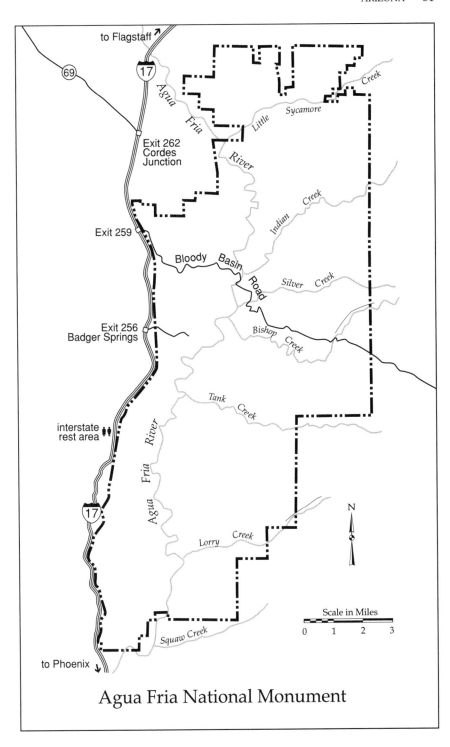

Agua Fria National Monument

Agua Fria National Monument offers a rugged terrain of cacti and other desert plants, with wide panoramic views. (photo by Chris Tincher, courtesy Bureau of Land Management)

today call neighborhoods. It was named for William Perry, who used the area for cattle grazing from 1880 to 1929. Black Mesa, on the west side of the river, comprised the suburbs of the metropolis, and included three much smaller settlements. All told, several thousand people probably lived on these mesas.

Archeologists say they have identified 450 prehistoric sites within the monument and nearby in the Tonto National Forest. Unfortunately, there has been much pot-hunting and vandalism, and one of the reasons for the national monument designation was to provide added protection to the sites, which, even with the existing damage, are considered some of the most significant late prehistoric sites in the Southwest.

The monument is under the jurisdiction of the Bureau of Land Management. Those planning to visit will also want to include in their itinerary a section of the adjacent Tonto National Forest, which is administered by the U.S. Forest Service.

In addition to the walls and assorted remains of a number of masonry villages, some with hundreds of rooms, there are rock runoff diversion systems and other farming structures. Perhaps the most interesting attractions of this monument, especially to those of us who are not gung-ho students of archeology, are the petroglyphs, which range from geometric designs to human figures and a variety of animals.

A prehistoric people archeologists call the Hohokam inhabited much of the Sonoran Desert of what is now south-central Arizona from sometime just before or after the first century A.D. to about 1450. The Perry Mesa area has evidence of Hohokam pit houses, including one pit house village about 0.25 mile long which was probably occupied around 1000.

The bulk of archeological sites in and near the monument are large stone blocks of rooms that were built in the 1300s. Although these have a definite Hohokam heritage, there are differences

Prehistoric petroglyphs are among the highlights of Agua Fria National Monument. (photo courtesy Bureau of Land Management)

between these and other Hohokam sites in that the structures here are primarily groupings of rooms. Hohokam villages built elsewhere during this period were usually compounds made up of rooms surrounding a plaza and specialized community rooms, including kivas (circular chambers traditionally used for religious rites by Southwestern tribes). Such community rooms are absent here.

These structures are essentially blocks of fairly large rectangular rooms, usually only one story high, with few doorways on the exterior walls (entrance was by ladder to openings in the roof). In modern terms we might think of these as a series of connected suites, simply a series of residential and storage units.

In addition, there appear to be outlying groups of structures that some archeologists refer to as guard villages or lookouts, which would have been used to provide early warning of outsiders approaching the villages.

At this time there is no definitive answer to the question of who these people were. At present the people who lived here are referred to as the "Perry Mesa Tradition."

Some of the easiest sites to visit are not actually in the national monument, but lie just to the east of the monument in the Tonto National Forest, along Forest Road 14. These include the Brooklyn Basin group, which had about 300 rooms total, and the Squaw Creek group, with from 150 to 200 rooms. Along cliffs between and slightly east of these two sets of ruins are some of the area's best petroglyphs.

Within the boundaries of the monument is the Perry Tank group, located in Perry Tank Canyon, which has about 300 rooms and some fascinating petroglyphs, including images of human-type figures and cute little ducks. The Baby

Canyon group, along Bishop Creek, contains about 100 rooms and a variety of geometric and abstract petroglyphs.

In addition to the prehistoric American Indian sites there are more recent historic ruins, such as the small stone shelter believed to have been built by a sheepherder, perhaps in the late 1800s, near the top of Joe's Hill.

At this writing there are no maintained hiking trails in and immediately outside the monument, but there are a number of sometimes difficult to follow jeep roads leading to mining claims, utility easements, and stock tanks. These roads are rough and rutted in good weather, becoming impassable mud bogs when wet, and it is strongly recommended that those planning trips into the monument and Tonto National Forest first check on current conditions with the appropriate government offices and obtain the latest maps.

Likewise, there are no developed and maintained campgrounds here, although there is one primitive campground (with no facilities) in the Tonto National Forest along Forest Road 14 near the Brooklyn Basin group. Backcountry camping is permitted in most areas of the national forest and in the monument.

Summers here are hot, with highs often reaching well above 100 degrees, when serious hiking is positively discouraged. Winters, however, are delightful, with high temperatures often in the 60s and 70s.

CANYON DE CHELLY NATIONAL MONUMENT

HOURS/SEASONS:	Overnight; year-round
BEST TIME TO VISIT:	Spring and fall
AREA:	83,840 acres
ELEVATION:	5,510 feet
FACILITIES:	Visitor center, interpretive exhibits, nature walk, picnic tables, restrooms, 96 campsites (no hookups), public telephone, RV dump station
ATTRACTIONS:	Hiking, photography, archeological sites, interpretive programs, bird-watching, wildlife viewing
NEARBY:	Hubbell Trading Post National Historic Site
ACCESS:	3 miles east of Chinle via Navajo Route 7

Sheer cliff walls of red sandstone stained with streaks of dark desert varnish provide a dramatic backdrop for cliff dwellings built almost 1,000 years ago. Here, in rugged, spectacularly beautiful land, modern explorers hike or ride through canyons that have attracted humans for thousands of years, including the ancient Archaic peoples and the Navajo, who arrived here about 1700 and continue to farm and ranch on the canyon floor.

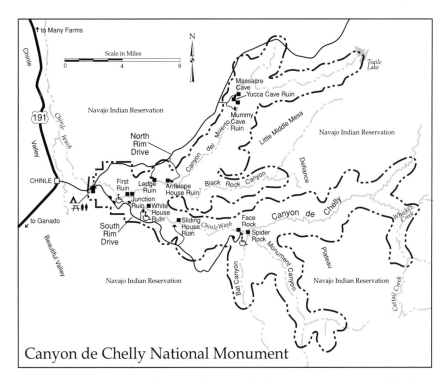

Canyon de Chelly National Monument

Although it is operated by the National Park Service, Canyon de Chelly is unique among national monuments in that all the land here is under the domain of the Navajo Nation, and so is essentially private. About 70 families live, ranch, and farm within the monument's boundaries; outsiders are restricted to certain areas and limited to travel with an official Navajo guide.

The monument's name (pronounced canyon de SHAY) comes from the Navajo word *tségi*, meaning "rock canyon." The monument actually includes two major canyons, Canyon de Chelly and Canyon del Muerto (Spanish for "Canyon of the Dead"), plus several smaller canyons. Like the rest of those in the Colorado Plateau, these canyons have been carved by the forces of uplift and erosion over millions of years. The sandstone's red color comes from iron oxide in the material that glues together the grains of sand, with additional iron oxide and manganese oxide producing the streaks of desert varnish on the canyon walls.

Most people see the monument by car. Each of its two rim drives stretches about 20 miles one-way. With stops these trips can easily take up to 3 hours each. Photographers find that the best time to see and photograph the ruins along the North Rim Drive is in the morning, when they're bathed in sunlight. Lighting is best on the South Rim during the afternoon. Photographers should ask permission before photographing the Navajo people, their homes, animals, or other property; payment is usually expected.

A view from the South Rim at Canyon de Chelly National Monument

The South Rim Drive climbs steadily along Canyon de Chelly's South Rim, and the canyon gets progressively deeper as the drive continues. Overlooks provide views of rugged canyons, the junction of Canyon del Muerto and Canyon de Chelly, and the Junction Ruin, with ten rooms and a kiva (a circular chamber traditionally used for religious rites by Southwestern tribes). The Junction Ruin was occupied from around 1100 until the Ancestral Puebloans disappeared shortly before 1300. Also visible is First Ruin, perched precariously on a narrow ledge, with twenty-two rooms and two kivas. Further along, White House Overlook offers splendid views into the canyon plus the only opportunity to hike into Canyon de Chelly without a guide or ranger. Sliding House Overlook, the next stop, offers a look at the ruins of dwellings that were built precariously on a narrow shelf and appear to be sliding into the canyon. Sliding House was inhabited from about A.D. 900 until 1200 and contained between thirty and fifty rooms. From the South Rim's final stop you have a spectacular view of Spider Rock, twin towers that rise 800 feet from the canyon floor.

The only trail into the canyon that is open to unescorted hikers is the White

House Ruins Trail, which provides impressive views of the monument's rock formations as it drops some 600 feet from the rim to the canyon floor, crosses Chinle Wash, and ends in front of the White House Ruins. Though hikers cannot enter the ruins, a great deal can be seen from the trail. Hikers are required to not leave the trail and respect the privacy of the Navajos living in the canyon. The 2.5-mile round-trip hike takes about 2 hours. It is a combination of slickrock and sand, steep in some sections, and is considered moderately strenuous. Hikers are advised to wear good hiking boots, carry drinking water, and be prepared for intense sun and heat during the summer and ice and possibly snow in winter. A trail guide is available at the visitor center.

Named White House for the white plastered walls in the ruin's upper section, these are among the largest Ancestral Puebloan dwellings in the canyon, and during their occupation from A.D. 1060 to 1275 probably housed up to a dozen families with a total of fifty to sixty people. Constructed both on the canyon floor and 50 feet up the cliff wall in a small cave, this complex once included about eighty rooms. Some of the lower rooms have been destroyed by stream erosion. Today there is evidence of about sixty rooms and four kivas, and several prehistoric pictographs can be seen on the cliff walls.

The North Rim Drive overlooks Canyon del Muerto. From viewpoints you'll see Ledge Ruin, which was occupied between A.D. 1050 and 1275, and a lone kiva nearby that was reached by means of toeholds cut into the sandstone cliff. Antelope House, once home to between twenty and forty people, takes its name from the Navajo paintings of antelopes on a nearby rock wall, believed to have been done in the 1830s. Further along the drive is the most impressive archeological site in the canyon. Named for two mummies discovered here, Mummy Cave is actually a giant amphitheater consisting of two caves that are believed to have been occupied from A.D. 300 to 1300. It includes a three-story structure similar to those found at Mesa Verde, and altogether there are eighty rooms. The final stop on the North Rim Drive is at Massacre Cave Overlook, where Spanish troops killed about 120 Navajo in 1805.

The national monument is a good bird-watching location. Swifts and swallows are plentiful along the cliffs and a variety of birds can be seen in the wet areas in the canyon bottom and in the campground. Permanent residents include prairie falcons, American kestrels, great blue herons, rock doves (common pigeons), mourning doves, yellow-bellied sapsuckers, Steller's jays, Clark's nutcrackers, common ravens, canyon wrens, mockingbirds, American robins, western bluebirds, ruby-crowned kinglets, starlings, house and song sparrows, western meadowlarks, and dark-eyed juncos. During summer also watch for yellow-rumped warblers, warbling vireos, red-winged blackbirds, violet-green swallows, white-throated swifts, spotted sandpipers, and black-chinned hummingbirds.

These canyons are also home to lizards and snakes, including the poisonous

Hiking the White House Overlook Trail at Canyon de Chelly National Monument

western rattlesnake. There are several species of squirrels and chipmunks, along with desert cottontails, black-tailed jackrabbits, spotted skunks, coyotes, ringtails, raccoons, porcupines, mule deer, and bobcats. Domestic dogs are sometimes present at overlooks. National Park Service officials say that these are not strays, but herding dogs that belong to local Navajo families, and they request that people not feed the dogs because it only encourages their begging.

Except for the White House Ruins Trail, discussed above, access to the floor of Canyon de Chelly is available only to those accompanied by a park ranger or other authorized guide. Navajo guides lead hiking parties into the canyon and conduct horseback tours or four-wheel-drive vehicle tours (you must usually provide your own vehicle, although a few do supply vehicles). Details are available from National Park Service offices in advance, or at the visitor center when you arrive.

The visitor center contains a bookstore and a small museum with exhibits on the geologic and human history of Canyon de Chelly. Rangers and National Park Service volunteers provide information on guided trips, and there's often a silversmith demonstrating Navajo jewelry-making. A 22-minute video offers a look at the various peoples that have made Canyon de Chelly their home. In front of the visitor center is an example of a traditional hogan, a hexagonal structure of logs and earth that Navajos use as both home and ceremonial center. Also just outside the visitor center is a short nature trail showcasing the monument's plant life. A Plant Walk guide is available in the visitor center.

During the summer the National Park Service offers regularly scheduled talks and other programs, including campfire programs several evenings each week. The monument also offers a Junior Ranger program; children complete activities in a brochure to earn badges and certificates.

Cottonwood Campground, near the visitor center, has shady sites that are surrounded by large boulders. Sites are good for tenters and those with pickup campers and other small RVs, but only a small number of sites are large enough for motor homes and larger trailers. Campsite parking areas are uneven, so those with RVs will need leveling blocks. Sites have grills and picnic tables; the campground has drinking water in summer but not in winter. There is also group camping for parties of fifteen to fifty tenters, but there are no group sites for those with RVs. Backcountry camping is permitted with an authorized Navajo guide (check at the visitor center).

Summer daytime temperatures are often in the 90s, and sometimes above 100 degrees. Temperatures drop into the upper 40s and 50s at night. Afternoon thunderstorms are common from July through September. In winter, daytime temperatures are usually in the 40s and 50s, with nighttime lows in the teens and 20s. Light snow is common in January and February.

Nearby attractions include Hubbell Trading Post National Historic Site, which is discussed in its own section in this book.

CASA GRANDE RUINS NATIONAL MONUMENT

HOURS/SEASONS:	8 A.M. to 5 P.M. daily; closed Christmas
BEST TIME TO VISIT:	Fall through spring
AREA:	472 acres
ELEVATION:	1,480 feet
FACILITIES:	Visitor center/museum, interpretive exhibits, bookstore, paved trail, picnic tables, restrooms, public telephone
ATTRACTIONS:	Archeological sites, interpretive programs, interpretive historical exhibits, bird-watching
NEARBY:	McFarland State Historic Park
ACCESS:	In Coolidge, Arizona, off AZ 87/287

Resting beneath what looks like a huge protective table, this four-story build-ing that is the main attraction at Casa Grande Ruins National Monument is the largest and most striking prehistoric structure remaining in the Southwest. Named *Casa Grande* (Big House) by Father Kino in 1694, it was built by the Hohokam people around 1350. But the building's exact purpose, and even the fate of its builders, continue to baffle archeologists.

Visitors today explore the remains of this massive structure, wander among the other ruins surrounding it in what once was a busy walled compound, and view from an observation deck the ruins of another nearby compound and ball court.

The Hohokam lived in the Sonoran Desert from at least 300 B.C. and are con-sidered the American desert's first farmers. At first they built primitive and somewhat fragile pit houses, but as their culture evolved they constructed more substantial structures above ground in walled compounds. By 1450, it appears that they had left the area. The name Hohokam comes from one of southern Arizona's modern tribes, the Pima, and is translated as "those who are gone." Hohokam villages were built along rivers, and at the height of their civi-lization their communities were spread over 45,000 square miles of the Sonoran Desert. They created beautiful shell jewelry and sturdy pottery with red geo-metric designs. Unlike most other ancient peoples of the region, they cremated most of their dead. On trips south they traded for colorful bird feathers and copper bells, and they traded with tribes to the west to acquire shells for their jewelry.

When the Hohokam inhabited this area, the land was relatively lush, with water available just 12 feet below ground. The Hohokam learned to make full use of everything the desert offered. Mesquite, paloverde, and ironwood pro-vided edible seeds, wood, and other products. They used poles to knock fruit from the tall saguaro cactus and ate the pads of prickly pear cactus after care-fully removing the sharp spines. They also fished and hunted jackrabbits and other small mammals.

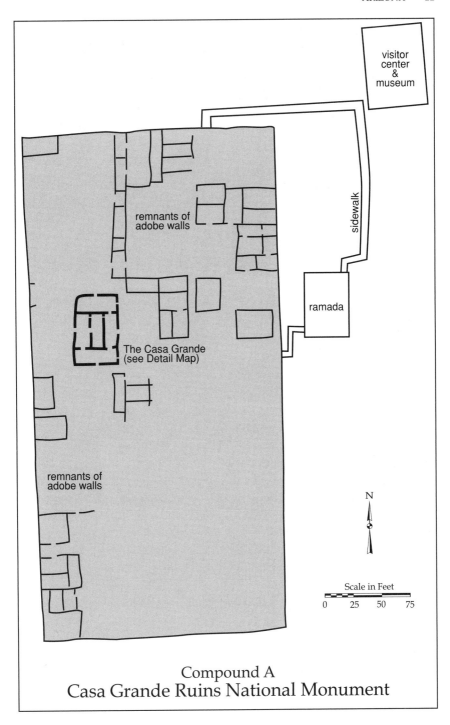

visitor
center
&
museum

sidewalk

remnants of
adobe walls

ramada

The Casa Grande
(see Detail Map)

remnants of
adobe walls

N

Scale in Feet

0   25   50   75

Compound A
Casa Grande Ruins National Monument

But it was their skill as engineers, which included their ability to construct
an elaborate and sophisticated irrigation system, that enabled the Hohokam to

The Big House at Casa Grande Ruins National Monument

survive here for more than 1,000 years. Without metal tools, wheels, or beasts of burden, they managed to dig more than 600 miles of canals and construct a series of dams and floodgates, sometimes carrying life-giving water as far as 10 miles from its source, usually the Gila or Salt Rivers. The Hohokam grew corn, beans, squash, cotton, and tobacco.

The Big House, the main attraction at Casa Grande Ruins, was constructed in the early fourteenth century using caliche, which lies about 3 feet beneath the earth's surface in this area. This rock-hard combination of sand, clay, and calcium carbonate was mixed with water to create mud, which was piled in layers up to 2 feet high and 4 feet thick at the base. When one layer dried another was added, eventually creating walls soaring 35 feet. Then trunks of pine, fir, and juniper trees were brought some 50 to 60 miles from the mountains to support the floors and ceilings. Saguaro cactus ribs and reeds were laid perpendicularly to them and topped with caliche.

As the largest Hohokam building known, it is generally agreed that the Big House was a very important structure, but archeologists are not entirely sure why. It may have been a government and religious center, and it is possible that religious leaders lived on the upper floors. The building also appears to have been an astronomical observatory, and, like England's famed Stonehenge, was used as a calendar. A small circular window in the west wall aligns perfectly with the setting sun on the summer solstice, the longest day of the year; openings

Square hole in upper wall aligns once
every 18½ years with the setting
moon at an extreme point in its cycle.

central
room
one
story
higher

equinox
sunrise
alignment

N

lunar
alignment

Small circular window in upper
wall aligns with the setting
sun on the summer solstice.

Detail Map
Casa Grande Ruins National Monument

are also aligned with the moon at significant times of the year.

So why, after all the work of creating an elaborate network of canals and building the huge Big House, did the Hohokam pack up and leave?

Archeologists don't know for sure, but think it may have been to do with erratic river flows. Dealing with changes in river flows was a constant challenge for the Hohokam, who had to adapt their farming to varying amounts of water and repair their canals, dams, and headgates because of periodic floods. It appears that much of the early 1300s was unusually dry, but suddenly, in 1358, rivers were running at record high levels. It may have been that these extremes simply became too much to make all the work worthwhile.

Some archeologists theorize that the Hohokam abandoned Casa Grande and their other villages to pursue a nomadic hunting and gathering existence. Others believe they just moved, and are seen today in their descendents—the Tohono O'odham (formerly called Papago) and the Pima. But most agree that we really don't know what happened to them, or where they went, and that the secrets of the Hohokam lie buried at Casa Grande and other sites in the Sonoran Desert.

In addition to the Great House and the ruins in its immediate area, from an observation platform in the monument's picnic area you can see ruins of another compound and what is believed to be a ball court, where a game similar to one played by Mexican Indians of the day was played. Unfortunately, no one left us the game's rulebook.

While at Casa Grande, be sure to keep your bird guide handy. A variety of species are found here, including year-round residents such as Gambel's quail, Inca doves, mourning doves, Gila woodpeckers, cactus wrens, verdins, European starlings, and house sparrows. During the winter you also might spot western meadowlarks, white-crowned sparrows, and yellow-rumped warblers. Summer visitors should be on the lookout for black-chinned hummingbirds, cliff swallows, and lesser nighthawks.

Operated by the National Park Service, Casa Grande Ruins receives most of its visitors from January through April, when daytime temperatures range from the 60s to the 80s. The scorching days of summer can see highs well over 100 degrees.

Start at the visitor center/museum, where you can see a variety of exhibits, and then walk out of the center's back door to stroll the 900-foot self-guided trail to and through the ruins. Guided tours are offered from January through April, and a Junior Ranger activity book is free to children who want to earn a Junior Ranger badge.

Special archeological tours are offered during Arizona State Archeology Month each March, and events are scheduled throughout the area during Native American Month each November.

Those who want to see history from a somewhat more modern era might consider a visit to McFarland State Historic Park in the town of Florence, a little over 10 miles east of the monument. This park—actually a museum—was the

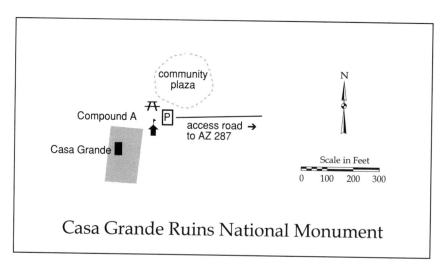

Casa Grande Ruins National Monument

county courthouse in the late 1800s, during the height of Arizona's Wild West days. Today its jail, hospital room, and other exhibits bring a bit of the real Old West to life.

CHIRICAHUA NATIONAL MONUMENT

HOURS/SEASONS:	Overnight; year-round
BEST TIME TO VISIT:	Spring and fall
AREA:	12,000 acres
ELEVATION:	5,400 feet
FACILITIES:	Visitor center/bookstore, interpretive exhibits, nature trail, scenic drive, picnic tables, restrooms, 25 campsites (no showers or hookups), group campsite, public telephone
ATTRACTIONS:	Hiking, wildlife viewing, bird-watching, interpretive programs, historical sites and exhibits
NEARBY:	Fort Bowie National Historic Site
ACCESS:	36 miles southeast of Willcox via AZ Highways 186 and 181

Rugged stone monoliths scattered among tall pines and streams tumbling over jumbles of fallen rocks create delightful opportunities for hiking, bird-watching, and camping at Chiricahua National Monument. In addition, the monument offers historic buildings, panoramic views, and a painless geology lesson. This National Park Service property, which was named for the Chiricahua Apaches who lived in these mountains, is 90 percent designated wilderness.

Chiricahua's spectacular scenery—this is a fantasyland of striking and often surreal rock sculptures—owes its creation in large part to a volcanic eruption that struck the region some 27 million years ago just 10 miles south of today's national monument boundary. The eruption is believed to have been about 1,000 times more powerful than the destructive 1980 eruption of Mount St. Helens in Washington State.

The Turkey Creek Caldera eruption spit tons of hot ash into the air, which fell to earth, cooled, and formed a layer of dark volcanic rock almost 2,000 feet thick. This rock, called rhyolite tuff, formed the basis of the Chiricahua Mountains, which were sculpted by the forces of water, ice, and wind over millions of years into the fascinating towers, columns, walls, and balanced rocks that led the Apaches to call this spot "the land of standing-up rocks."

The 8-mile Bonita Canyon Drive winds through forests of oak, juniper, and pine to Massai Point, named for Apache warrior Bigfoot Massai, who is said to have stolen a horse from a local ranch and disappeared from a pursuing posse in this area. At Massai Point is an overlook that offers excellent scenic views, including a panorama of natural rock sculptures and a look at the Cochise Head formation, said to resemble the famous Apache chief. This drive also provides access to a number of hiking trails, and has about a half-dozen pullouts (all on the right as you head back to the visitor center) with exhibits and good views of rock formations.

Chiricahua has about 17 miles of maintained day-use hiking trails, ranging from less than 0.25 mile to about 8.5 miles round trip, and from flat and easy to steep and rocky. No overnight hiking or backcountry camping is permitted. Most trails are also open to horseback riders, but all trails are closed to mountain bikes. Because terrain can be rocky, hiking boots with good ankle support are recommended.

The 0.25-mile round-trip Massai Point Nature Trail is easy, although it involves climbing some steps and has uneven footing in some spots. Signs discuss the area's geology and the trail offers panoramic views and a look at a large balanced rock. Another short, easy walk is the 0.5-mile one-way Bonita Creek Trail, which follows the intermittent creek between the Bonita Creek Picnic Area and Faraway Ranch. It offers good chances of seeing white-tailed deer, javelina (also called collared peccaries), and a variety of birds.

An especially scenic hike is the Echo Canyon Loop, 3.3 miles round trip, which combines the Echo Canyon, Hailstone, and Ed Riggs Trails on a moderate to difficult hike among spectacular rock formations and into a densely wooded area. The Natural Bridge Trail, 4.8 miles round trip, is a good choice for bird-watchers, as it climbs through groves of oak, juniper, and pine to a small natural rock bridge. The hike is rated moderate to difficult and gains almost 650 feet.

The difficult Heart of Rocks Loop, which includes a side trip to Inspiration Point, offers a bit more challenge. The 8.5-mile round trip hike gains more than 1,000 feet in elevation. It combines the Ed Riggs, Mushroom Rock, and Big Balanced Rock Trails and leads to views of a huge balanced rock and delightful formations such as Punch and Judy, Duck on a Rock, Mushroom Rock, Cochise Head, Old Maid Rock, and Camels Head Rock. The Heart of Rocks Loop also boasts some of the best panoramic views in the monument. There are a number of other trails in the monument as well, and plans are underway for a new trail that will start in the monument and extend into the adjacent Coronado National Forest and to the base of Cochise Head. When completed, this mostly moderate trail will be about 3 miles each way.

Chiricahua is a premier wildlife viewing and bird-watching area where you might see animals and birds more common to the Sierra Madre Mountains of Mexico than the United States. Surrounded by desert, but with the largest forested areas in the region, the Chiricahua Mountains provide a cool, moist oasis where a wide variety of species prosper.

Animals to watch for include white-tailed deer, javelina (also called collared

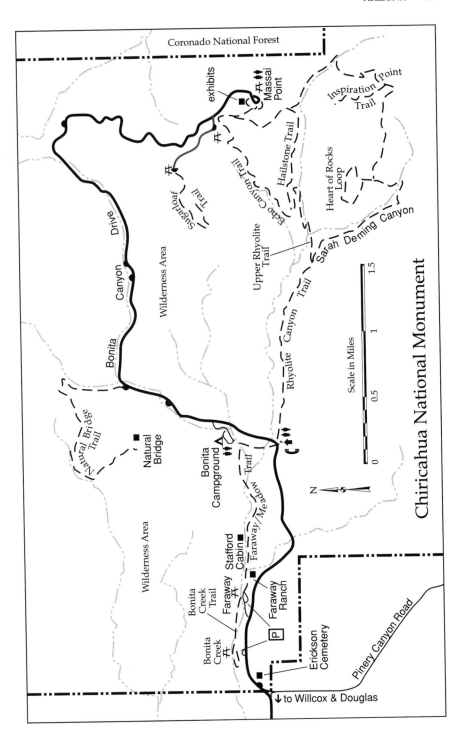

Chiricahua National Monument

Hiking the Ed Riggs Trail at Chiricahua National Monument

peccaries), hog-nosed and hooded skunks, and Chiricahua fox squirrels. The coatimundi, also called the white-nosed coati, is also seen in the monument. A relative of the raccoon, the coatimundi has a long, pointed nose with a white facial mask, white ears, a mostly brown body, and a long, thin tail. Females and young often travel in groups of several dozen, and the young are sometimes seen chasing each other up and down trees. There are also bears and mountain lions in the monument, although most visitors don't see them.

Numerous birds can be seen at Chiricahua, especially in the area of Bonita Creek and other water sources. Commonly seen year-round residents include Gambel's quail, mourning doves, acorn woodpeckers, gray-breasted jays, white-breasted nuthatches, and black-throated sparrows. During summer watch for black-throated, magnificent, and black-chinned hummingbirds as well as solitary vireos, Cassin's and western kingbirds, Scott's orioles, red-faced warblers, hepatic tanagers, and western wood-peewees. Winter residents include dark-eyed juncos and ruby-crowned kinglets. Prairie falcons sometimes nest in the cliffs along Bonita Canyon Drive, and red-tailed hawks and golden eagles have been seen above the meadows near the monument entrance.

Various reptiles also inhabit the monument, including mountain spiny lizards, striped plateau lizards, and tree lizards. Nonpoisonous bullsnakes and Sonoran whipsnakes are found at Chiricahua, as are several poisonous rattlesnakes—the Mojave and rock.

The views from Massai Point at Chiricahua National Monument.

These mountains were home for about 400 years to the Chiricahua Apaches, who fiercely resisted the invasion of white settlers that began in the mid-1800s. Although their more than 30 years of raids on the settlers may have slowed the so-called "civilization" of the region, the Apaches were eventually defeated, and the Indian Wars officially ended with the surrender of Geronimo in 1886.

Just 2 years after Geronimo's surrender, Swedish immigrants Neil and Emma Erickson homesteaded a farm and cattle ranch in Bonita Canyon. Around 1920, one of the Erickson's daughters, Lillian, turned the homestead into a guest ranch, which she called Faraway Ranch, because, as she put it, "it was so god-awful far away from everything." She and her husband, Ed Riggs, explored the mountains, built trails, named many of the formations, and took guests out on horseback to see what they called "the wonderland of rocks."

The Riggs took photographs and promoted their "wonderland," which in 1924 became Chiricahua National Monument by presidential proclamation. Ed was hired to map the area and lay out trails, while Faraway Ranch became a popular base for those who wanted to explore the new monument. Ed died in 1950 and Lillian, although blind and deaf, continued to manage the guest ranch until she was incapacitated by a heart attack in 1973. After her death the ranch was purchased by the National Park Service, which restored the ranch house and finally opened it to the public in 1988.

Today, Faraway Ranch is furnished with historic artifacts, and tells the story of the ranch's beginnings as an 1880s pioneer homestead and its evolution as a cattle ranch and finally a twentieth-century guest ranch. Guided tours of the main ranch house are given daily, and a variety of special events, including a

Christmas open house and Mother's Day ice cream social, are also scheduled.

The monument's visitor center offers an audiovisual program, a computer information station, and a variety of exhibits. Talks, including evening programs at the campground amphitheater, and guided walks are offered from March through November. Schedules are posted at the visitor center and campground.

The monument's Bonita Campground certainly lives up to its name—*bonita* is Spanish for "pretty"—with its abundance of trees and mostly well-spaced sites. The campground is an easy walk to the visitor center. There is also camping nearby in the Coronado National Forest (a map and other information can be obtained at the monument's visitor center).

The busiest season here is spring, particularly from March through May, when daytime temperatures are usually in the 70s. Summer high temperatures are often in the upper 90s, with lows in the 50s. During the winter, days are often in the 50s and 60s with nighttime temperatures dropping into the upper teens or low 20s. Daily thunderstorms are common from July through September, and the monument also gets its share of winter and early spring snow.

Nearby attractions include Fort Bowie National Historic Site, which is discussed in its own section of this book.

CORONADO NATIONAL MEMORIAL

HOURS/SEASONS:	Visitor center 8 A.M. to 5 P.M. daily. Closed Thanksgiving and Christmas
BEST TIME TO VISIT:	Spring and fall
AREA:	4,750 acres
ELEVATION:	5,230 feet
FACILITIES:	Visitor center, interpretive exhibits, nature trail, picnic tables, restrooms, public telephone
ATTRACTIONS:	Hiking, spelunking, bird-watching, wildlife viewing, interpretive programs, historical exhibits
NEARBY:	Coronado National Forest
ACCESS:	21 miles south of Sierra Vista via AZ 92 and Coronado Memorial Highway

This national memorial, which was established to commemorate the 1540 expedition by Spanish explorers into what would eventually become the United States, offers historical exhibits, opportunities for hiking and cave exploring, and spectacular panoramic views. Operated by the National Park Service, Coronado National Memorial is located along the United States–Mexico border, within sight of a river valley through which Francisco Vásquez de Coronado led a group

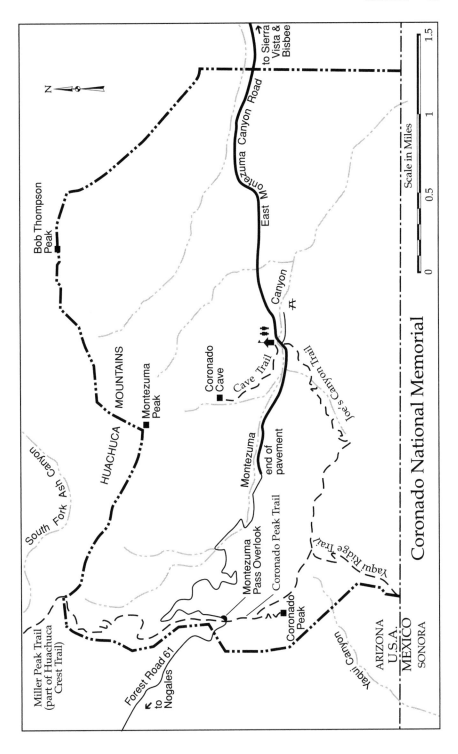

Coronado National Memorial

of soldiers and priests in search of the fabled Seven Cities of Gold.

Stories of vast riches in what would become the states of Arizona, New Mexico, Texas, and even Kansas lured Spanish explorers north from Mexico City, in what was then New Spain, in the early 1500s. Coronado's task was to follow up on earlier reports, claim whatever he found for Spain, and bring Christianity to the natives.

However, his 2-year expedition failed to find the wealthy cities "with houses of many stories, and doorways studded with emeralds and turquoise" that some earlier explorers had claimed existed. Instead, he found mud and stone pueblos and natives who did not welcome them with open arms. It didn't help Coronado's cause that, when negotiations with the Indians for food and supplies were unsuccessful, his troops simply attacked them, killing or driving them away from their homes. After his failed mission, Coronado returned to Mexico City, and 10 years later died in relative obscurity at the age of 42.

Although there are exhibits and a video presentation on Coronado's trip, the national memorial's real claims to fame are its hiking and cave exploring opportunities, plus the drive up to 6,575-foot Montezuma Pass for splendid and seemingly unending 360 degree views. From the visitor center the road to the pass is paved for 1 mile but then becomes a narrow, gravel mountain road for the remaining 2 miles. The road is steep in spots, with tight switchbacks, and vehicles over 24 feet are prohibited. From Montezuma Pass the road continues west into the Coronado National Forest, and after much wandering ends up at AZ 82, which leads to Nogales, which is 55 miles west of the memorial.

Joe's Canyon Trail, which links the visitor center and Montezuma Pass Overlook, is moderate to difficult. From the visitor center, the 3.1-mile trail gains 1,000 feet in its first mile, climbing among oak, piñon, and juniper to a ridge that offers splendid views into Mexico, which is about 1 mile south. Just past the halfway point, the Yaqui Ridge Trail branches south off Joe's Canyon Trail for a moderate 1-mile (each way) side trip to the Mexican border and an historic international boundary marker that dates from the late 1800s. The Yaqui Ridge Trail is the southernmost part of the planned 750-mile Arizona Trail, which is to extend from Mexico to Utah. Back on Joe's Canyon Trail, hikers continue along Smuggler's Ridge, which joins with the Coronado Peak Trail for the last 600 feet to Montezuma Pass.

From Montezuma Pass, the easy to moderate Coronado Peak Trail gains about 300 feet as it climbs to the top of Coronado Peak. Along its 0.4 mile (each way) are signs describing Coronado's expedition, with quotations from the explorers.

The longest trail here, at 5.3 miles one-way, is the Miller Peak Trail, which goes north from Montezuma Pass, leaving the memorial and entering the Coronado National Forest. Rated moderate to difficult, it climbs more than 2,900 feet to the summit of Miller Peak and also offers access to other trails in the Miller Peak Wilderness. The Miller Peak Trail is actually the southern section of the

Hiking the Cave Trail at Coronado National Memorial

Huachuca Crest Trail, and climbs through grasslands, passes old mines, enters forests of Douglas fir, and clings to a steep mountainside before ascending a series of switchbacks to the peak. Miller Peak, at 9,466 feet, is the highest point in the Huachuca Mountains and offers breathtaking views in all directions

For those who want to combine hiking and cave exploring, the Coronado Cave Trail is ideal. Although the moderately rated hike is short—only 0.75 mile each way—the trail from the visitor center up to the cave entrance is steep and rocky and gains about 500 feet in elevation. When you get to the cave entrance you'll need to scramble over some boulders to get in, but after that the cave is easy to explore. Permits, which are available for free at the visitor center, are required for those who plan to enter the cave.

The limestone cave contains two connected rooms and is about 600 feet long, some 20 feet high, and about 70 feet wide. It is also dirty and dark, so each person going into the cave should carry a powerful flashlight. Rangers say that those going alone to the cave should carry two flashlights. Inside you'll see a variety of cave formations, ranging from draperies just inside the entrance to stalagmites, stalactites, helictites, cave coral, and rimstone dams, which are ridges of calcite that sometimes hold pools of water.

According to legend, the famous Apache leader Geronimo used the cave as a hideout during the Indian Wars of the late 1800s. There is a narrow shaft in the cave that Geronimo supposedly used as an escape route when soldiers caught up with him, and graffiti on the cave ceiling dates to the late nineteenth century. You're also likely to see several species of bats. The cave is sometimes home to white-nosed coatis (or coatimundi) and ringtails (both relatives of the raccoon), but they're only occasionally seen.

It is estimated that fewer than 5,000 of the park's 95,000 annual visitors actually get into the cave, but even that relatively small number of people can have an impact. Rangers say that people should not touch any formations because the oils and acids from human skin can discolor them and actually stop the "live" formations from growing. In addition, cave visitors should not disturb any bats they see, particularly hibernating bats, which may die if they are awakened.

A variety of birds and other wildlife can be seen throughout the memorial. Among the more than 140 species of birds reported to have been seen, some of the most common are the acorn woodpecker, bridled titmouse, chipping sparrow, red-shafted flicker, painted redstart, gray-breasted jay (also called the Mexican jay), Montezuma quail, white-winged dove, dark-eyed junco, northern mockingbird, phainopepla, pyrrhuloxia, ruby-crowned kinglet, and white-breasted nuthatch. Especially at Montezuma Pass, watch for red-tailed hawks and turkey vultures.

The memorial is also home to desert cottontails, white-tailed deer, coyotes, gray foxes, javelina (also called collared peccaries), mountain lions, and black bear. Several lizards are commonly seen, including the desert-grassland whiptail, a species that includes only females and which reproduce quite effectively without any assistance from males. There are several species of poisonous snakes, including the western diamondback rattlesnake and banded rock rattlesnake.

The visitor center has displays that describe Coronado's trek and include authentic and replica weapons and armor (that visitors can try on), a short video on Coronado's expedition, and exhibits on the memorial's birds and other wildlife. There is also a bookstore, and just outside the visitor center is a short nature trail where you can learn about the flora and fauna of the Upper Sonoran Desert. During the memorial's busy season, generally from January through April, rangers offer guided tours of Coronado Cave, as well as other history and nature programs. Junior Naturalist Programs for kids are also sometimes scheduled.

Summers here are hot, with daytime temperatures usually in the 90s or above.

Winter days are often in the 40s and 50s, with freezing temperatures at night. Thunderstorms, with the possibility of flash flooding and lightning hazards, are common from late June through early September, and light snow is possible in winter.

Although there is no camping at the memorial, there is camping to the west and north of the memorial in Coronado National Forest, which also has a number of good hiking trails and fishing at Parker Canyon Lake.

FORT BOWIE NATIONAL HISTORIC SITE

HOURS/SEASONS:	Trail sunrise to sunset daily; visitor center 8 A.M. to 5 P.M. daily, closed Christmas
BEST TIME TO VISIT:	Spring and fall
AREA:	1,000 acres
ELEVATION:	5,000 feet
FACILITIES:	Visitor center, interpretive exhibits, interpretive trail, picnic tables, restrooms
ATTRACTIONS:	Hiking, historical exhibits, bird-watching, wildlife viewing
NEARBY:	Chiricahua National Monument
ACCESS:	Parking area and trailhead are 13 miles south of Bowie on Apache Pass Road

Fort Bowie National Historic Site is one of the few National Park Service sites that requires a hike just to get to the visitor center and main attraction. It tells the poignant story of the defeat of the Chiricahua Apaches in one of the last of the American West's Indian Wars. The ruins of the fort, which operated from 1862 to 1894, and a visitor center are accessed by a 3-mile round-trip hike, which generally follows a nineteenth-century wagon road to the fort. In addition to helping today's visitors understand how soldiers felt in this isolated outpost, the trail passes by several historic sites and provides a good chance of seeing a wide variety of birds and other wildlife.

The United States military built the fort to safeguard Apache Pass, and more importantly the reliable year-round water source of Apache Spring. The pass, which is between the Chiricahua and Dos Cabezas (Spanish for two heads) Mountains, was the scene of several confrontations between whites and the Chiricahua Apaches, who had lived and hunted in these mountains for at least 300 years.

The tragedy is that the first confrontation, which led to continued and greater hostilities, was all a stupid mistake. In 1861 a band of Apaches raided a ranch belonging to John Ward along the Mexican border, near the present town of Nogales. They stole some horses and oxen and abducted the son of Ward's wife.

Ward mistakenly believed that the raiders were Chiricahua Apaches under the leadership of Cochise, and at the rancher's insistence the army sent fifty-four soldiers under Lt. George Bascom to Apache Pass to get the boy and livestock back.

Bascom arranged a meeting with Cochise, accused him of the raid and kidnapping, and told Cochise that he would be held captive until the boy was returned. Cochise, knowing he was innocent, was furious, and, cutting his way out of the tent in which they were meeting, escaped into the surrounding hills. Several other Apaches at the meeting, including Cochise's brother, failed to escape and were arrested. Sporadic fighting over the next few weeks led to deaths on both sides, which escalated to years of hostilities. It turns out that the boy had actually been abducted by an entirely different group of Apaches—the Western Apaches. He was raised by them and later worked as an interpreter and scout for the army.

Meanwhile, the Civil War had begun, and in 1862 a troop of Union soldiers from a California regiment were on their way to battle Confederate troops that were threatening Arizona and New Mexico. As they reached Apache Pass they

Remains of the old fort at Fort Bowie National Historic Site

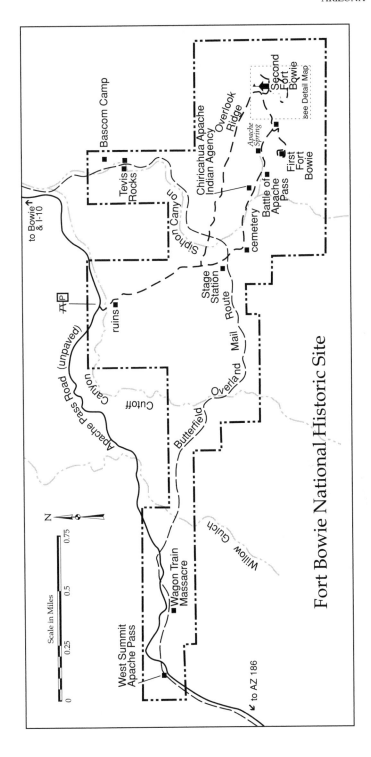

Fort Bowie National Historic Site

were ambushed by Cochise and at least 100 Chiricahua Apache warriors, who were trying to keep the soldiers away from Apache Spring. However, the Apaches were no match for the army's two howitzers, and soon the Indians fled, ending what came to be known as the Battle of Apache Pass. This attack, however, convinced the army of the importance of the pass and its water supply, and within a month work began on the fort, which was named for the California regiment's commanding officer, Col. George Washington Bowie.

The fort evolved gradually. The troops first slept in tents, then partial dugouts in hillsides, and finally some adobe structures. But the fort was hardly anything to brag about, and in 1868 work began on a completely new fort about 900 feet east of the first one. This second Fort Bowie included a parade ground surrounded by adobe barracks, officers' houses, a store, a hospital, a bakery, a kitchen, a school, a telegraph office, storage buildings, stables, and corrals. At its peak, the fort had 38 buildings, about 300 troops, its own brass band, and even tennis courts.

Fort Bowie was the staging area for campaigns against the Chiricahua Apache, and its reason for being essentially ended in 1886 when Chiricahua leader Geronimo surrendered and the Chiricahuas were loaded aboard a train and shipped to Florida and then Alabama. The fort remained active for 8 more years, and after it was finally closed in 1894 area settlers began scavenging

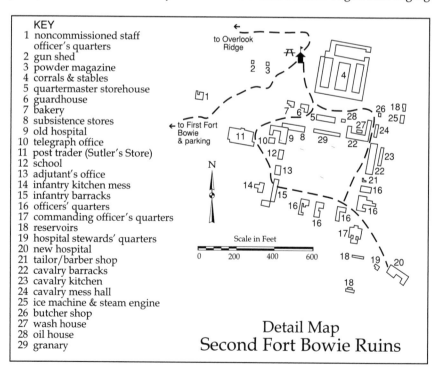

KEY
1 noncommissioned staff officer's quarters
2 gun shed
3 powder magazine
4 corrals & stables
5 quartermaster storehouse
6 guardhouse
7 bakery
8 subsistence stores
9 old hospital
10 telegraph office
11 post trader (Sutler's Store)
12 school
13 adjutant's office
14 infantry kitchen mess
15 infantry barracks
16 officers' quarters
17 commanding officer's quarters
18 reservoirs
19 hospital stewards' quarters
20 new hospital
21 tailor/barber shop
22 cavalry barracks
23 cavalry kitchen
24 cavalry mess hall
25 ice machine & steam engine
26 butcher shop
27 wash house
28 oil house
29 granary

to Overlook Ridge

← to First Fort Bowie & parking

N

Scale in Feet
0   200   400   600

Detail Map
Second Fort Bowie Ruins

the buildings for lumber, doors, windows, fixtures, and whatever else could be hauled away.

The ruins that visitors see today are primarily preserved adobe walls, but enough of the past remains to give visitors some insight into what this fort was like more than 100 years ago, when it sat in the middle of nowhere surrounded by hostile Apaches.

A 1.5-mile (one-way) moderate trail leads from a parking area to the visitor center and ruins of the second fort, passing through high desert terrain of cactus, yucca, manzanita, and mountain mahogany, where cottonwoods and willows line stream banks. Wet winters produce an abundance of desert marigolds, globemallows, bladderpods, and other spring and summer wildflowers. The lower end of the trail is a loop, so many hikers follow a ridge, from which there are panoramic views of the fort and battle site, to return to the trailhead. On windy days, however, the unprotected ridge experiences extremely fierce winds.

Hikers may see deer, gray foxes, coyotes, coatis, javelina (also called collared peccaries), lizards, and possibly even a mountain lion. Rattlesnakes are also occasionally seen. Birds to watch for include chipping sparrows, dark-eyed juncos, and ruby-crowned kinglets in winter; and western kingbirds, lark sparrows, black-chinned hummingbirds, and western wood-peewees in summer. Year-round residents include a lot of Gambel's quail, plus mourning doves, acorn woodpeckers, gray-breasted jays, white-breasted nuthatches, Bewick's wrens, and black-throated sparrows.

Also along the trail are stone ruins of a Butterfield Stage Station, which operated here from 1858 to 1861; the fort cemetery; Apache Spring, the site of the Battle of Apache Pass, with a marker discussing the battle; a reconstructed Apache wickiup; ruins from the first Fort Bowie; and several other ruins. Those with mobility impairments can make advance arrangements to get to the visitor center and second fort via a dirt maintenance road.

At the trailhead on Apache Pass Road are a parking area, picnic tables, vault toilet, and a sign with information on the trail and the national historic site. Picnic tables and restrooms are also located near the visitor center, which contains a small museum with artifacts from the fort, displays on military life, a computerized slide program, and a small bookstore.

Summers are hot, with daytime temperatures often rising above 100 degrees. Because practically all visitors will be hiking 3 miles, sun protection and drinking water are highly recommended. Winters are cool with occasional light snow. High winds with below-freezing wind chills are common from October through April.

Camping is not permitted at the historic site, but is available, along with excellent hiking trails and spectacular scenery, at nearby Chiricahua National Monument, which is discussed in its own section of this book.

GRAND CANYON–PARASHANT NATIONAL MONUMENT

HOURS/SEASONS: Overnight; year-round
BEST TIME TO VISIT: Summer
AREA: 1,014,000 acres
ELEVATION: About 2,000 feet to more than 8,000 feet
FACILITIES: None
ATTRACTIONS: Hiking, wildlife viewing, bird-watching, historical sites, four-wheeling (high-clearance vehicles)
NEARBY: Grand Canyon National Park, Pipe Spring National Monument, Lake Mead National Recreation Area, Zion National Park
ACCESS: Southwest of Fredonia via AZ 389 and Mount Trumball Road; or south of St. George, UT via Quail Hill Road

Stark buttes and mesas, deep canyons, rangelands, piñon and juniper, and rugged mountains make up one of America's newest and most remote national monuments. The Grand Canyon–Parashant National Monument, which was created by presidential proclamation in January 2000, protects a vast, mostly inaccessible, strikingly beautiful part of the American West. With spectacular

The rugged terrain at Grand Canyon–Parashant National Monument (photo courtesy Bureau of Land Management)

views into the Grand Canyon, this is not a typical national monument suitable for a weekend family outing, but rather a place where the seasoned adventurer will find miles of rugged dirt roads and backcountry to explore.

Miles from the nearest paved road, the monument is currently accessible only to those willing and able to brave a wild and mostly natural area that has changed little since ranchers and miners sought its riches more than 100 years ago, or when ancestors of today's Pueblo Indians lived here more than 8,000 years ago. The monument encompasses part of Lake Mead National Recreation Area, and is bounded by Grand Canyon National Park on the south and the state of Nevada on the west.

To those with the means (a high-clearance four-wheel-drive vehicle) and the inclination, the Grand Canyon–Parashant National Monument offers spectacular western scenery, unlimited backcountry hiking and camping opportunities, and historic sites. What it does not offer are any facilities, established trails or camp-grounds, or even maintained roads. Those who come here are on their own, and need to be prepared with a good map, plenty of fuel and water, extra food, blankets, raingear, and a spare tire.

The awe-inspiring landscape was created by volcanic activity—some going back 9 million years—and the sculpting power of water and wind. In addition, the monument represents two quite different ecosystems—the arid Mojave Desert and the higher-elevation Colorado Plateau—whose extremes have helped nurture a vast variety of plant and animal life, including a number of threatened and endangered species.

Archaic hunter-gatherers who lived between 300 B.C. and 7000 B.C. are among the earliest peoples to have been here, according to archeologists. They were followed by Ancestral Puebloans (also called the Anasazi), the Southern Paiutes, and finally Spanish and Anglo explorers and settlers.

Hidden among the canyons and mesas are unexcavated sites of prehistoric villages, as well as mining sites from the 1870s, old ranch buildings and corrals, and water tanks. An historic schoolhouse has been reconstructed and is open to the public.

There are also ruins of sawmills built by Mormon pioneers, who cut and milled timber from 8,000-foot Mount Trumbull during construction of the Church of Jesus Christ of Latter-day Saints' temple in St. George, Utah. Completed in 1877, it was the first Mormon temple west of the Mississippi River and is the oldest still in use in the world.

The monument has no maintained trails, but there are ample opportunities for backcountry hiking. Motorized and mechanized vehicles (jeeps and mountain bikes) are restricted to existing roads, all of which are dirt.

The numerous species of wildlife to be seen include mule deer, the delightful tufted-ear Kaibab squirrel (a subspecies of the Abert's squirrel), desert cottontails, coyotes, mountain lions, and several species of bats. Watch for wild turkeys in the meadows and species such as the willow flycatcher, peregrine falcon, bald eagles, and the rare Mexican spotted owl. Bureau of Land Management officials say that the California condor has also been seen in the monument.

Because of the great variations in elevation, weather differences throughout the monument can be extreme. In the eastern section, summers are hot and dry at lower elevations, with temperatures often exceeding 100 degrees, while winters are relatively mild. In the mountains, however, winters are snowy and cold while summer days are warm. Summer highs are commonly in the upper 80s and 90s and nights are pleasantly cool, with temperatures dropping into the 50s and low 60s.

Adjacent to the monument are the Grand Canyon National Park North Rim, Lake Mead National Recreation Area, and Pipe Spring National Monument. Zion National Park is nearby. All of these areas are discussed in their own sections of this book.

The monument is managed jointly by the Bureau of Land Management and National Park Service. Although it has no visitor center or other visitor contact station as of this writing, maps and other information, such as the very important current road conditions, can be obtained at the visitor centers at Pipe Spring National Monument and Lake Mead National Recreation Area and at the Bureau of Land Management offices in Arizona and Utah.

HUBBELL TRADING POST NATIONAL HISTORIC SITE

HOURS/SEASONS: 8 A.M. to 6 P.M. daily in summer; 8 A.M. to 5 P.M. daily in winter. Closed Thanksgiving, Christmas, and New Year's Day (Note: Hubbell Trading Post is within the Navajo Reservation, which, unlike the rest of Arizona, observes Daylight Saving Time)

BEST TIME TO VISIT: Summer

AREA: 160 acres

ELEVATION: 6,340 feet

FACILITIES: Operating trading post, visitor center, interpretive exhibits, picnic tables, restrooms, public telephone

ATTRACTIONS: Historic trading post experience, shopping for American Indian arts and crafts, interpretive programs, guided tours, historical exhibits

NEARBY: Petrified Forest National Park and Canyon de Chelly National Monument

ACCESS: 1 mile west of Ganado

John Lorenzo Hubbell was one of the good guys. In an era when Indian traders and most other whites were best known for their mistreatment and

Navajo rugs and other crafts on display at Hubbell Trading Post National Historic Site

disparaging attitude toward American Indians, Hubbell was different—he was a trader who not only respected his Navajo and Hopi customers but believed that it was his duty as a trader to help the Indians improve their lives.

Located within the boundaries of the Navajo Reservation, Hubbell's trading post and home are now a national historic site under the jurisdiction of the National Park Service. The trading post he started in the 1870s continues in operation and is managed by the nonprofit Southwest Parks and Monuments Association. Little changed since its beginnings, the trading post continues its role of buying and selling. Today's visitors often stand shoulder to shoulder with Navajos, Hopis, and members of other tribes who barter for basic necessities such as flour, as well as top-quality Navajo rugs, baskets, or jewelry.

Hubbell was born in 1853 in the village of Pajarito, New Mexico, just south of Albuquerque. The son of an Anglo father and Spanish mother, he grew up speaking both English and Spanish. He was mostly self-educated and learned about the Navajos as a young man while working as a clerk for early traders in Navajo country, and then as a Spanish–English interpreter for the army.

Hubbell began trading with the Navajos in the mid-1870s, and bought an existing trading post at Ganado in 1878. He married an Hispanic woman, Lina Rubi, and built a handsome home on the trading post property. He and Lina had four children—two girls and two boys. Work began on a new trading post in 1883, and the old trading post buildings were torn down in the 1920s.

Hubbell's is the oldest continuously operating trading post on the Navajo Reservation. It was managed by the Hubbell family until 1967, when it was sold to the National Park Service. John Hubbell's children and then their spouses participated in the business, which at one time included more than thirty trading posts, two wholesale outlets, several curio shops (including one in Hollywood, California), bean farms, apple orchards, a freight business, and a livery service.

Called "Don Lorenzo" by Anglos and Hispanics and "Old Mexican" or "Eyeglasses" by Navajos, John Lorenzo Hubbell is credited with doing more to popularize the weaving and silversmithing of the Navajo people than any other person. Hubbell believed that what was good for him was good for the Navajo, and vice-versa. Not only did he actively promote Navajo arts and crafts across the country, he advised weavers on what rug designs and even colors would fetch the highest prices, and reportedly was one of several traders who brought in Mexican silversmiths to teach Navajos how to improve their silverwork.

Hubbell gained the respect and admiration of the Navajos, and even to the present day Navajos use him as an example of what they want from the outsiders who come to the reservation to trade with them. Hubbell hired many Navajos, often acted as an intermediary between the Navajos and federal government, and even sometimes mediated family and tribal disputes. In 1886,

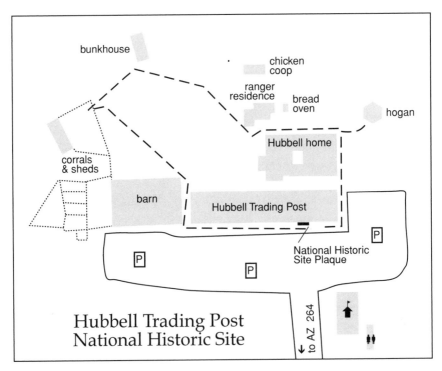

when a smallpox epidemic struck the reservation, Hubbell turned his home into a hospital and personally helped care for the sick.

The National Park Service provides a quotation from Hubbell on his philosophy: "The first duty of an Indian trader is to look after the material welfare of his neighbors; to advise them to produce that which their natural inclinations and talent best adapts them; to treat them honestly and insist upon getting the same treatment from them . . . to find a market for their products and vigilantly watch that they keep improving in the production of same, and advise them which commands the best price."

Hubbell was active in politics most of his life. He was a local sheriff, participated in the movement to gain statehood for Arizona, and later served as a state senator. He also was considered quite progressive for his time, supporting the right to vote for women and opposing English-only laws. He also favored prohibition. His main vice, it seems, was gambling, but his wife reportedly put an end to that fairly early in their marriage when, after a particularly large loss in a card game, she threatened to leave him if he didn't quit.

Trading posts such as Hubbell's were more than simply stores, and for many years Hubbell's was the main gathering spot where Navajos and members of other tribes would meet people from other parts of their reservations as well as non-Indians. It is here that they would learn the news of the day, such as what was happening in tribes elsewhere in the Southwest, or what new program or problem the United States government was creating for them.

The main room of the trading post, like other trading posts of the late 1800s, is called the "bullpen." It looks much like the central room of an old-fashioned general store, with a creaky wooden floor, a wood stove, shelves piled with containers of flour, sugar, coffee, and an assortment of canned goods, and counters where a wide variety of items are displayed, ranging from medicines to candy. There are also bolts of cloth used by Navajo women for sewing their traditional skirts and blouses. Hardware and other larger items hang from the ceiling.

Other rooms include one devoted to jewelry, baskets, kachinas, and paintings and the colorful rug room, which is filled almost to overflowing with traditional and contemporary Navajo rugs. Simple 12-inch-by-18-inch rugs usually sell for under $100, but larger rugs with more intricate designs can cost thousands of dollars.

The visitor center has a small bookstore and exhibits on the history of the trading post. In addition, Navajo weavers are usually at work creating rugs, and talks and other presentations are occasionally given. The National Park Service offers regularly scheduled guided tours of the inside of the Hubbell home, which show how a fairly well-to-do trader lived 100 years ago. The house tour is also worthwhile, if only to see the Hubbell family's personal collection of art, Navajo baskets, and rugs. Self-guided tours of the home are not permitted.

Guided tours of the grounds are offered occasionally, and a self-guided walking tour booklet, available at the visitor center, directs visitors around the grounds of the trading post, past the Hubbell's home, a hogan-style guest house, a large outdoor bread oven, an adobe chicken coop, and the garden. The large barn also served as a blacksmith shop, and brand marks can still be seen on the wooden doors. The easy, mostly level trail is only a few hundred yards long, but can be muddy in spots.

During the summer, daytime temperatures are often in the 80s and 90s, while winter daytime temperatures usually range from the teens to the upper 30s. Thunderstorms are common in July and August, and winters can be snowy. Spring weather is fickle, ranging from wintry to beautiful, although it is often windy.

Nearby are Petrified Forest National Park and Canyon de Chelly National Monument, which are discussed elsewhere in this book.

MONTEZUMA CASTLE NATIONAL MONUMENT

HOURS/SEASONS:	8 A.M. to 7 P.M. daily in summer; 8 A.M. to 5 P.M. daily in winter
BEST TIME TO VISIT:	Fall through spring
AREA:	840 acres
ELEVATION:	3,200 feet
FACILITIES:	Visitor center/museum/bookstore, interpretive exhibits, interpretive trails, restrooms, picnic tables, public telephone
ATTRACTIONS:	Archeological sites, interpretive programs, bird-watching
NEARBY:	Tuzigoot National Monument, Fort Verde State Historic Park
ACCESS:	Montezuma Castle accessible from I-17 exit 289 (follow signs for 3 miles); Montezuma Well accessible from I-17 exit 293 (follow signs for 4 miles)

Compared to other prehistoric peoples of the American Southwest, the Sinagua of the Verde Valley had it pretty good. The climate here is relatively moderate, there is a long growing season, and best of all, this area has plenty of water. At Montezuma Castle and nearby Montezuma Well we can marvel at the Sinaguas' buildings, see their artifacts, and wonder why they ever left. Short trails take us to the remains of their homes and through the rich environment in which they lived.

This national monument, which is managed by the National Park Service, protects one of the best-preserved prehistoric cliff dwellings in the Southwest. It also includes a nearby detached unit with additional ruins and a lake with remains from an elaborate irrigation system.

The cliff dwelling, an impressive five-story, twenty-room structure, was mistakenly named Montezuma Castle by early European-American settlers to the area, who thought it must have had something to do with the Aztec emperor Montezuma. In truth, it was built long before Montezuma was born, and he never traveled this far north.

The name Sinagua comes from the Spanish *sin agua,* which means "without water." The label is appropriate for the members of other branches of the Sinagua people who lived to the north in what is now the Flagstaff area (see the descriptions of Walnut Canyon and Wupatki National Monuments, elsewhere in this book), but conditions here in the Verde Valley were much better. Not only did these people have more than adequate water for farming and domestic uses, but the reliable water sources brought them an abundance of wild plants, deer and other game, as well as tall sycamore trees for their roof beams.

The Sinagua built their homes into cliffs for several reasons, not the least of which was that building into an existing cave means that your top roof and several walls are already there. It is believed that they also did not want to waste flat land for housing when it could be better used for farming; they grew corn, beans, squash, and cotton. Also, building too close to the river would leave them

Cliff dwellings at Montezuma Castle National Monument

vulnerable to floods. The major disadvantage of living on the side of a cliff is that you have to haul everything you need, such as water, either up or down.

The structures here were built about A.D. 1100 or 1200, possibly by people who had left the pueblos of what is now the Flagstaff area due to overpopulation there. By about 1450, however, they had abandoned their "castles" here, as well. As with many of the other mass migrations of that time, it remains a mystery as to why the inhabitants left the area. It is believed that the Sinagua may have gone to the east and north, and in fact several of today's Hopi groups trace their ancestors to Montezuma Well.

A level, paved 0.3-mile loop trail provides good views of Montezuma Castle, which may not be entered, and

A squirrel poses along the Cliffside at Montezuma Castle National Monument

interpretive signs describe the site's human and natural history. The castle is built into a shallow cave about one-third of the way up a cliff that towers over Beaver Creek, which is lined with Arizona sycamore trees, hackberry, and numerous other bushes and grasses.

Just west of Montezuma Castle, along the same trail, are the remains of another pueblo, which archeologists have named "Castle A." Built against the base of the cliff, it once was a six-story structure with about forty-five rooms, and may have housed about a hundred people. Unfortunately Castle A is not nearly as well preserved as Montezuma Castle, in part because a fire destroyed much of the interior sometime in the late 1400s. What remains are sections of several walls and a partially reconstructed foundation.

Less than 6 miles upriver (11 miles on today's roads), Montezuma Well has a paved 0.3-mile interpretive loop trail that leads over an easy but somewhat hilly route to the edge of Montezuma Well, a small lake about 370 feet across and 55 feet deep, that is actually a limestone sink hole filled with water from a continuously flowing spring. The trail also offers views of a pit house and other prehistoric buildings, plus remains of the Sinaguan's irrigation system. Signs name the flora along the way, which includes an abundance of mahonia (also called desert holly or barberry) and poison ivy.

The same water sources and plant life that made the Verde Valley appealing to the Sinagua also make it attractive to wildlife today, especially birds. Year-round residents include canyon wrens, rock wrens, Gambel's quail, mourning doves, bushtits, and northern cardinals. During spring and summer, watch for violet-green and cliff swallows swooping and gliding along the cliff sides. Other birds you might see in spring and summer include black-throated sparrows, yellow warblers, Lucy's warblers, phainopepla, yellow-breasted chats, and common ravens. American robins are often seen from summer through winter, and white-crowned sparrows are seen in abundance from fall through spring. Rock squirrels seem to be everywhere in the vicinity of the castle.

The Montezuma Castle site has a visitor center/bookstore with a museum that contains artifacts discovered at the site. At Montezuma Well there is a contact station and there are descriptive signs. Ranger-led walks and talks are offered periodically at Montezuma Castle.

Summers here are usually fairly hot, with daytime temperatures in the 90s, while winters are pleasantly moderate, with daytime temperatures often in the 50s and 60s. Short afternoon thunderstorms are common in summer and early fall. Tour buses frequently stop at the Montezuma Castle site between 10 A.M. and 1 P.M., so planning your visit either before or after that time period is a good idea.

Nearby is Tuzigoot National Monument (which is discussed later in this section) and Fort Verde State Historic Park, which consists primarily of buildings that remain from a late-nineteenth-century military fort used by the U.S. Army in its efforts to subdue the area's American Indians.

NAVAJO NATIONAL MONUMENT

HOURS/SEASONS:	Overnight; year-round (Note: the monument is within the Navajo Reservation, which, unlike most other parts of Arizona, observes Daylight Saving Time)
BEST TIME TO VISIT:	Spring through fall
AREA:	360 acres
ELEVATION:	7,300 feet
FACILITIES:	Visitor center/museum, interpretive exhibits, nature trail, picnic tables, restrooms, 44 campsites (no showers or RV hookups), group campsites, amphitheater, public telephone
ATTRACTIONS:	Archeological sites, interpretive programs, hiking, bird-watching
NEARBY:	Grand Canyon National Park, Monument Valley Navajo Tribal Park
ACCESS:	30 miles west of Kayenta via US 160 and AZ 564

Several of the region's best-preserved prehistoric cliff dwellings are protected at Navajo National Monument. Betatakin can be seen at a distance from a viewpoint along a short hike or up close after a fairly strenuous ranger-led hike. Keet Seel can only be seen on a full-day or overnight hike.

Navajo National Monument is operated by the National Park Service in conjunction with the Navajo tribal government. The name of the monument is somewhat misleading. Although the Navajos live here now, the cliff dwellings that are the monument's main attraction were constructed centuries before the Navajos' arrival by a group of Ancestral Puebloans called the Kayenta, who are believed to be the ancestors of today's Hopi and other Pueblo peoples.

The cliff dwellings here were occupied for only a brief period in the thirteenth century, and why these well-built structures were abandoned is unclear. Archeologists suggest that it may have been at least partly due to changes in weather patterns that made the Kayenta's farming existence unproductive.

Betatakin, a Navajo word for "ledge house," perches in a large protective alcove in a canyon wall. It was occupied from about 1250 to 1300, and at its peak may have housed 125 people. The easy, paved, 1-mile round-trip Sandal Trail, which has an elevation change of about 200 feet, leads to several overlooks offering good views of the ruin; binoculars are recommended.

Those with more time and ambition would do well to arrive at the monument early for the strenuous 5-mile round-trip ranger-led Betatakin hike. It takes about 6 hours and involves descending more than 700 feet to the floor of Tsegi Canyon and later hiking back up to the rim. The hike is conducted once each day from late May through early September. Sign up for this popular hike is first come, first served and the tour is limited to twenty-five people.

The site of Keet Seel, which is Navajo for "remains of square houses," was occupied as early as A.D. 950, but the pueblo here today was built later, over the period from 1250 to about 1275. At its height Keet Seel may have been home to 150 people. However, by 1300 it had been abandoned.

The strenuous 17-mile round-trip Keet Seel hike can be accomplished in one long day by experienced hikers in excellent physical condition, but most hikers stay overnight at a primitive campground near the ruins. You must carry enough water for your trip, since none is available along the trail, and wood fires are prohibited. Rangers stationed at the ruins provide guided tours.

Only twenty people a day are given permits for the Keet Seel hike, and all hikers are required to attend a briefing before setting out. Permits are available in advance from the park office. The trail is open only from Memorial Day to Labor Day.

The monument has a fourth trail that does not offer views of any ruins. The Aspen Forest Overlook Trail instead provides a look at an ancient forest of aspen and fir, with signs identifying the area's plant life. This 1-mile round-trip moderate hike drops 300 feet in elevation, which you then have to hike back up.

Although Navajo National Monument wouldn't be considered a prime birdwatching destination—you'll want to head to southern Arizona for that—it does have a surprising number of bird species. The best bird-watching season is

The Betatakin Ruin at Navajo National Monument

from late spring through summer, when visitors might see chipping sparrows, rufous-sided towhees, American robins, rock and canyon wrens, scrub jays, violet-green swallows, hairy woodpeckers, white-throated swifts, broad-tailed hummingbirds, and mourning doves.

You'll also probably see turkey vultures, which from a distance look a lot like golden eagles. One way to tell them apart is that turkey vultures are adept at riding air currents, which enables them to glide for long periods without flapping their wings. Golden eagles exhibit more wing movement.

The national monument's visitor center has displays on the Kayenta and Navajo cultures, with exhibits of pottery, stone tools, and numerous other artifacts excavated from Tsegi Canyon. There is also a replica of a Tsegi family home and an exhibit on tree-ring dating techniques.

Several audio-visual programs are offered, including a 20-minute video on Betatakin. Navajo artists often give demonstrations of their jewelry-making and other skills, and a gift shop sells Navajo jewelry, pottery, weavings, and other crafts. Just outside the visitor center, near the beginning of the Sandal Trail, are replicas of a traditional fork-stick Navajo hogan, a sweat house, and a wagon that was among those built in the early 1900s specifically to be sold to Navajos at area trading posts.

From late May through early September rangers present nightly campfire talks at the campground amphitheater. Also during that period talks are presented regularly at the visitor center. A Junior Ranger program offers a booklet of activities that kids complete to earn Junior Ranger badges.

The monument's main campground, with an abundance of piñon and juniper, has thirty-one sites, and an additional fourteen sites are available Memorial Day through Labor Day in an overflow campground. The main campground has restrooms and drinking water, but the overflow campground does not. RVs more than 25 feet long are not permitted in either campground.

In addition, a primitive campground near Keet Seel Ruins is available, with a permit, to those hiking to the ruins.

Summer weather is generally very pleasant, although afternoon thunderstorms are common in July and August. Daytime highs in summer are usually in the 80s and occasionally the 90s, while nighttime temperatures often drop into the 50s. Winters, on the other hand, are cold and snowy, with daytime highs sometimes reaching the upper 40s and 50s and nighttime temperatures usually falling below—sometimes well below—freezing. Spring weather varies considerably, and spring winds can be biting. Fall usually has warm days and cool nights.

Nearby attractions include Monument Valley Navajo Tribal Park, about 53 miles to the northeast, with classic western scenery of majestic stone towers and lonely windswept buttes. Also relatively close by is the north rim of Grand Canyon National Park, which is discussed elsewhere in this book.

ORGAN PIPE CACTUS NATIONAL MONUMENT

HOURS/SEASONS:	Overnight; year-round
BEST TIME TO VISIT:	Late fall through early spring
AREA:	330,689 acres
ELEVATION:	1,670 feet
FACILITIES:	Visitor center, interpretive exhibits, amphitheater, nature trails, picnic tables, restrooms, 212 campsites (no showers or hookups), campground amphitheater, group campground, public telephone, RV dump station
ATTRACTIONS:	Hiking, scenic drives, wildlife viewing, bird-watching, interpretive programs
ACCESS:	22 miles south of Why via AZ 85, along the United States–Mexico border

With excellent hiking trails, two scenic driving loops, a delightful campground, a rugged backcountry, and an abundance of birds and other wildlife, Organ Pipe Cactus National Monument is a wonderful destination for those who want to explore the rugged Sonoran Desert.

Operated by the National Park Service, the monument is named for the organ pipe cactus, a large cactus of multiple stalks that is common in Mexico but

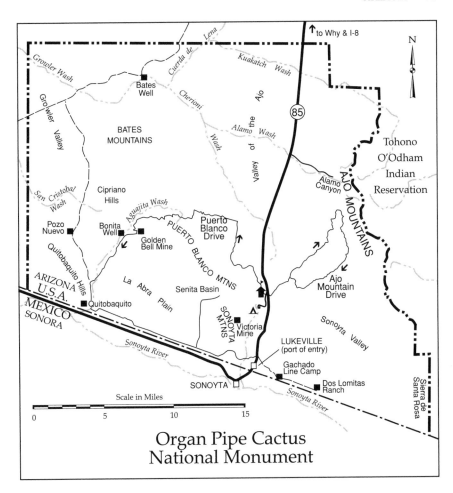

Organ Pipe Cactus
National Monument

rare in the United States. In fact, Organ Pipe Cactus National Monument contains the bulk of the species in the United States. The reason is climate: Organ pipes demand sun and heat and thrive on the south-facing slopes here that seldom see the severe frosts that are common almost everywhere else in the United States—and which would be fatal to them.

The monument is more than one particular plant, though. It is an ideal spot to experience a classic Sonoran Desert terrain, with its more than two dozen species of cacti and numerous other plants and animals that have adapted to this parched land of little rain, much sun, and extreme heat.

Throughout the monument organ pipe and saguaro cacti dominate the skyline as they tower over the other desert plants. At first glance they appear similar, especially the younger plants, but the two are actually fairly easy to distinguish: Organ pipe branches, or arms, are generally smaller in diameter; organ pipes have multiple arms that all grow from the base. Saguaros, however, have

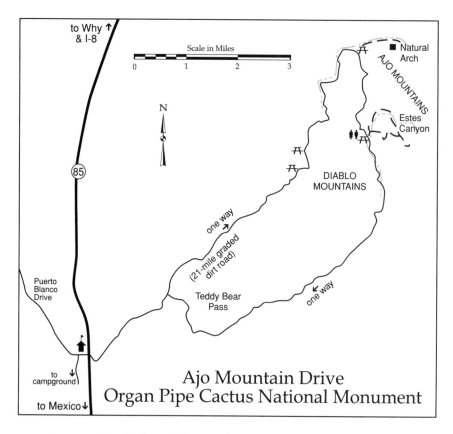

to Why ↑
& I-8

Scale in Miles

0   1   2   3

N

85

Puerto
Blanco
Drive

Natural
Arch

AJO MOUNTAINS

Estes
Canyon

DIABLO
MOUNTAINS

one way →

(21-mile graded
dirt road)

Teddy Bear
Pass

← one way

to
campground ↓

to Mexico ↓

Ajo Mountain Drive
Organ Pipe Cactus National Monument

one tall, somewhat thick trunk from which its arms emerge at varying heights above the ground.

Two scenic one-way loop drives provide relatively easy access to some of the monument's best scenery. Both roads are graded dirt, hilly and winding, with a few sections of washboard. They are also prone to flooding from July through October, so check with the visitor center before setting out. Otherwise, though, these roads are usually passable by standard passenger vehicles. However, they are not recommended for vehicles with low ground clearance, motor homes more than 25 feet long, and vehicles towing trailers. There are picnic tables and pit toilets along each route. Guidebooks are available at the visitor center and at the beginning of each drive.

Ajo Mountain Drive wanders for 21 miles along the base of the Ajo Mountains, affording good views of desert terrain, including a variety of cacti, a natural arch, and 4,408-foot Mount Ajo, the highest point in the monument. Allow about 2 hours for this trip.

The 53-mile Puerto Blanco Drive circles the Puerto Blanco Mountains, partly following the United States–Mexico border. It provides access to several trails, including a short walk to Quitobaquito Oasis, a pond and springs that is a rare

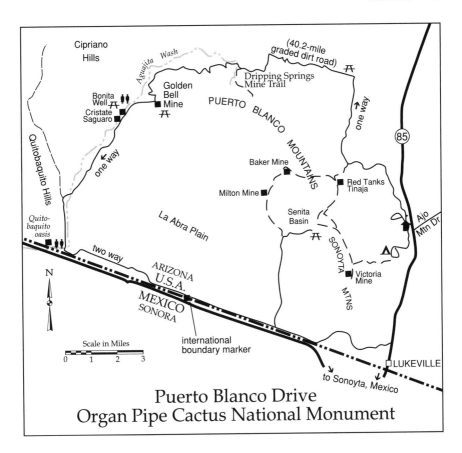

Puerto Blanco Drive
Organ Pipe Cactus National Monument

desert wetland. At another stop a short trail leads to several very odd-looking saguaros. They have abnormalities that botanists call cristates—curling, fan-shaped growths from the saguaro's trunk or arms. The Puerto Blanco Drive, including a few stops, takes most people a half day.

Visitors with high-clearance four-wheel-drive vehicles can explore a bit more of the backcountry on several unimproved dirt roads that lead to old ranch sites and abandoned mines. Information is available at the visitor center.

There are a half dozen maintained trails plus numerous opportunities for cross-country hiking here. Because of the extreme heat in the summer, the best times for hiking are from October through April, and even then hikers should avoid overexertion and overexposure to the sun and carry a gallon of water per person per day. In addition, rangers warn hikers to watch out for cactus spines and poisonous desert creatures such as rattlesnakes, Gila monsters, and scorpions. Those hiking or even walking around the campground after dark should use flashlights to avoid stepping on rattlesnakes, which are mostly nocturnal.

The monument's easiest walk is the wheelchair-accessible 0.1-mile round-trip Visitor Center Nature Trail, which meanders among a variety of Sonoran desert plants, including the park's namesake organ pipe cactus, saguaro, chainfruit and teddy bear cholla, ocotillo, and creosote bush. A trail guide is available at the trailhead.

Another fairly flat and easy walk through the desert, particularly recommended just after sunrise or before sunset, is the 1-mile round-trip Campground Perimeter Loop, which, not surprisingly, loops around the monument's main campground.

The 2.6-mile round-trip Palo Verde Trail connects the main campground with the visitor center on an easy walk that has a slight elevation change of about 150 feet. There are benches along the trail, plus a variety of cacti and other desert vegetation. This is also often a good area for seeing birds and lizards, and the trail offers good views of the rugged Ajo Mountains to the northeast.

An excellent trail for an easy to moderate walk of an hour or two is the Desert View Nature Trail, a 1.2-mile round-trip loop that climbs a short, steep hill through rugged desert terrain with numerous organ pipe and saguaro cacti. From the trail's highest point, a climb of about 300 feet from the trailhead, there are splendid views out across the national monument and of the mountains of Mexico to the south. Signs identify plants along the way and describe how people have used the plants over the years.

The Victoria Mine Trail, about 4.5 miles round trip, is a moderate hike that climbs about 300 feet through rolling hills to a 100-year-old gold and silver mine. Along the way it passes paloverde, mesquite, and cacti before arriving at the site of the mine, where there are sealed mineshafts, glory holes (short tunnels used to search for minerals), rusted smelting equipment, and the stone ruins of an old general store. From here, hikers either return on the same route or head out, with the use of a topographic map, for a view of an old stone cabin.

Combining the Estes Canyon and Bull Pasture Trails produces a 4.1-mile loop that includes a strenuous climb to a high plateau, but also the possibility of seeing bighorn sheep, javelina (also called collared peccaries), and other wildlife. It also passes among jojoba bushes and juniper trees, and provides a look at Bull Pasture, which was used by prehistoric Hohokam and more recent Tohono O'odham but was named for its use by ranchers as a winter range for their cattle. The route is a bit more gradual and less demanding when you take the Estes Canyon Trail up and the Bull Pasture back down, but either way there is an 800-foot elevation gain.

In addition to these fairly well-marked and popular trails, there are a number of routes through the backcountry that were created years ago by miners and ranchers. These are not maintained, are often difficult to follow, and require good map-reading skills. A trail guide and topographic map can be purchased at the visitor center.

Like most National Park Service properties, Organ Pipe has regulations that treat bikes as motor vehicles, which means they are prohibited from using hiking trails or going cross country. But here there are a number of dirt roads that

A strange cristate saguaro stands next to a normal saguaro in Organ Pipe Cactus National Monument

are ideal for mountain bikes, including the 21-mile Ajo Mountain Drive, which is discussed above. Information on other dirt roads open to bikes is available at the visitor center.

Horseback riders also must stay off of hiking trails, but are permitted on dirt roads in the backcountry and can also ride cross country. There is neither water nor the requisite certified weed-free feed available in the monument, so you must bring all the horses' needs with you. It is recommended that equestrians discuss their plans with rangers before traveling to the monument.

Organ Pipe Cactus National Monument is a natural botanical garden, and again visitors can see far more than its namesake organ pipe cactus here. Throughout the monument are a wide variety of plants. March through July is usually the best time to see wildflowers, with annuals such as lupine and the Ajo lily blooming first and perennials appearing later. The earlier perennials include paloverde, fairy duster, and ocotillo; these are followed by colorful cacti, including hedgehogs, cholla, saguaro, and organ pipes. The wildflower display varies greatly from year to year depending on the weather, so it's best to call ahead if wildflowers are an important reason for your visit.

About 275 species of birds have been seen in the monument, and more than 60 species are known to breed here. Year-round residents include Gambel's quail, American coots, mourning doves, greater roadrunners, Gila woodpeckers, ladder-backed woodpeckers, gilded flickers, verdins, cactus wrens, rock wrens, black-tailed gnatcatchers, northern cardinals, rufous-crowned sparrows, black-throated sparrows, and house finches. Also, watch year-round for red-tailed hawks, Harris' hawks, turkey vultures, American kestrels, and ravens.

In addition, those visiting Organ Pipe in the winter are likely to see white-throated swifts, Costa's hummingbirds, red-shafted flickers, ruby-crowned kinglets, American robins, northern mockingbirds, phainopepla, loggerhead shrikes, orange-crowned warblers, yellow-rumped warblers, green-tailed towhees, white-crowned sparrows, and green-winged teal.

The monument's mammal population, in addition to humans, includes desert bighorn sheep, mule and white-tailed deer, pronghorns, ringtails, raccoons, mountain lions, coyotes, bobcats, several types of squirrels, antelope and black-tailed jackrabbits, and desert cottontails. Javelina, also known as collared peccaries, are sometimes seen at the monument, and you're almost sure to see the mouth-shaped cutouts left in the pads of prickly pear cactus from the javelina's bite.

There are more than a dozen species of lizards in this area, including the poisonous Gila monster, which can grow up to 2 feet long. The Gila monster has a beaded-looking appearance, a dark brown on beige banded design, a rounded head, and a thick tail. The monument also has about two dozen species of snakes, including six species of poisonous rattlesnakes.

The endangered Quitobaquito pupfish, just over an inch long, lives in Quitobaquito pond and spring, partway around the Puerto Blanco scenic drive. The females are gray, while the males have a blue tint that becomes bright blue during breeding season each spring.

The visitor center has a bookstore and a variety of exhibits on the Sonoran Desert. A 15-minute slide program is presented throughout the day. From December through mid-April rangers offer guided walks plus daytime and evening talks. The monument also has a Junior Ranger program in which kids complete activities in a booklet to earn Junior Ranger badges.

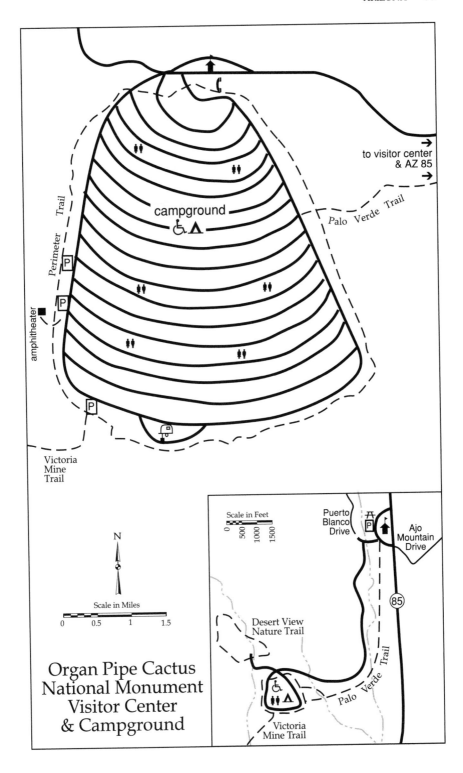

to visitor center & AZ 85

Palo Verde Trail

campground

Perimeter Trail

amphitheater

Victoria Mine Trail

N

Scale in Miles
0   0.5   1   1.5

Organ Pipe Cactus
National Monument
Visitor Center
& Campground

Scale in Feet
0   500   1000   1500

Puerto Blanco Drive

Ajo Mountain Drive

85

Desert View Nature Trail

Palo Verde Trail

Victoria Mine Trail

Birds such as this mourning dove congregate in the campground at Organ Pipe Cactus National Monument.

The spacious main campground has sites separated by typical desert vegetation, such as paloverde and creosote bush, with an abundance of cacti. It offers panoramic views, which are especially photogenic at sunset; easy access to several hiking trails; and a variety of birds. There are grills and picnic tables. A small number of sites have designated tent pads, while tenters using other sites are asked to pitch their tents in the cleared areas next to the picnic tables. RV units over 35 feet are prohibited.

Four campsites for tenters are also available in Alamo Canyon Primitive Campground, which does not have drinking water and is closed to motor homes and vehicles towing trailers. Backcountry camping is also permitted. Free permits, available at the visitor center, are required for both backcountry camping and Alamo Canyon Primitive Campground. Camping is not allowed along the scenic drives.

Summers here are hot, with daytime temperatures often exceeding 105 degrees. Winter days are usually delightful, with temperatures commonly in the 70s. Nights are usually considerably cooler than days year-round, with winter nighttime temperatures in the upper 30s and 40s and summer temperatures dropping into the 70s and sometimes even the 60s. Thunderstorms are common in August and September, and there are occasional light rains from December through March.

Visitation is highest from February through April, when hordes of retirees from northern climes (called snowbirds) descend on Organ Pipe. The quietest months at the monument are June through September.

PIPE SPRING NATIONAL MONUMENT

HOURS/SEASONS: 7:30 A.M. to 5:30 P.M. daily in summer, with Winsor Castle guided tours on the hour and half hour from 8 A.M. to 5 P.M.; 8 A.M. to 4:30 P.M. daily in winter, with Castle tours on the hour and half hour from 9 A.M. to 3:30 P.M. (Note: the monument is on Mountain Standard Time year-round.)

BEST TIME TO VISIT: Summer

AREA: 40 acres

ELEVATION: 4,990 feet

FACILITIES: Visitor center/museum, interpretive exhibits, interpretive trail, restrooms, public telephone

ATTRACTIONS: Historical exhibits, interpretive and living history programs

NEARBY: Grand Canyon–Parashant National Monument, Kaibab–Paiute Indian Reservation

ACCESS: 14 miles west of Fredonia via US 89A and AZ 389

This national monument preserves the impressive stone headquarters of a large cattle ranch and transports visitors back to the genuine Old West of the 1800s with guided tours and demonstrations of pioneer living.

Pipe Spring was one of many settlements established at the direction of Brigham Young, leader of the Church of Jesus Christ of Latter-day Saints, whose members are often called Mormons, which was headquartered in Salt Lake City. Dubbed "Winsor Castle" for early ranch superintendent Anson Perry Winsor, the ranch house was the headquarters of the church's southern Utah tithing herd, the cattle contributed by Mormon families as one-tenth of their incomes.

Built in 1870, the ranch house, actually two stone houses joined by high walls and sharing a spring, was constructed as a fort because just 4 years earlier Mormon settlers here had been killed by Navajo raiders. Happily, the thick rock walls, constructed of stone quarried from the red sandstone cliffs just west of the fort, never had to withstand an attack.

Visitors today see what is in many ways a typical nineteenth-century western ranch, located as close as possible to a reliable water source, constructed of whatever materials were at hand, and fortified to protect its inhabitants from attack.

From the visitor center, a 375-foot trail leads to the ranch house and other historic buildings, passing an orchard and gardens as well as ponds that have been used to irrigate the gardens since the 1880s. In addition to the large ranch house, there are two cabins that served as housing during construction of the main ranch house and then in 1871 as sleeping quarters for explorer John Wesley Powell's survey crew.

Also on the grounds is a corral made of juniper logs, complete with longhorn cattle. There is also the site of a dugout, built in 1863, which is considered the first permanent dwelling built at Pipe Spring.

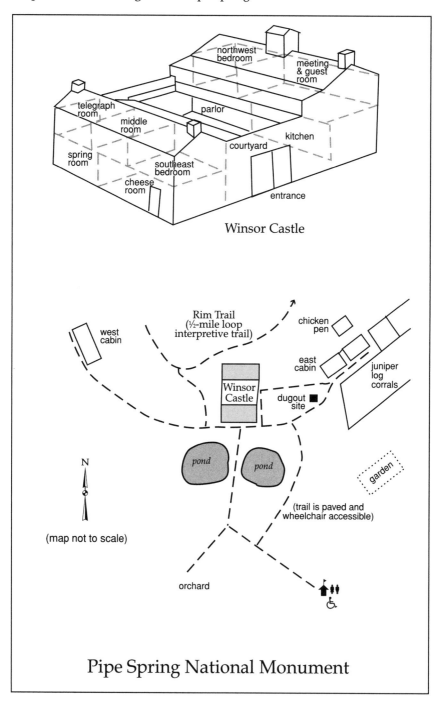

Winsor Castle

Pipe Spring National Monument

The interior of the ranch house, completely furnished as it would have been in the late 1800s, can be seen only on guided tours. Visitors see the bedrooms, the comparatively elegant parlor, a meeting room that doubled as a guest bedroom, the fully equipped cheese-making room, and the telegraph room, which served as the Arizona Territory's first telegraph office.

Perhaps the most interesting room in the house is the all-important kitchen/dining room, with the table set in Mormon fashion with plates upside down and chairs facing away from the table to facilitate kneeling for prayers.

Starting behind the ranch house, the Rim Trail, an easy 0.5-mile loop, leads up sandstone cliffs to the canyon rim, gaining about 150 feet and offering panoramic views of the surrounding countryside. Along the way are exhibits that describe the interaction of humans with the land. From the rim the trail returns through a piñon-juniper forest.

The monument's visitor center/museum has exhibits depicting the lives of both the Mormon settlers and the Navajos, Paiutes, and other American Indians of the area. A short video program describes the site's history. There is also a separate, well-stocked bookstore, a gift shop, and a snack bar operated by the Kaibab–Paiute tribe.

During the summer rangers offer guided nature walks through the grounds in addition to the tours inside Winsor Castle. A variety of talks and demonstrations of pioneer life—often in period costume—are also offered. Although topics vary, in recent years they have included weaving, quilting, yucca

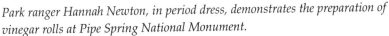

Park ranger Hannah Newton, in period dress, demonstrates the preparation of vinegar rolls at Pipe Spring National Monument.

soap-making, cheese-making, and using a woodstove to bake a tasty cinnamon-bun-type delicacy called a vinegar roll.

Summer days here are often hot, with temperatures reaching the mid-90s, and afternoon thunderstorms are common in July and August. Winters are cool to cold, with high temperatures averaging about 40 degrees; there is occasional snow. Spring weather is variable and unpredictable, and fall is usually quite pleasant.

Although the summer here is a bit warmer than most of us would like, it is the best time to visit. The monument receives its highest visitation in summer and therefore schedules most of its demonstrations and nature walks at that time. It is almost always pleasantly cool inside the stone walls of Winsor Castle even in the summer months.

Nearby is the Grand Canyon–Parashant National Monument, which is discussed elsewhere in this book. Surrounding the monument is the Kaibab–Paiute Indian Reservation, which offers a 1-mile guided hike to a canyon where a variety of petroglyphs can be seen. A campground, operated by the Kaibab–Paiute tribe, is located 0.25 mile north of the monument.

SUNSET CRATER VOLCANO NATIONAL MONUMENT

HOURS/SEASONS:	Monument dawn to dusk daily; visitor center 8 A.M. to 5 P.M. daily; closed Christmas
BEST TIME TO VISIT:	Summer through early fall
AREA:	3,040 acres
ELEVATION:	6,690 feet
FACILITIES:	Visitor center, interpretive trails, scenic drive, 42 campsites (U.S. Forest Service; no hookups or showers), picnic tables, restrooms, public telephone
ATTRACTIONS:	Interpretive exhibits, hiking, interpretive programs, wildlife viewing
NEARBY:	Wupatki and Walnut Canyon National Monuments and Grand Canyon National Park
ACCESS:	12 miles north of Flagstaff via US 89 to the scenic drive connecting Sunset Crater Volcano and Wupatki National Monuments; Sunset Crater Volcano Visitor Center 2 miles further east along this road

What must they have thought?

It was the fall of A.D. 1064, and the residents of what is now northern Arizona would have been preparing for winter—grinding corn into meal, drying fruits and berries, gathering firewood, and perhaps sewing rabbit pelts together.

Suddenly the ground began to tremble and then to shake violently. Finally, the earth swelled and opened, shooting smoke, ash, and molten lava into the sky, blanketing the region with cinders and hot lava. Sunset Crater Volcano had been born.

The eruptions continued for months, throwing ash and cinders over an area of 700 square miles, destroying homes and burying crops. After a while the eruptions subsided, but they returned periodically for at least 130 years, and by the time the eruptions stopped, sometime before 1250, a cone 1,000 feet high had been created. Unfortunately, the Sinagua and other prehistoric people of the area left no written account of their experience. It is possible that they had seen or heard of other smaller volcanos in the area, and likely that they explained it in religious terms.

While it seems logical to assume that they took the eruption as a bad omen—perhaps believing that the gods were angry with them for some reason—we don't have any proof of this. In fact, it seems curious that they would have stayed under these circumstances, but they did. Although they wisely fled from approaching lava and falling rocks, these prehistoric people didn't go far. In fact, nearby Wupatki Pueblo prospered during the times of volcanic activity, and was not abandoned until after the volcano became dormant. One recent theory is that the people stayed because they were attracted by the power of the volcano, and interpreted the end of volcanic activity as a sign that it was time to move on.

Today, Sunset Crater, operated by the National Park Service, offers an intimate view of a dormant volcano and its beautiful, rugged landscape of black basalt that has been twisted and molded into shapes both whimsical and grotesque. The volcano, surrounded by a forest of ponderosa pine and a few hardy aspen, has a cone about 1 mile in diameter at its base and a crater at its top about 300 feet deep.

Although the terrain here is primarily dark gray and black—a striking, shiny black after a rain—the crater is more colorful than might be expected. A heavy concentration of iron has left the rim of the crater a rich red, while gypsum and other minerals are credited with adding shades of yellow, purple, and green. Explorer John Wesley Powell visited in 1885 and, noting that from a distance the red rocks appeared to be on fire, named the cone Sunset Peak, from which its current name evolved.

Color also comes from the plants that struggle for life among the rocks. Lichen provides a yellow-green blanket to the dark lava, and the landscape is enlivened by bright yellow rabbitbrush and green grasses. In summer, look among the black volcanic rocks for the delicate pink flowers of the penstemon and the bright red trumpet-shaped skyrocket. Fall turns the aspen leaves from green to brilliant yellow.

The Sunset Crater Volcano Visitor Center, with exhibits on volcano formation, is among the first stops on the 36-mile scenic loop drive that also include

Wupatki National Monument, views across northern Arizona's Painted Desert, and several lava flows.

Within the monument are several trails, including the 1-mile round-trip Lava Flow Nature Trail, an easy to moderate loop that meanders through a section of the Bonito Lava Flow. Numbered signs correspond to sections in a booklet available at the visitor center, describing volcanic formations, such as the aptly named squeeze-ups, plus plants and other aspects of the lava flow.

Those who want to hike to the top of a cinder cone can choose the 1-mile round-trip Lenox Crater Trail, which, although short, is steep and considered moderate to difficult. Backcountry hiking is permitted in most parts of the monument, but backcountry hikers are advised that lava is sharp and unstable, and caution as well as sturdy thick-soled hiking boots are needed. Hiking is not permitted on Sunset Crater Volcano.

Wildlife to watch for includes Abert's squirrels, cottontail rabbits, jackrabbits, coyotes, and pronghorns. Birds you're likely to see include noisy, bright blue Steller's jays, hairy woodpeckers, white-breasted nuthatches, mountain chickadees, and violet-green swallows.

Bonito Campground, operated by the U.S. Forest Service, is located across the road from the visitor center just outside the monument entrance. It is usually

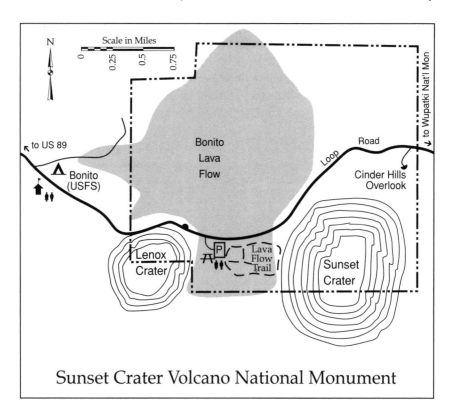

Sunset Crater Volcano National Monument

open from late May through mid-October, and often fills by mid-afternoon from June through August. Maximum vehicle length allowed at the campground is 35 feet.

Ranger programs are usually presented in June, July, and August. These might

Snow stands out against the jet-black lava along the Lava Flow Nature Trail at Sunset Crater Volcano National Monument.

include talks on volcano formation and other subjects at either the visitor center or Bonito Campground, or a guided walk on the Lava Flow Nature Trail.

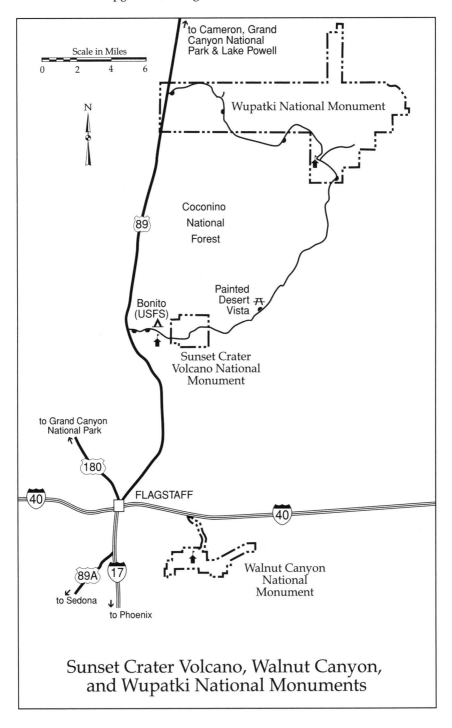

Sunset Crater Volcano, Walnut Canyon, and Wupatki National Monuments

There is also a Junior Ranger program in which kids complete activities in a booklet to earn a Junior Ranger badge.

Conditions here are windy most of the year, and abrupt weather changes should be expected at any time. Summer days often see temperatures in the 80s and occasionally higher, and short afternoon thunderstorms are common from July through September. Autumn and spring days are usually mild, and winters are cool to cold, although sunny days can be very pleasant. Heavy snow is possible from fall through spring.

The monument, created in 1930, owes its existence at least in part to Hollywood. Plans by filmmakers in 1928 to set off a landslide at the volcano so outraged the people of Flagstaff that they pressured the federal government to step in, which it did with the creation of the national monument.

Nearby attractions include Wupatki and Walnut Canyon National Monuments and Grand Canyon National Park, which are discussed elsewhere in this book.

TONTO NATIONAL MONUMENT

HOURS/SEASONS:	8 A.M. to 5 P.M. daily; closed Christmas
BEST TIME TO VISIT:	Winter
AREA:	1,120 acres
ELEVATION:	2,805 feet
FACILITIES:	Visitor center, bookstore, interpretive exhibits, picnic tables, restrooms, public telephone
ATTRACTIONS:	Archeological sites, interpretive programs, hiking, bird-watching, wildlife viewing, wildflower viewing
NEARBY:	Tonto National Forest and Apache Trail Scenic Byway
ACCESS:	Just south of Roosevelt Lake on AZ 88

Cliff dwellings dating back 700 years, birds and other wildlife, and hiking trails that zigzag up saguaro-studded hillsides are the lures at this National Park Service facility. This was the home of the ancient Salado culture, a skilled and adaptable people who learned to survive, and even prosper, in the harsh and unforgiving Sonoran Desert. They lived here only for about three centuries and, as with many other prehistoric Southwestern cultures, little is known about where they came from or where they went.

This area had been inhabited by the Hohokam (see the section on Casa Grande National Monument) from as early as the late eighth century A.D., but by 1150 the residents differed greatly from the Hohokams of the past and their contemporary Hohokam neighbors to the south. Their pottery was significantly different, their construction techniques differed, and perhaps most significant, the Salado buried their dead while the Hohokam cremated theirs.

Archeologists have offered several theories about the Salado. Some argue that they were a group of Puebloans who came from the north and displaced the Hohokam, while others theorize that the Salado migrated from the south, from present-day Mexico. There are also theories that they were a blending of Hohokam with other cultures, and some recent archeologists believe that the Salado were direct descendants of the Hohokam whose different lifestyles were simply a result of the different terrain and climate in this region compared to the main Hohokam stronghold further south.

Like the Hohokam the Salado used irrigation for farming, and grew corn, beans, squash, amaranth, and cotton. They also ate the fruits of cactus, prickly pear cactus pads, and the beans and seeds of various desert plants, such as mesquite. The Salado hunted primarily deer and rabbits, but they also hunted bighorn sheep, prairie dogs, gophers, woodrats, fish, birds, and even snakes and lizards.

The Salado women created beautiful polychrome pottery, and it is believed that the men were the weavers, creating sandals and baskets from yucca and agave leaves and shirts and other clothing from the cotton they grew. Archeologists believe that some of the textiles and pottery were created specifically for trade with other groups.

The heart of the Salado culture was in the Tonto Basin, a wide valley where the Salt River and Tonto Creek converge, as well as the surrounding mountains. They built multistoried pueblos, both in the open and in protected caves. Although ruins of pueblos with up to 150 rooms have been discovered, most had

The prehistoric cliff dwellings at Tonto National Monument

fewer than 20 rooms. The weather took its toll on the unprotected structures, and pot hunters and vandals contributed a great deal of damage in the late 1800s

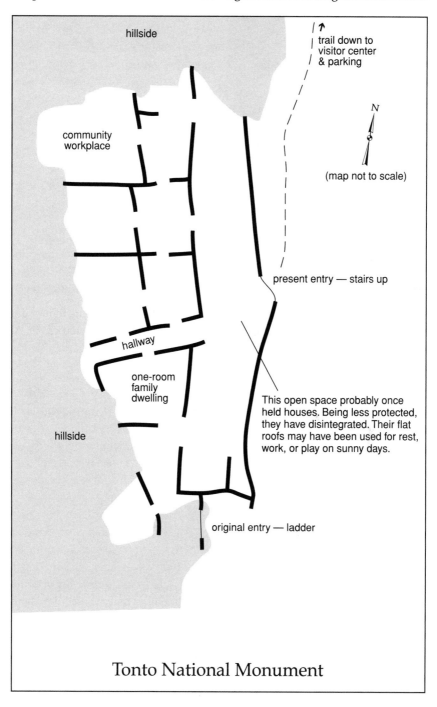

hillside

trail down to
visitor center
& parking

community
workplace

N

(map not to scale)

present entry — stairs up

hallway

one-room
family
dwelling

This open space probably once
held houses. Being less protected,
they have disintegrated. Their flat
roofs may have been used for rest,
work, or play on sunny days.

hillside

original entry — ladder

Tonto National Monument

Saguaro and other cacti cover the hillside that leads to the prehistoric cliff dwellings at Tonto National Monument

and early 1900s. In addition, much of the Salado's past is now buried beneath the surface of Roosevelt Lake, created by the construction of a dam in 1911.

The best preserved Salado sites are the stone and mud cliff dwellings at Tonto National Monument, built in the 1300s.

The Lower Ruin, which is easily seen from the monument's parking lot, contains about twenty rooms built into a shallow cave that welcomed the low winter sun but shaded the rooms from the hot summer sun, which is higher in the sky. It is believed that from forty to sixty people lived here, and along its walls, some blackened by cooking and heating fires, are marks left by the residents' hands and fingers from smoothing wet mud plaster. About 300 feet north of the Lower Ruin are the much-weathered remains of what archeologists believe was an annex of about a dozen additional rooms.

The Lower Ruin is accessed by a 1-mile round-trip self-guided trail (a booklet is available at the visitor center). The trail is moderately difficult, and although paved it gains 350 feet and offers little shade. Benches along the trail offer a welcome respite from the climb as well as panoramic views of the valley stretched out below. Allow at least an hour for this walk. The hike must be started by 4 P.M.

The Upper Ruin, the largest of the national monument's sites, contains about forty rooms—thirty-two on the ground floor and eight on the second story. Because the cave floor slopes steeply, rooms are built on terraces, so the rooms at the back of the cave are up to 20 feet higher than the ones closer to the opening.

Access to the Upper Ruin is on ranger-guided hikes only. These hikes along an unpaved 3-mile round-trip trail gain 600 feet in elevation and are rated moderate to difficult. The guided hikes are offered several times a week from November through April only, and are limited to fifteen people. Reservations are required and fill quickly. Allow 3 to 4 hours for this hike. Sturdy hiking boots are recommended.

The cliff dwellings were likely occupied for only a hundred years or so, and by 1450 the Salado were gone. It is not known why they left, although a number of prehistoric peoples left their homelands during this period, possibly because of climate changes. There are theories that the Salado joined either the Hopi to the north or the Zunis to the northeast, and some archeologists speculate that they moved south into Mexico.

This is also a good area for wildlife viewing; more than 100 bird species and a variety of mammals and reptiles are found here.

Commonly seen year-round are Gambel's quail, mourning doves, Gila woodpeckers, Say's phoebes, common ravens, verdins, cactus and canyon wrens, curved-billed thrashers, northern cardinals, canyon towhees, black-throated sparrows, brown-headed cowbirds, and house finches. During spring and fall also watch for Bell's vireos, northern mockingbirds, and western kingbirds.

Mammals you might see include jackrabbits and cottontails, whitetail and mule deer, coyotes, javelina (also called collared peccaries), chipmunks, skunks, and several species of squirrel. Also present, although seldom seen, are mountain lions, bobcats, and ringtails. There are more than a dozen types of snakes, including three species of rattlesnakes, plus Gila monsters and other lizards.

A variety of wildflowers often bloom from February through March, while barrel cacti usually bloom between April and June.

There is a 1-mile road from the monument boundary to the visitor center and trailhead parking lot. The picnic area is located along the entrance road about 0.5 mile from the park boundary, and visitors with especially long vehicles, such as motor homes over 30 feet that are also towing a vehicle, are advised to leave them in the picnic area parking lot and walk the remaining half a mile to the visitor center because the visitor center parking lot has a limited turning radius.

The visitor center has exhibits on the Salado and presents an 18-minute video program. A variety of talks and guided walks are offered from January through April (in addition to the guided hikes discussed above), and the monument also has a Junior Ranger program in which children can earn badges and certificates by completing various activities.

The busiest time at the monument is during the mild winters, when high temperatures are usually in the 60s and lows in the 30s. Summer sees low temperatures in the 70s and highs often between 100 and 120 degrees. The sun can be intense, and hikers are advised to wear hats, use sunscreen, and carry water.

Nearby is the Tonto National Forest, with hiking, mountain biking, and camping opportunities, plus fishing and boating at Roosevelt Lake. The Apache Trail Scenic Byway offers a beautiful drive from the Phoenix area to the monument, which is partly paved but also includes 22 miles of maintained gravel road that wind through the national forest and past several lakes, including Roosevelt Lake.

TUMACÁCORI NATIONAL HISTORICAL PARK

HOURS/SEASONS: 8 A.M. to 5 P.M. daily; closed Thanksgiving and Christmas
BEST TIME TO VISIT: Fall through spring
AREA: 46 acres
ELEVATION: 3,260 feet
FACILITIES: Visitor center/museum, interpretive exhibits, historic trail, picnic tables, restrooms, public telephone
ATTRACTIONS: Historic sites and exhibits, interpretive programs, hiking, bird-watching
NEARBY: Tubac Presidio State Historic Park
ACCESS: Follow signs from I-19 exit 29, about 45 miles south of Tucson

This historic site tells the story of the first Europeans to come to what is now Arizona and their relationship with the native Pima people who were already here. The park, which is operated by the National Park Service, has a museum, a garden, an historic cemetery, bird-watching opportunities, and a trailhead for the Juan Bautista de Anza National Historic Trail (for hiking and horseback riding). However, its main attraction is the massive adobe mission church, *San José de Tumacácori,* built in the early 1800s.

The first mission here—in fact the first in what is now Arizona—was established in 1691 by Father Eusebio Francisco Kino, an Italian-born Jesuit priest. Over the years additional missions were built, there were several Pima revolts, and the Jesuits were replaced by the Franciscans.

In 1794 Franciscan Father Narciso Gutiérrez arrived at Tumacácori and began planning the construction of a large new church to replace the modest one that had been built years earlier by the Jesuits. Work began about 1800, but lack of money caused delays and the walls rose very slowly. It was not until 4,000 head of the mission's cattle were sold in 1821, a year after Father Gutiérrez's death, that work resumed in earnest and the church was finally ready to welcome its first parishioners. Even then, though, the church bell tower was never finished.

Visitors to the church today see an imposing adobe structure that is really a mixture of styles, including Egyptian-style columns and Roman and Moorish statue niches. The nave (the main central hall) is 75 feet long, with a choir loft, elaborate main altar, and four side altars. There are no pews, as the parishioners stood or knelt during services. Much of the interior plaster and decorations are gone, as the church was abandoned and roofless for more than 70 years.

Behind the nave is a domed sanctuary, and the still unfinished bell tower stands to the east, its fired red bricks contrasting with the main building's tan adobe. Adjoining the church is a patio, which is surrounded by the ruins of the

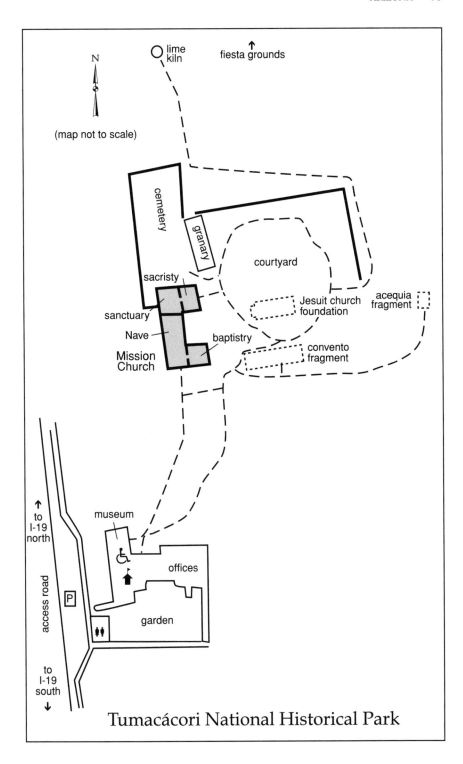

N

(map not to scale)

lime kiln

fiesta grounds

cemetery

granary

courtyard

sacristy

sanctuary

Nave

baptistry

Mission Church

Jesuit church foundation

acequia fragment

convento fragment

to I-19 north

access road

P

to I-19 south

museum

offices

garden

Tumacácori National Historical Park

priest's lodgings, workrooms, and store rooms. There are also the remains of an earlier church, a cemetery, and a lime kiln.

The visitor center/museum, contained in an historic building constructed in 1937, has exhibits on the Spanish missionaries and local Pima and Apache Indians. These include several statues of saints, including St. Francis, that were carved in Mexico in the 1700s. There is also a variety of American Indian pottery, baskets, and other crafts. Look for the attractive Pima coiled baskets, created of bear grass, strips of yucca, and black devil's claw pod.

There are also "Please Touch" exhibits containing materials from the church construction, plus the components of a stick game played by Pima children. A 14-minute video shows what life here was like 200 years ago.

Just outside the museum, a shady courtyard contains a fountain and a garden that includes many of the types of fruit trees, herbs, and other plants that would have been cultivated here by the mission priests. Although these have primarily been reintroduced by the National Park Service, a fig tree along the garden's east wall is believed to be a descendent of the mission's original fig trees, brought here by Father Kino in the 1690s.

Guided tours of the park are offered daily during the winter; on weekends from September through May local crafts workers demonstrate the making of a variety of items, including baskets, pottery, paper flowers, and tortillas.

Annual events include a two-day fiesta the first weekend in December, with crafts, foods, children's activities, and music from the Hispanic and American

An impressive early nineteenth-century Spanish mission is one of the highlights at Tumacácori National Historical Park.

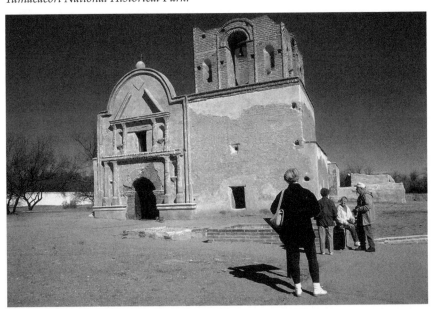

Indian cultures of the area. Occasionally, the park is opened in the evening during a full moon.

Twice a year, in March or April and October, High Mass is celebrated in the church, with a local priest and traditional music. All participants are required

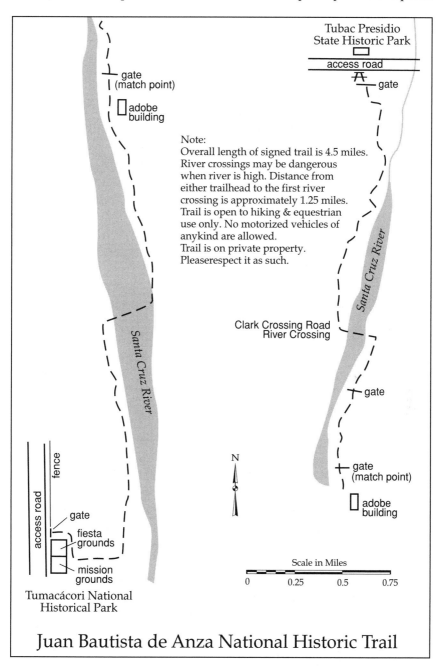

Note:
Overall length of signed trail is 4.5 miles. River crossings may be dangerous when river is high. Distance from either trailhead to the first river crossing is approximately 1.25 miles. Trail is open to hiking & equestrian use only. No motorized vehicles of anykind are allowed.
Trail is on private property. Pleaserespect it as such.

Tubac Presidio State Historic Park

access road

gate

gate
(match point)

adobe building

Santa Cruz River

Clark Crossing Road
River Crossing

gate

N

gate
(match point)

adobe building

Santa Cruz River

fence

access road

gate

fiesta grounds

mission grounds

Tumacácori National Historical Park

Scale in Miles

0   0.25   0.5   0.75

Juan Bautista de Anza National Historic Trail

to dress in traditional Spanish or American Indian clothing. Because attendance is limited, advance reservations are required.

The Anza Trail, a 4.5-mile hiking and horseback riding trail, leads from Tumacácori to Tubac Presidio State Historic Park, (which is discussed later in this section. The trail follows a portion of the route taken by Spanish explorer Captain Juan Bautista de Anza of Tubac in 1776 from Culiacan, Sinaloa to California, in an expedition that culminated with the founding of San Francisco. Informational displays are set up along the flat, easy trail, which involves fording the Santa Cruz River several times.

Numerous riparian and desert plants are seen along the trail, including stands of elderberry, mesquite, desert willow, cottonwood, desert grasses, and cactus. There are also numerous lizards and birds. Hikers should carry drinking water, as the river water is not safe to drink.

This short trail is only a very small part of what will eventually be the Juan Bautista de Anza National Historic Trail, expected to run 600 miles from within Mexico, through Arizona, and west to San Francisco, following as closely as possible the more than 1,800-mile route of de Anza's 1775 journey. There is also a section of the trail now open in Anza-Borrego Desert State Park in southern California, and additional sections are being developed from Rio Rico to Tumacácori and between Tubac and Green Valley.

Although Tumacácori's best bird-watching is along the Santa Cruz River, almost anywhere in the immediate park vicinity provides good bird-watching possibilities.

Among the many species to watch for year-round are mourning and white-winged doves, Gambel's quail, great blue herons, Gila woodpeckers, vermilion flycatchers, Say's phoebes, verdins, white-breasted nuthatches, brown creepers, Bewick's wrens, mockingbirds, curved-billed thrashers, ruby-crowned kinglets, phainopepla, loggerhead shrikes, yellow-rumped warblers, western meadowlarks, red-winged blackbirds, cardinals, and pyrrhuloxia. Red-tailed hawks, American kestrels, turkey vultures, ravens, and roadrunners are also seen year-round. From spring through fall watch for a variety of hummingbirds, including black-chinned, broad-billed, broad-tailed, and rufous.

Temperatures at the park are especially pleasant from late fall through early spring, with daytime highs often in the 60s and 70s. On the other hand, summers are hot, with temperatures often soaring over 100 degrees, with monsoon rains common in July and August.

Nearby attractions include Tubac Presidio State Historic Park, which is about 4.5 miles north via I-19 or about 3 miles along the frontage road, or the Anza Trail. The state park contains the eroded adobe ruins of an early Spanish fort, built after a Pima Indian revolt against Spanish domination in 1751. The park has an impressive underground exhibit that shows the fort's foundation, lower walls, and floor. A museum has exhibits that include detailed models of the original presidio, displays on the local Pima and Apache Indians, the Spanish missions and military, and daily life here in the 1700s.

TUZIGOOT NATIONAL MONUMENT

HOURS/SEASONS: 8 A.M. to 7 P.M. daily in summer; 8 A.M. to 5 P.M. daily in winter; closed Christmas

BEST TIME TO VISIT: Fall through spring

AREA: 42 acres

ELEVATION: 3,545 feet

FACILITIES: Visitor center/museum/bookstore, interpretive exhibits, interpretive trails, restrooms, public telephone

ATTRACTIONS: Archeological sites, interpretive programs, hiking, bird-watching

NEARBY: Montezuma Castle National Monument, Dead Horse Ranch State Park, Jerome State Historic Park

ACCESS: I-17 exit 287, then west on AZ 260 to Cottonwood, follow Main Street (AZ 279) toward Clarkdale and follow signs

Tuzigoot was home to the southern branch of the Sinaguan people from about A.D. 1000 until about 1400. The ancient village is perched on a hilltop and has a commanding view in all directions. Excavated in the 1930s, the village is open to exploration via a paved trail, and another short trail provides excellent bird-watching along the edge of a marsh. The monument's name, Tuzigoot (pronounced TWO zee goot) is derived from an Apache word for "crooked water," which refers to nearby Peck's Lake.

This national monument, managed by the National Park Service, provides a close-up look at the lives of the Sinagua, who are believed to have emigrated here from the San Francisco Peaks area near present-day Flagstaff. They built the first dozen rooms, on the hill's highest point, just before A.D. 1000. Then, over the next few hundred years, additional rooms and several separate structures were added, until at its height the pueblo stood three stories high with an enclosed courtyard and 110 rooms housing several hundred people.

The structure is made from limestone and sandstone rocks that were cemented together with clay mud, and roofs were made of mud, grasses, reeds, and bark supported by poles and sticks of cottonwood, sycamore, juniper, and pine. Interior walls were plastered with a reddish clay, and rooms were entered through roof openings, which also provided light and ventilation.

Visitors to the site today might think this must have been a scenic but lonely spot, sitting atop a hill in the middle of nowhere. But Tuzigoot was not an isolated outpost. In its time there were about fifty pueblos throughout the

A typical room of the prehistoric Sinagua people, as depicted in the museum at Tuzigoot National Monument

Verde Valley, spaced approximately every 1.7 miles along the Verde River and its tributaries. Apparently this was also a popular stop for more distant groups as well. Decorated pottery, clay figurines, shells, feathers, and other items found during the excavation show that a lively trading network existed with cultures to the north and south.

Like the other Sinagua of the Verde Valley, the residents of Tuzigoot were relatively well off, at least in terms of life in the prehistoric American Southwest. The Verde River provided plenty of water and they had generally better weather than their Sinagua cousins and the Ancestral Puebloans to the north, and the Salado, Hohokam, and Mogollon peoples to the south. The reliable water sources of the Verde Valley—*verde* is Spanish for green—plus a growing season of almost 200 days, made this an ideal farming location. There was also an abundance of native plants and wild animals.

Although residents of Tuzigoot were primarily farmers, by necessity they were also potters, creating plain but functional brown or reddish-brown storage containers. They also made stone tools including knives, axes, hammers, drills, and arrow points. They were especially skilled weavers, producing blankets, sleeping mats, and baskets. They also created attractive jewelry of shells from the Gulf Coast (which they received in trade) decorated with turquoise and other stones.

The 0.25-mile Ruins Loop Trail winds from the visitor center/museum to and through the Tuzigoot Pueblo. Interpretive signs along the route discuss the construction of the structures, the daily life of the Sinaguans, and identify vari-

The hilltop ruins at Tuzigoot National Monument

ous plants, explaining how they were used by prehistoric people. A trail guide is available at the visitor center/museum.

Another 0.25-mile round-trip trail, which also starts at the visitor center/museum, is a joint effort with the Arizona Department of Game and Fish. The hard-surface Tavasci Marsh Overlook Trail leads to views of Tavasci Marsh, one of Arizona's few freshwater marshes, where you're likely to see a wide variety of birds and other wildlife.

Birds to look for near the marsh and elsewhere in the monument include year-round residents great blue herons, wood ducks, common mergansers, pied-bill grebes, red-tailed hawks, Gambel's quail, American coots, rock and Bewick's wrens, European starlings, red-winged blackbirds, and song sparrows. During winter also watch for Brewer's blackbirds, great-tailed grackles, dark-eyed juncos, white-crowned sparrows, and American robins. Birds dropping by in summer include violet-green and cliff swallows, Bell's vireos, yellow warblers, mourning doves, and black-chinned hummingbirds.

Mammals seen in the marsh include river otters, beaver, muskrats, and even deer and javelina (also called collared peccaries).

Tuzigoot's visitor center/museum, built in the 1930s, is a full-fledged museum with excellent exhibits, including many of the artifacts recovered from the Tuzigoot excavation. Rangers present frequent talks and guided tours of the pueblo, and a Junior Ranger Program offers an activity guide for kids.

Summer daytime temperatures often reach the 90s and winters are moderate, with daytime temperatures usually in the 50s and 60s. Short afternoon thunderstorms are common from June through October.

Among nearby attractions are Jerome State Historic Park, which explores a different period of this region's history—the Wild West mining days of the late 1800s. Dead Horse Ranch State Park, from which you can see Tuzigoot in the distance, offers camping, hiking, bird-watching, and fishing. Also nearby is Montezuma Castle National Monument, which is discussed elsewhere in this book.

WALNUT CANYON NATIONAL MONUMENT

HOURS/SEASONS:	9 A.M. to 5 P.M. daily December through February; closed Christmas; 8 A.M. to 5 P.M. daily March through May; 8 A.M. to 6 P.M. daily June through August; 8 A.M. to 5 P.M. daily September through November
BEST TIME TO VISIT:	Summer
AREA:	3,541 acres
ELEVATION:	7,000 feet
FACILITIES:	Visitor center/museum, interpretive exhibits, interpretive trails, picnic tables, restrooms, public telephone
ATTRACTIONS:	Archeological sites, hiking, bird-watching, wildlife viewing, interpretive programs
NEARBY:	Sunset Crater Volcano and Wupatki National Monuments
ACCESS:	7.5 miles east of Flagstaff via I-40, take exit 204 and go south 3 miles on the access road

It would seem that the name says it all—*Sinagua*—Spanish for "without water." But the story of these prehistoric people, who built their homes in caves in this 400 foot-deep canyon far from any reliable year-round water sources, is much more complicated. And, in addition to protecting these 800-year-old cliff dwellings and teaching about the Sinagua, Walnut Canyon National Monument offers hiking, a surprising range of plant habitats, and opportunities to see a wide variety of birds and other wildlife.

Although Walnut Canyon was likely a summer stopping point for prehistoric peoples who hunted in the area thousands of years ago, it was not until about 1125 that the canyon had its first and only year-round residents—the Sinagua. As with most other cultures of this period it is not clear exactly who the Sinagua were or where they came from. They may have been immigrants from elsewhere or possibly broke away from another local group, such as the Ancestral Puebloans (also called Anasazi), Hohokam, or Mogollon.

Actually, the Sinagua had been in the area since before A.D. 600, living in one-room pit houses and using dry farming techniques to grow corn, beans, and squash. In the late eleventh century there was a marked increase in the Sinaguan population and their architecture evolved from simple pit houses to above-ground pueblos (see the section on Wupatki National Monument below), to the cliff dwellings here in Walnut Canyon.

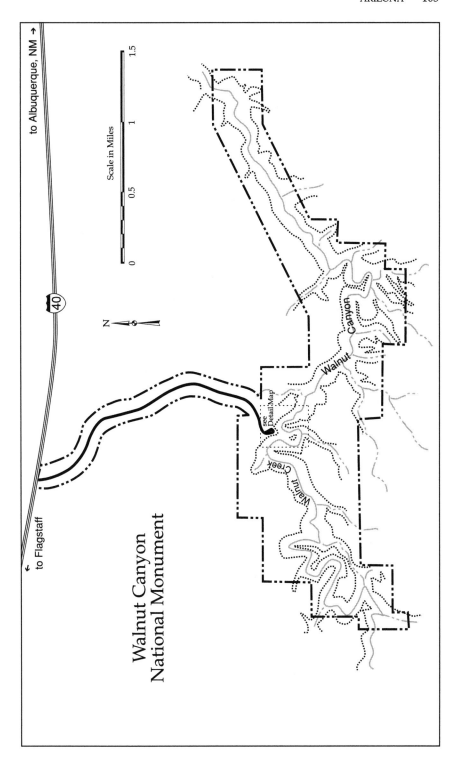

to Albuquerque, NM →

to Flagstaff ↓

40

Scale in Miles

0   0.5   1   1.5

N

Walnut Canyon
National Monument

see
DetailMap

Walnut Canyon

Walnut Creek

Hikers pause to examine the ruins of the cliff dwellings at Walnut Canyon National Monument.

It was first theorized that the Sinagua's good fortune was related to an eruption of nearby Sunset Crater Volcano in 1064–65, which would have made the land more fertile. But recent studies indicate that climate changes—specifically more rain—plus the introduction of more sophisticated farming techniques and an increase of trade with other prehistoric peoples—may have led to population increases.

Even after the construction of the canyon cliff dwellings, the Sinagua continued to farm along the canyon rims. The main water source, Walnut Creek, probably did not flow year-round, but the Sinagua captured as much water as possible by building rock dams across the mouths of washes. In addition, water was retrieved from pockets in the canyon's bedrock floor, and the Sinagua made large ceramic water storage jars that could hold up to 35 gallons each. The Sinagua also protected their crops from sometimes ferocious winds, and the evaporation winds cause, by constructing windbreaks of rock and brush.

In addition to their crops, the Sinagua likely ate the fruits and berries of more than a dozen wild plants, including wild grape, serviceberry, elderberry, prickly pear cactus, and Arizona black walnut, for which the canyon is named. The piñon provided firewood, lumber, nuts, and sap, which was used as both an adhesive and dye. The yucca was the source of fibers, food, and soap. The Sinagua also hunted mule deer, bighorn sheep, rabbits, squirrels, and even packrats.

In addition to hunting, farming, and hauling water, the Sinagua weaved. They made the mats they used for beds and wove their clothing. They also created simple but functional pottery, usually deep brown or reddish brown, and various types of jewelry from shell and turquoise. Their jewelry materials, as well as their cotton, came from another major activity of the Sinagua—trading. Archeologists believe that the Sinagua were some of the area's most prominent merchants, trading not only for things they wanted for themselves, but also to acquire goods that were then traded to other groups.

At its peak, there were probably several hundred people living in Walnut Canyon. Curiously, they stayed for only a little over 100 years before relocating to Anderson Mesa, just a few miles to the southeast, and by 1250 Walnut Canyon was deserted. It is generally believed that the Sinagua were eventually assimilated into the Hopi culture.

The main attraction of the monument, which is operated by the National Park Service, is its dozens of cliff dwellings, which are built in shallow caves along the faces of limestone cliffs. Archeologists believe that these homes were built by the Sinagua women, who constructed the walls by cementing crudely shaped limestone rocks together with clay and plastering them with more clay. Wood from the canyon's juniper trees was used to reinforce the small, T-shaped doorways. Most of the homes faced south or east to catch the warming rays of the sun, and archeologists speculate that the few homes that face north or west were used only in the summer months.

There are two paved trails at Walnut Canyon. The fairly level Rim Trail is an easy way to get excellent views of the ruins and canyon scenery from above, as it follows the canyon's north rim to several viewpoints. It then continues through a piñon-juniper forest past a small pueblo and pit house. The round-trip distance is about 0.75 mile.

The significantly more strenuous Island Trail is only about 0.9 mile round trip, but it drops 185 feet into the canyon and the 240 steps back up to the rim can be tiring, especially for those not used to the 7,000-foot elevation. This loop hugs the canyon wall as it circles a promontory called Third Fort Island, providing access to twenty-five cliff dwelling rooms plus views across the canyon

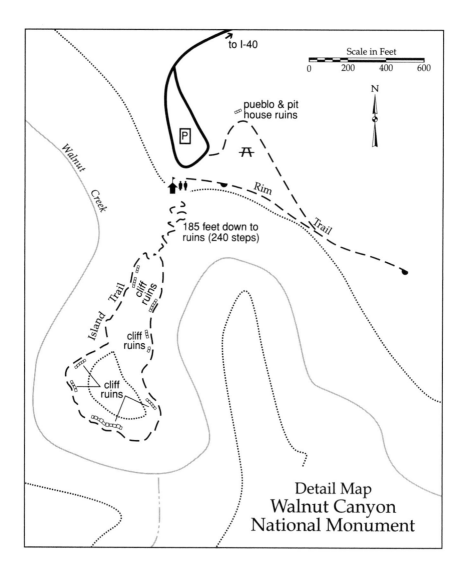

Detail Map
Walnut Canyon
National Monument

to additional homes. The Island Trail also takes you through a variety of habitats, ranging from the Upper Sonoran Desert, where you'll see yucca and cactus, to a cooler and more lush forest of mixed conifers, such as Douglas fir, that you would expect to see in the Pacific Northwest. Entrance to the trail closes 1 hour before the park closes.

From June through August, usually on weekends and sometimes Wednesdays, the Park Service offers a variety of organized activities, ranging from half-hour talks at a rim overlook to guided off-trail hikes to cliff dwellings and other historic sites in areas of the park that are usually off limits. Reservations may be required for the guided hikes, and the number of participants is limited. No independent backcountry hiking is permitted.

Because of a wide variety of life zones that were created by great differences in sunlight and available moisture, you'll find plants here that are usually seen as far north as Canada or as far south as Mexico. Watch for cliffrose, columbine, Rocky Mountain iris, sego lily, fourwing saltbush, Indian paintbrush, evening primrose, golden aster, goldeneye, sunflower, and a variety of ferns and grasses.

There is also a rich variety of wildlife, including desert cottontails and black-tailed jackrabbits, several species of squirrels and chipmunks, Ord's kangaroo rats, coyotes, gray foxes, three species of skunks, mule deer, and pronghorn. Also present, although you're unlikely to see them, are mountain lions. Rangers say that mountain lion attacks are rare, but have occurred, and advise visitors to travel in groups and not allow children to run ahead on the trails.

Practically every Walnut Canyon visitor at any time of year will see Steller's jays, American robins, and the plain titmouse. Also spotted fairly often year-round are red-tailed hawks, wild turkeys, northern flickers, acorn and hairy woodpeckers, mountain chickadees, white-breasted nuthatches, mountain bluebirds, western bluebirds, and rufous-sided towhees. During summer you might also see western tanagers and turkey vultures. Those visiting in winter should be on the lookout for Townsend's solitaires and dark-eyed juncos.

Your first stop at the monument should be the visitor center/museum to examine the exhibits and ask about recent wildlife sightings. Then head out on one of the trails (both trailheads are at the visitor center) to see the ruins first-hand. Vehicles towing trailers or other vehicles with a combined length of more than 40 feet, may have a problem turning in the somewhat tight parking lot.

The busiest time at the monument is summer, when days will be hot in the sun but pleasantly cool in the shade. Winters are cold, and snow and ice may temporarily close the Island Trail. Spring and fall are usually mild, but snow can occur. Windy conditions are common year-round.

Close by are Wupatki and Sunset Crater Volcano National Monuments, which are discussed in their own sections of this book, and the famed Grand Canyon National Park.

WUPATKI NATIONAL MONUMENT

HOURS/SEASONS: Monument dawn to dusk daily; visitor center 9 A.M. to 5 P.M. daily; closed Christmas

BEST TIME TO VISIT: Spring through fall

AREA: 35,253 acres

ELEVATION: 4,900 feet

FACILITIES: Visitor center, interpretive exhibits, interpretive trails, scenic drive, picnic tables, restrooms, public telephone.

ATTRACTIONS: Archeological sites, hiking, interpretive programs, bird-watching, wildlife viewing

NEARBY: Sunset Crater Volcano and Walnut Canyon National Monuments and Grand Canyon National Park

ACCESS: 12 miles north of Flagstaff via US 89 to the scenic drive connecting Sunset Crater Volcano and Wupatki National Monuments; the Wupatki Visitor Center is 21 miles north along this road

Wupatki National Monument is a bit of a puzzle. Generally considered an archeological site from the prehistoric Sinaguan culture, there is also evidence of the presence of other peoples of the day. These impressive ruins and artifacts are not from any one particular culture, but are representative of practically every group that was living in the Southwest in the first 300 or so years of the last millennium. What we seem to have is a prehistoric melting pot, or at least a crossroads where various cultures met and to some extent intermingled.

At Wupatki you'll see the traditional Sinagua undecorated reddish-brown pottery, but archeologists have cataloged well over 100 other types of pottery as well. The Wupatki Pueblo architecture itself is a mixture, with masonry work and T-shaped doorways common to Ancestral Puebloan (Anasazi) builders, a ball court that looks a lot like those the Hohokam built, and a circular amphitheater one would expect at a Sinaguan pueblo.

It is generally agreed that this was a major trading center, and the exchange of goods was also likely to mean the exchange of ideas, but archeologists cannot agree on just what was happening here. Were these different cultures working and living side by side, or did the Sinagua copy others' architectural styles and simply import their pottery and other crafts?

Another mystery is just how the residents of this area reacted to the eruption of nearby Sunset Crater in the winter of A.D. 1064–65. It likely started with tremors, but soon the ground exploded, raining rocks and cinders, and burying their farmland in lava and ash. Periodic eruptions continued for well over 100 years.

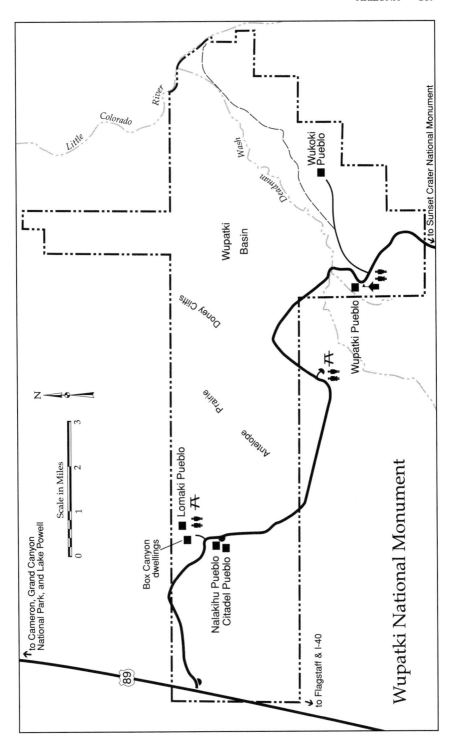

Wupatki National Monument

A trail provides easy access to the remains of Wupatki Pueblo at Wupatki National Monument.

The people naturally would have immediately fled from the falling rocks and molten lava, and from our modern perspective, realizing that these prehistoric people did not have the knowledge to understand what was happening, we might conclude that they were terrified and ran as far away as possible, never to return. But they did return, and in fact did not leave until the volcanic activity had ceased in the mid-thirteenth century.

The monument, managed by the National Park Service, protects numerous archeological sites, and visitors can see five stone pueblos, hike several short trails, and watch for birds and other wildlife.

The main attraction is Wupatki Pueblo, a 100-room apartment building, three stories high in places, that in the 1100s was the largest building for at least 50 miles in any direction. It was built into a sandstone outcropping and constructed of the materials at hand—red sandstone slabs, blocks of pale beige limestone, and chunks of brown basalt, cemented neatly together with clay. Beams of fir and pine were hauled from nearby mountains, and roofs were covered with brush, bark, and mud. Walls on the pueblo's north and west sides protected it from the prevailing winds, and rooms were aligned south and east to take advantage of the warming winter sun. Ground-level rooms had no doorways, but were entered through roof openings using ladders.

Construction is believed to have begun in about 1106, with more rooms added every 20 to 40 years, but by 1250 the pueblo was deserted. There is little agreement on why the residents of Wupatki Pueblo left. It may have been because of climate changes, or internal strife, possibly a spiritual quest, or maybe a combination of these and other factors. One intriguing theory is that it was the power of the Sunset Crater Volcano that attracted the Wupatki Pueblo residents, and when volcanic activity ceased they interpreted that as a sign to move on. It is believed that some relocated to other Sinaguan communities to the south, while others were assimilated into the Hopi and Zuni cultures to the east. The name Wupatki is a Hopi word that means "long cut house."

Access to Wupatki Pueblo is via the Wupatki Ruins Trail, an easy 0.5-mile round-trip walk that starts at the visitor center. The trail takes you around the pueblo ruins, allowing entry into one room (where early park personnel actually lived) and the adjacent amphitheater, ball court, and blowhole. The latter is a strange geological phenomenon in which a small opening in the earth, connected to large underground fractures, appears to breathe, sucking air in and blowing it out. A trail guide is available, keyed to numbers along the paved walkway. The pueblo ruins can also be viewed from an overlook.

The Lomaki Ruins Trail is an easy 0.5-mile round-trip walk that leads past several small ruins to the Lomaki ruins, which include the remains of nine rooms. The name Lomaki comes from the Hopi word for "beautiful house."

Ruins of three other smaller pueblos can be seen from short (0.2-mile) paved walks along the monument's 36-mile loop road, which connects both Wupatki and Sunset Crater Volcano National Monuments to US 89. Among these is the impressive Wukoki Pueblo, which has about a half dozen rooms, including a three-story structure almost 20 feet tall that appears to be a tower. An archeologist who explored the site in the late 1800s described Wukoki as resembling "an old castle as it looms above the plain." It is believed that two or three families lived at Wukoki. The name is Hopi for "Big House."

Hikers looking for scenic views should head for the Doney Mountain Trail, a 1-mile round-trip hike to the top of 5,589-foot Doney Mountain. The easy to moderate trail starts at the picnic area, at the sign "View Point and Lunch Area."

No independent backcountry hiking is permitted in the monument, although in recent years a guided Discovery Hike into the desert backcountry has been offered Saturdays in summer. Contact the monument office for the current schedule. In summer rangers occasionally present talks on the ruins and their builders, and also in summer rangers are usually stationed at the major sites to discuss the ruins and answer questions. The visitor center provides information on programs and includes a museum with exhibits on the geologic and human history of the area.

Although Wupatki National Monument is not a prime wildlife viewing destination, you may see desert cottontails, prairie dogs, and maybe even a mule deer. More common, though, are collared, fence, big spiny, and whiptail lizards, plus gopher snakes and birds such as northern orioles, sage sparrows, cinnamon teals, and mountain bluebirds. Those visiting in spring—generally April and May—and again in late summer should be on the lookout for colorful bunches of small wildflowers, including globemallow and fleabane.

Wupatki receives most of its visitors during summer, when daytime temperatures often reach the 90s and occasionally exceed 100 degrees. Short afternoon thunderstorms are common from July through September. Autumn and spring days are usually mild, and winters are cool to cold, with occasional snow. Conditions are often windy from spring through fall.

Nearby are Sunset Crater Volcano and Walnut Canyon National Monuments, as well as Grand Canyon National Park, all of which are discussed elsewhere in this book.

Right: *Numerous lakes at Rocky Mountain National Park provide double views of the snowcapped mountains.*

COLORADO

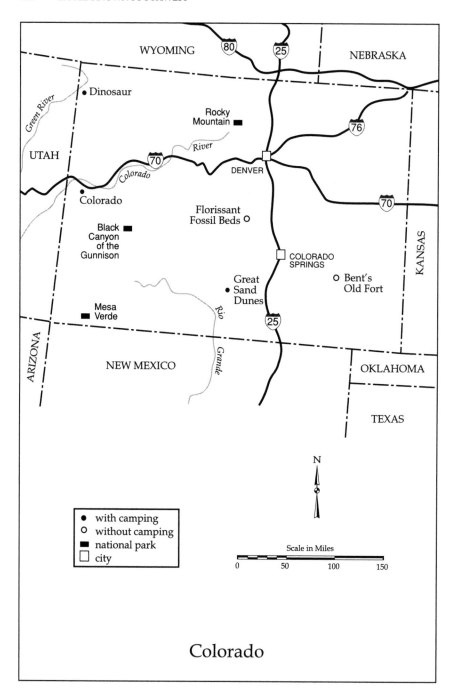

Colorado

To many people, Colorado is the Rocky Mountains—and with good reason. The Rockies are the backbone of North America, and Colorado embraces their heart. In the more than fifty peaks that soar above 14,000 feet, there are forests of fir and pine, clear streams and rivers, and a wealth of wildlife. These mountains are perfect for all sorts of outdoor recreation throughout the year, from hiking and rafting to skiing and snowshoeing.

But Colorado is not only mountains. Its 104,247 square miles also encompass the wheat and corn fields of the vast eastern prairies and the high plateau country of the west. The state's name, Spanish for "red," comes from its picturesque red rocks and soil, especially evident at places such as Colorado National Monument. Colorado also offers much for those interested in history, from the remains of ancient dinosaurs to prehistoric American Indians to nineteenth-century pioneers.

Federal park lands here include the famous Rocky Mountain National Park, known for its scenic beauty and abundance of wildlife, and Mesa Verde National Park, which contains awe-inspiring cliff dwellings. Colorado is also home to a new national park, the appropriately named Black Canyon of the Gunnison. Other little-known but fascinating destinations include the giant sand box of Great Sand Dunes National Monument and Bent's Old Fort National Monument, an historic frontier trading post.

COLORADO'S NATIONAL PARKS

The national parks of Colorado, taken as a group, offer an extremely wide range of experiences, from hiking above tree line to exploring villages built hundreds of years ago.

ROCKY MOUNTAIN NATIONAL PARK

Picture-perfect Rocky Mountain National Park is one of the most beautiful spots in America, with scenic views that literally take your breath away. Here you can see and explore snowcapped peaks, shimmering alpine lakes, and lush valleys where deer and elk graze. Covering 415 square miles, the park contains seventeen mountains over 13,000 feet elevation, including its highest, Longs Peak, at 14,255 feet.

But scenic beauty is only part of the story here. What really sets the park apart is its variety of plants and animals. As you rise and descend in altitude, the landscape, flora, and fauna change dramatically.

The lower areas, from about 7,500 to 9,000 feet, contain lush forests of pine and juniper on southern slopes and Douglas fir on the cooler northern slopes. Blue spruce and lodgepole pine cling to streamsides, there are occasional groves

Elk are seen frequently, especially in the early fall, at Rocky Mountain National Park.

of aspen, and elk and mule deer are abundant. As you move higher you reach a subalpine zone, which is dominated by forests of Engelmann spruce and subalpine fir interspersed with meadows of wildflowers. This is also home to bighorn sheep, the unofficial mascot of the park. Climbing above 11,500 feet, you'll find the air gets thinner and trees become gnarled and stunted, finally disappearing altogether as you reach the forbidding alpine tundra, a bleak, rocky world with many of the same plants found in the Arctic.

Although this is a wonderful destination for hikers and backpackers, with dozens of splendid trails for virtually all ability levels, Rocky Mountain National Park is also a good destination for those disinclined or not physically able to hit the trail.

Trail Ridge Road, the park's primary east-west thoroughfare, is one of America's most scenic highways and, with a high point of 12,183 feet, the highest continuously paved road in the United States. It offers scenic viewpoints galore and access to both major trails and short, relatively easy walks. The road is usually open from Memorial Day into October, depending on snowfall. Motorists should allow 3 hours one-way for the 48-mile drive.

Among the many trails, an especially scenic easy walk is the short trail around Sprague Lake, where you often see towering, snowcapped mountain peaks and glaciers not only in the flesh, so to speak, but also reflected in the lake. There are numerous day-hiking possibilities, such as the beautiful Emerald Lake Trail. Probably the most challenging but also rewarding overnight trek is the hike/climb up the east side of Longs Peak.

The park is home to herds of elk, which often congregate in meadows and on mountainsides, plus mule deer, beavers, coyotes, river otters, moose, bighorn sheep, and numerous songbirds and small mammals, including chipmunks and squirrels.

The park has several visitor centers, with interpretive exhibits, bookstores, and rangers who can help prospective hikers plan their excursions. A variety of guided walks and hikes—including snowshoe hikes in winter—are scheduled, and evening campground programs take place regularly.

There are five campgrounds in the park, plus additional camping just outside the park on national forest lands.

MESA VERDE NATIONAL PARK

Mesa Verde is the largest archeological preserve in the United States and has by far the most impressive cliff dwellings in the Southwest. The park's earliest known inhabitants built underground pit houses on the mesa tops, but during the thirteenth century moved into shallow caves and constructed complex cliff

Mesa Verde National Park preserves what many consider the finest examples of prehistoric cliff dwellings in the Southwest.

dwellings. Although a massive construction project, these homes were only occupied for about a century; they were abandoned in about 1300 for reasons as yet undetermined.

The Cliff Palace, the park's largest site, is a four-story apartment building set neatly into a cave under the protective rim of a cliff. Accessible by guided tour only, it is reached by a 0.25-mile downhill path. Another ranger-led tour climbs a ladder to explore the interior of Balcony House. These tours are given only in summer and early fall.

Several other sites are accessible only in summer, but winter visitors have the advantage of being able to take a ranger-led tour to Spruce Tree House, another major cliff-dwelling complex, which is also open to self-guided tours year-round.

None of the trails to the Mesa Verde sites are strenuous, but the 7,000-foot elevation can make the treks tiring for visitors who are not used to the altitude. For those who want to avoid hiking and climbing, the 12-mile Mesa Top Road makes a number of pit houses and cliff-side overlooks easily accessible by car.

Although the main reason to come to Mesa Verde is to see the ancient cliff dwellings and other archeological sites, which involves a bit of walking and climbing, the park does offer several longer day hikes into scenic Spruce Canyon and one of its side canyons. Hikers are required to register at the ranger's office before setting out.

The park's Chapin Mesa Museum, open daily year-round, houses artifacts and exhibits related to the history of the area, including those from other nearby prehistoric sites. Morefield Campground, which is usually open from mid-April to mid-October, has almost 500 sites, and during the summer rangers give nightly campfire programs.

BLACK CANYON OF THE GUNNISON NATIONAL PARK

A national monument since 1933, the Black Canyon of the Gunnison became a national park on October 21, 1999, in a ceremony in which President Bill Clinton called the Black Canyon a "true natural treasure;" adding, "its nearly vertical walls, rising a half mile high, harbor one of the most spectacular stretches of wild river in America."

This deep chasm, carved by 2 million years of erosion, ranges in depth from 1,730 to 2,700 feet, but its width at its narrowest point along the Gunnison River is only 40 feet. The canyon was avoided by early American Indians and later Utes and Anglo explorers, who believed that no human could survive a trip to its depths. The deepest and most spectacular 14 miles of the 53-mile canyon make up the national park, which, at 30,300 acres, is among the United States' smallest.

The canyon can be viewed from the South Rim Road, site of the visitor center, and the lesser-used North Rim Road. Short paths branching off both roads lead to splendid overlooks with signs explaining the canyon's unique geology.

Considered totally inaccessible by early explorers, this still-forbidding canyon is now Black Canyon of the Gunnison National Park.

There are hiking trails along both rims, backcountry hiking routes down into the canyon, and excellent trout fishing for anglers willing to make the trek to the canyon floor.

This is a good place for wildlife viewing, and you are likely to see chipmunks, ground squirrels, badgers, marmots, and mule deer. Although they are not frequently seen, there are also black bear and cougars. Peregrine falcons can sometimes be spotted along the cliffs, and you may also see red-tailed hawks, golden eagles, and white-throated swifts.

The park provides challenges for experienced rock climbers who tackle its sheer canyon walls. In winter, much of the park is closed to motor vehicles, but it is a delight for cross-country skiers and snowshoers. There are campgrounds on both rims; these are usually open from May through October.

Adjacent to Black Canyon of the Gunnison is Curecanti National Recreation Area. This recreation area is made up of three very different reservoirs and is a paradise for boaters and anglers. There are boat rentals, boat tours, and a variety of hiking trails, often with splendid views of the lakes. This is also a good wildlife-viewing destination, and anglers catch rainbow, brown, and Mackinaw trout and kokanee salmon. There are four major campgrounds plus several smaller campgrounds, and backcountry and boat-in camping is also permitted.

COLORADO'S NATIONAL MONUMENTS AND OTHER LESSER-KNOWN FEDERAL LANDS

Colorado possesses the smallest number of national monuments and historic sites of the four states coverered in this book. These sites offer an extremely large range of experiences and variety of scenery.

BENT'S OLD FORT NATIONAL HISTORIC SITE

HOURS/SEASONS: 8 A.M. to 5:30 P.M. daily June through August; 9 A.M. to 4 P.M. daily September through May. Closed Thanksgiving, Christmas, and New Year's Day

BEST TIME TO VISIT: Summer

AREA: 768 acres

ELEVATION: 4,000 feet

FACILITIES: Visitor center, interpretive exhibits, picnic tables, restrooms, public telephone

ATTRACTIONS: Historical sites and exhibits, guided tours, living history and interpretive programs, bird-watching

NEARBY: Koshare Indian Museum and Kiva

ACCESS: 7 miles east of La Junta via Colorado Highways 109 and 194

Bent's Fort must have been a very welcome sight to travelers along the Santa Fe Trail in the mid-1800s. This imposing adobe trading post, with two corner towers that gave it a castlelike appearance, was the only permanent white

The imposing fort at Bent's Old Fort National Historic Site stands watch over the plains of eastern Colorado.

settlement between Missouri and the towns of Santa Fe and Taos, in what was then northern Mexico. Bent's Fort has been carefully reconstructed by the National Park Service and furnished with reproductions, and a visit to this oasis on the plains of eastern Colorado will take you back to the very early days of the Old West, when the white man's presence was just beginning to be felt.

Brothers Charles and William Bent and partner Ceran St. Vrain built this trading post along the north bank of the Arkansas River, then the boundary between the United States and Mexico, to provide a trade network connecting eastern U.S. merchants, Rocky Mountain fur trappers, Cheyenne and other Plains Indians, and Mexican settlers in Santa Fe and Taos.

Charles Bent and St. Vrain, both Missouri men who had become fur trappers and traders, joined forces in 1830 to haul goods from Missouri to sell in Santa Fe, a distance of more than 800 miles. They began trading with the local Cheyenne, primarily for buffalo skins, at a stockade near present-day Pueblo, Colorado. In 1833, the two men and Charles' younger brother William decided to build a trading post closer to the Cheyenne's hunting grounds.

Due mainly to a lack of lumber, the trading post was built of adobe bricks, made of mud mixed with straw and dried in the sun, each measuring 19 inches by 9 inches by 4 inches. Mexican workers, skilled in this type of construction, were brought up from Taos to build the fort in the style of Mexican haciendas. The resulting design was of a large square compound with rooms along the perimeter and opening onto a central courtyard. The project was completed in 1834 and named Fort William, for the younger Bent Brother who had supervised

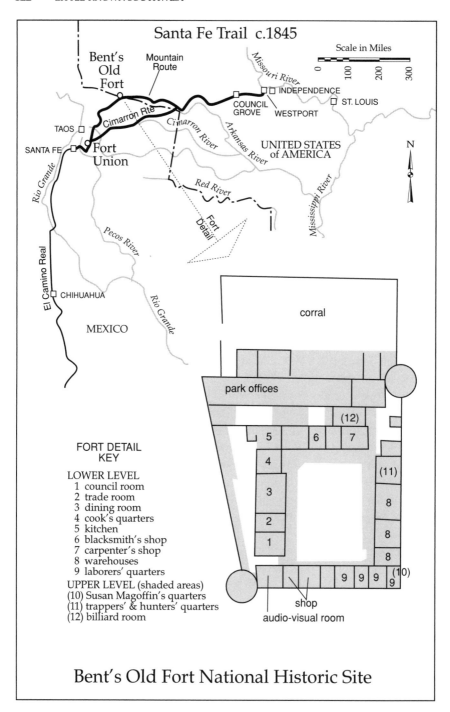

Santa Fe Trail c.1845

Bent's Old Fort National Historic Site

FORT DETAIL KEY

LOWER LEVEL
1 council room
2 trade room
3 dining room
4 cook's quarters
5 kitchen
6 blacksmith's shop
7 carpenter's shop
8 warehouses
9 laborers' quarters
UPPER LEVEL (shaded areas)
(10) Susan Magoffin's quarters
(11) trappers' & hunters' quarters
(12) billiard room

construction and later directed the trading activities at the fort. The trading post later came to be called Bent's Fort.

Charles Bent spent much of his time on the Santa Fe Trail, transporting goods between Missouri and the Mexican settlements, and St. Vrain established and ran stores in Santa Fe and Taos. During the Mexican-American War in 1846, the fort became a staging area for the U.S. military. Under the leadership of Col. Stephen Kearny the fort hosted more than 1,600 troops, along with their horses, wagons, and other equipment and supplies. With Charles Bent's scouting help, Kearny captured Santa Fe without firing a shot, and then appointed Charles as the first U.S. governor of the territory. However, Bent's government career didn't last long—he was assassinated in Taos during a short-lived rebellion in 1847.

After Charles' death, William and St. Vrain continued in business for several years until St. Vrain sold his share of the company to William and moved permanently to New Mexico. Then in 1849, after the breakout of a cholera epidemic among the Cheyenne and several other problems, William abandoned the fort. However, he built a new stone trading post about 40 miles down river in 1853. The new trading post came to be known as Bent's New Fort, while the original trading post took on the name Bent's Old Fort.

The old adobe fort was subsequently used by several other traders, for a while acted as a stage station, and became headquarters for several cattle ranches. However, by the early 1900s the fort had been abandoned, and many of its adobe bricks and other building materials had been carted off by local settlers.

In 1926 the site was given to the Daughters of the American Revolution, who later transferred it to the Colorado Historical Society. The site eventually came under the jurisdiction of the National Park Service, which conducted a thorough archeological excavation before completely reconstructing the trading post in 1976.

The fort's thirty-three rooms include a kitchen with an adjoining pantry, a cook's room, and a dining room; a trade room with robes, pelts, and blankets; blacksmith and carpenter shops; William Bent's office and bedroom; quarters for Mexican laborers, trappers, and soldiers; and a billiard room. There is a small, square watchtower over the main gate, as well as two cylindrical corner towers. The fort's defenses include two 6-pound cannons.

Of particular human interest is the upstairs corner room in which trader Samuel Magoffin and his 18-year-old wife Susan stayed in late July 1846 while traveling from Missouri to Santa Fe. Susan suffered a miscarriage, and during her recovery at the fort took meticulous notes in her diary, including the observation that the fort "fits my idea of an ancient castle." She also noted that the trading post was extremely noisy. "Col. Kearny has arrived," she wrote, "and it seems the world is coming with him."

A 0.25-mile walk on a paved path leads from the parking lot and entry station to the fort. Although the fort is open year-round, the best time to visit is during summer, when hosts in period costume greet visitors and there are demonstrations of frontier life, such as blacksmithing, adobe-making, trapping,

Park ranger Jennifer Leezer, in period dress, makes her way through the courtyard at Bent's Old Fort National Historic Site.

cooking, and medical and survival skills. Historically accurate reproduction trade goods plus a variety of publications, including a book based on Susan Magoffin's diary, are sold in the fort's trade room.

A 20-minute film, "Castle of the Plains," is shown year-round. From June through August 45-minute guided tours, beginning on the hour, are offered daily. Annual events include a children's program called Kid's Quarters in mid-June, the Santa Fe Trail Encampment in late July, and an 1840s Christmas celebration in early December.

Because of the proximity of the Arkansas River, this is a good spot for bird-watching, with recorded sightings of well over 100 species. Watch for various ducks and geese, plus great blue herons, American kestrels, ring-necked pheasants, killdeer, mourning doves, common nighthawks, western kingbirds, barn swallows, American robins, European starlings, common yellowthroats, blue grosbeaks, lazuli buntings, lark sparrows, house sparrows, and red-winged blackbirds.

Summer daytime temperatures at the historic site range from the low 80s to just over 100 degrees. Short afternoon thunderstorms, sometimes accompanied by hail, are fairly common in the summer. Winter days are usually sunny, but daytime temperatures vary greatly—from zero to 65 degrees—and although snowfall is usually light, heavy snow is not unheard of.

Nearby, in La Junta, the Koshare Indian Museum and Kiva exhibits one of the finest collections in the Southwest of works by early-twentieth-century Taos artists, plus an excellent selection of other works featuring American Indians both as artists and subjects. The Koshare Dancers, a nationally acclaimed troop of Boy Scout Explorers, perform in the museum's own Great Kiva, a circular chamber traditionally used for religious rites by Southwestern tribes.

COLORADO NATIONAL MONUMENT

HOURS/SEASON:	Overnight; year-round
BEST TIME TO VISIT:	Fall
AREA:	20,454 acres
ELEVATION:	5,787 feet
FACILITIES:	Visitor center/bookstore, interpretive exhibits, nature trails, picnic areas, restrooms, 80 campsites (no showers or hookups), public telephone
ATTRACTIONS:	Hiking, wildlife viewing, bird-watching, rock climbing, horseback riding, biking, photography, interpretive programs, camping, cross-country skiing
ACCESS:	West entrance is 15 miles west of Grand Junction at I-70 exit 19; east entrance is 5 miles southwest of Grand Junction via Horizon Drive

The 32 square miles of Colorado National Monument, much of it more than 2,000 feet above the Colorado River Valley, is a colorful maze of red, steep-walled canyons filled with an array of delicately sculpted sandstone monoliths. The monument is part of the Colorado Plateau, which also includes such stellar areas as Grand Canyon and Bryce Canyon National Parks. The rock sculptures and sheer walls here are the result millions of years of water and wind erosion that have combined with a series of upward lifts to create striations on the canyon walls.

Much of this National Park Service property can be appreciated from viewpoints easily reached by car or bike. The 23-mile Rim Rock Drive, which was built during the Great Depression, snakes through dramatic Fruita Canyon and offers panoramic views of fanciful and bizarre natural stone monuments as well as the cliffs and mesas beyond.

However, the best way to truly experience this rugged land is on foot or cross-country skis, and the monument offers trails varying in length from several hundred yards to 17 miles round trip. Many of the short, easy trails lead

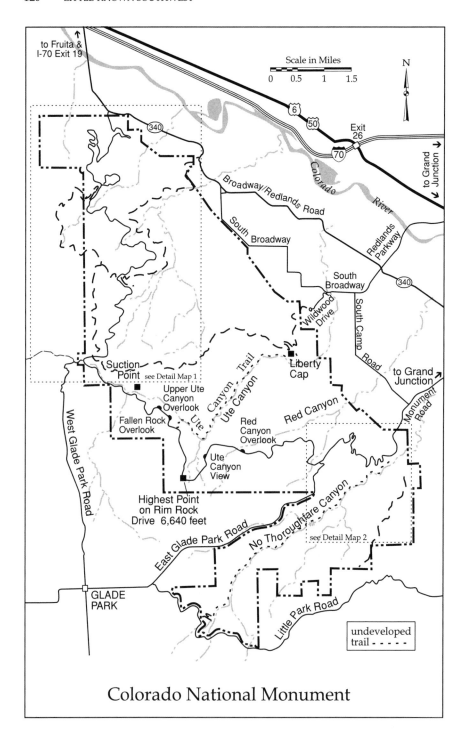

Colorado National Monument

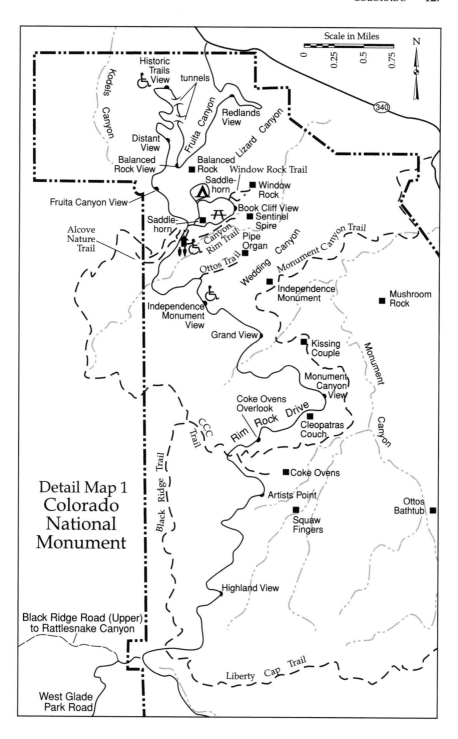

Scale in Miles

0   0.25   0.5   0.75

N

340

Kodels Canyon

Historic Trails View   tunnels

Redlands View

Fruita Canyon

Lizard Canyon

Distant View

Balanced Rock View

Balanced Rock

Window Rock Trail

Saddle-horn

Window Rock

Fruita Canyon View

Book Cliff View

Saddle-horn

Sentinel Spire

Alcove Nature Trail

Canyon Rim Trail

Pipe Organ

Wedding Canyon

Monument Canyon Trail

Ottos Trail

Independence Monument

Mushroom Rock

Independence Monument View

Grand View

Kissing Couple

Monument Canyon View

Monument Canyon

Coke Ovens Overlook

Rim Rock Drive

Cleopatras Couch

CCC Trail

Black Ridge Trail

Coke Ovens

Detail Map 1
Colorado
National
Monument

Artists Point

Ottos Bathtub

Squaw Fingers

Highland View

Black Ridge Road (Upper) to Rattlesnake Canyon

Liberty Cap Trail

West Glade Park Road

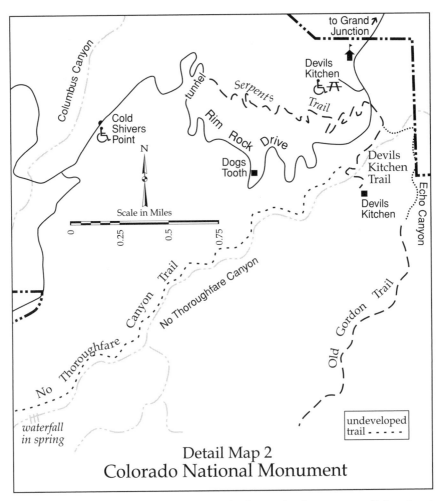

Detail Map 2
Colorado National Monument

to spectacular canyon overlooks, while the longer backcountry trails head out across the mesas or down into the canyons. Strange formations such as Window Rock, the massive rounded Coke Ovens, the boulder-strewn Devils Kitchen, the barely touching Kissing Couple, and the free-standing Independence Monument—which can be seen from the road—are easily reached by foot. All of the trails can be accessed from trailheads along Rim Rock Drive, and distances mentioned below are round trip.

For an easy 1-hour walk, head out on the 1-mile Canyon Rim Trail, which follows the edge of a cliff to spectacular views of the colorful rock formations in Wedding Canyon. An even shorter walk, the easy 0.5-mile Window Rock Trail, winds through a piñon-juniper woodland to an overlook with impressive views of Wedding Canyon, as well as a number of the monument's more spectacular rock formations.

The fairly easy 1-mile Ottos Trail has gentle inclines as it leads to an overlook with dramatic views of a number of towering rock formations. The Coke Ovens Trail, also 1 mile and fairly easy, winds to an overlook of the huge Coke Ovens formations.

Moderately rated trails include the 2-mile Alcove Nature Trail, a self-guided nature trail along a bench, and the 4.5-mile Serpents Trail, built in the 1920s, which climbs steadily over more than fifty switchbacks.

To get down into the monument, rather than viewing the canyons from above, hikers need to tackle one of the longer backcountry trails. The relatively difficult 12-mile Monument Canyon Trail drops 600 feet from the plateau into the canyon, passing by many of the monument's more dramatic rock formations, including the aptly named Kissing Couple and the stately Independence Monument.

If you'd like some panoramic views of the countryside, even to the canyonlands of Utah, try the Black Ridge Trail. This is the national monument's highest-elevation trail, reaching to more than 7,000 feet. It follows an old road through rugged terrain, climbing slowly to Black Ridge and offers views into Devils Canyon. Allow about 6 hours for the moderate 11-mile hike, but avoid it in wet weather when the clay surface becomes slippery.

The monument's longest hike is 17-mile No Thoroughfare Trail, which drops from the canyon rim on a maintained trail but soon becomes an undeveloped route through a beautiful wilderness canyon with sheer 400-foot walls and two delightful waterfalls that appear during spring runoff and after summer thunderstorms. There is a 1,600 foot elevation change on this hike. Allow two days for this moderate to difficult backpacking trek.

The backcountry is hot and dry and has little shade, so be sure to carry plenty of water.

Horseback riding is permitted on the monument's longer backcountry trails. However, some trails have steep and narrow sections that may make riding unsafe, so those with horses should discuss their plans with rangers before setting out. Rock climbing is also permitted in the monument, but because of safety considerations, climbers should check with rangers on the best spots before going.

Those visiting in winter can sometimes trade in their hiking boots for cross-country skis. Especially good, assuming there's enough snow, is Liberty Cap Trail, which meanders across gently sloping Monument Mesa through a piñon-juniper forest and sagebrush flatlands. The trail is 14 miles round trip, but cross-country skiers may want to turn back before the last mile and a half, which drops sharply into the Grand Valley.

Mountain lions and bighorn sheep are among the monument's residents, although they are only occasionally seen. However, most visitors have a good chance of spotting mule deer, desert cottontails, antelope ground squirrels, rock squirrels, and chipmunks. There are also numerous lizards. Watch for collared lizards—identified by its black and yellow neck ring—as well as whiptails, side-blotched, and sagebrush lizards. Rangers warn that the monument is also home to rattlesnakes and poisonous scorpions, so you'll want to watch where you put your feet and hands.

Birders should be on the lookout for Gambel's quail, violet-green swallows, canyon wrens, piñon jays, and white-throated swifts. There are also peregrine falcons, ravens, turkey vultures, red-tailed hawks, and golden eagles. Bald eagles are occasionally seen in the area during the winter.

Near the western entrance is the national monument headquarters and visitor center/bookstore, which features exhibits on geology and history and a slide show. During the summer there are back porch talks and other interpretive programs, plus campfire programs Friday evenings.

The monument's Saddlehorn Campground, located in a piñon-juniper forest near the visitor center, has a mixture of sunny and shaded sites. Backcountry camping (with a free permit) is permitted in most areas of the monument.

While the monument is worth visiting at any time of year, the best time is fall, when the air is crisp but not cold, the cottonwood trees turn a brilliant gold, and the summer crowds have departed. Summers are usually hot and dry, with high temperatures ranging from 80 to 100 degrees, while winter days are relatively mild, with temperatures ranging from 20 to 40 degrees. Those visiting in May and June will want to carry insect repellent to combat the clouds of gnats that invade at that time.

DINOSAUR NATIONAL MONUMENT

HOURS/SEASONS:	Overnight; year-round
BEST TIME TO VISIT:	Summer through fall
AREA:	210,000 acres
ELEVATION:	4,500 to 9,000 feet
FACILITIES:	Visitor centers (one with a dinosaur quarry), interpretive exhibits, nature trails, picnic tables, boat ramps, restrooms, 132 campsites (no showers or hookups), public telephone
ATTRACTIONS:	Dinosaur quarry, hiking, scenic drives, whitewater boating, fishing, horseback riding, wildlife viewing, bird-watching, interpretive programs, archeological and historic sites
NEARBY:	Flaming Gorge National Recreation Area
ACCESS:	Colorado entrance is 2 miles east of the town of Dinosaur via US 40; Utah entrance is 20 miles east of Vernal via US 40 and UT 149

There is a tremendous amount to do at this national monument, from hiking and backpacking to whitewater rafting and examining the bones of ancient di-

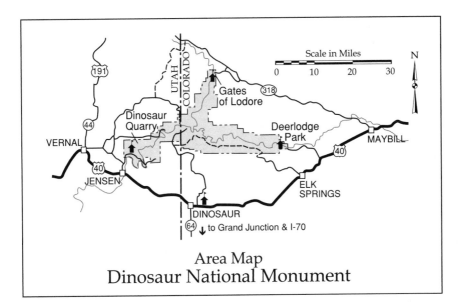

Area Map
Dinosaur National Monument

nosaurs. Dinosaur National Monument, which is operated by the National Park Service, is in many ways two separate parks, divided by the Utah–Colorado border. In the Utah section it offers a close-up look at the world of dinosaurs; in Colorado the monument is a scenic delight of colorful rock, deep river canyons, and a Douglas fir forest.

Both sides, though, have hiking trails, scenic drives, camping opportunities, an abundance of wildlife, and visitor centers with exhibits, bookstores, and rangers who can help you make the most of your visit.

One hundred and fifty million years ago this area was warm and dry, with adequate vegetation that made it a good habitat for dinosaurs, both mild-mannered vegetarians and their aggressive carnivorous cousins. As they died, most of their skeletons decayed and disappeared, but in at least one spot floodwaters washed their carcasses into a river channel, where they were preserved under a layer of sediment.

This Dinosaur Quarry, in the Utah section of the monument, contains the remains of many long-vanished species in one of the world's most concentrated and accessible deposits of the fossilized remains of dinosaurs, crocodiles, turtles, and clams.

One area in the quarry has bones you can touch and models that show what paleontologists believe these dinosaurs looked like when they had their skin. Sometimes visitors can see workers in the paleontology laboratory carefully chiseling away the hard rock to expose more bones, and park naturalists are on hand to explain the process. The quarry is the only place in the monument to view dinosaur bones.

However, visitors who limit their Dinosaur National Monument trip to its

Dinosaur National Monument is THE place to see dinosaur bones, right where they were discovered.

namesake dinosaur quarry miss quite a bit. The monument encompasses 325 square miles of stark canyons at the confluence of the Yampa and Green Rivers in Colorado, and in this vast land there are numerous hiking trails and scenic drives to explore, spectacular panoramic vistas, and opportunities to enjoy the thrill of whitewater rafting.

The Tour of the Tilted Rocks, a 24-mile round-trip drive on the Cub Creek Road in the monument's Utah section, provides scenic views of the Green River and Split Mountain, plus opportunities to see prehistoric rock art and the site of a pioneer homestead. It is suitable for all vehicles, although the last 2 miles are unpaved. A road guide is available at both visitor centers.

An easy way to see a lot of the Colorado section of the monument in a 2- to 4-hour road trip is on the scenic Harpers Corner Drive. This paved 62-mile round-trip drive, suitable for all vehicles, has several overlooks offering panoramic views into the gorges carved by the Yampa and Green Rivers, a look at the derby-shaped Plug Hat Butte, and close-ups of a variety of other colorful rock formations. The drive, for which a road guide is available at both visitor centers, also offers access to several trails.

The monument's dirt roads are also fun to explore, and provide access to some of Dinosaur's less-visited areas. However, they are usually impassable when wet, and even under the best of conditions are dusty and rough in spots. These roads include the 26-mile round-trip Echo Park Road, which takes you past some petroglyphs to the confluence of the Green and Yampa Rivers in the Colorado section; the 62-mile round-trip Island Park Road, in the Utah section, which winds through a colorful badlands; and the 25-mile (one-way) Yampa Bench Road, which provides access into an extremely rugged area with numerous backcountry hiking and backcountry camping possibilities, and for which a high-clearance vehicle is recommended.

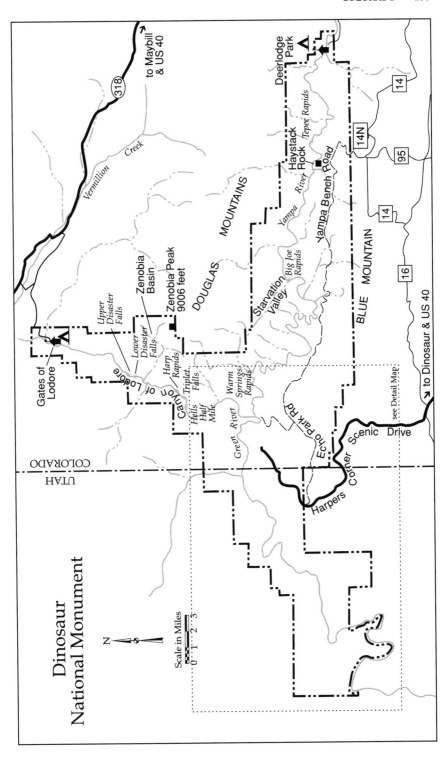

Dinosaur
National Monument

N

Scale in Miles
0 1 2 3

Although you can see a lot from the roadside viewpoints, a better way to appreciate Dinosaur National Monument is to get away from the pavement, either on one of the established trails or, with compass and map in hand, on a trek into the backcountry.

Among the monument's maintained trails in the Colorado section is the easy 0.25-mile round-trip Cold Desert Trail, a self-guided nature trail through desert shrub terrain. The Plug Hat Nature trail, another easy 0.5-mile round-trip walk in the Colorado section, offers an introduction to the plants and animals of a piñon-juniper forest, along with splendid panoramic views.

Also in the Colorado section, the moderate 2-mile round-trip Harpers Corner Trail is highly recommended for a magnificent view of the deep river canyons, as well as a variety of other geologic features. The 1.5-mile round-trip Gates of Lodore Nature Trail is an easy hike that offers spectacular views of the red rock Canyon of Lodore and its sculptor, the Green River. Trail guides for both of these trails are available at either visitor center.

In the Utah section of the monument, the moderately rated Desert Voices Nature Trail is 1.5 miles round trip and has signs describing the desert environment, including a series of signs made for children by children. It also offers sweeping panoramic views across the desert. There is little shade, and in summer it is best to hike early or late in the day to avoid the midday heat.

Also in the Utah section, the easy 1-mile round-trip Hog Canyon Trail crosses a small creek several times as it leads into a canyon where you'll see the remains of homesteader Josie Morris's cabin, which she built in 1933. The canyon received its name because Morris fenced its narrow ends to corral her pigs. Nearby, the Sounds of Silence route is not a marked trail and is sometimes difficult to follow. It is a challenging 3-mile round-trip hike that involves locating a series of landmarks, and considered a good training ground for beginning backcountry desert hikers.

The Jones Hole Trail, also in the Utah section, is a moderate 8-mile round-trip hike that some consider the prettiest in the monument. Starting at the Jones Hole National Fish Hatchery, it follows Jones Hole Creek through a spectacular canyon to the Green River. The trail passes 1,000-year-old rock art and a prehistoric American Indian shelter, and goes through habitat where you might see bighorn sheep, mule deer, and a variety of smaller animals and birds.

In addition to these developed trails, experienced hikers with the appropriate maps and skills can explore miles of unspoiled canyons and rock benches.

Mountain bikes are not permitted on hiking trails, but can be used on the paved and unpaved roads in the monument, and the less-traveled unpaved roads are preferred. The best choices are the 12- to 17-mile Island Park Road ride in the Utah section and the 13-mile Echo Park Road and the 50-mile Yampa Bench Road rides in the Colorado section.

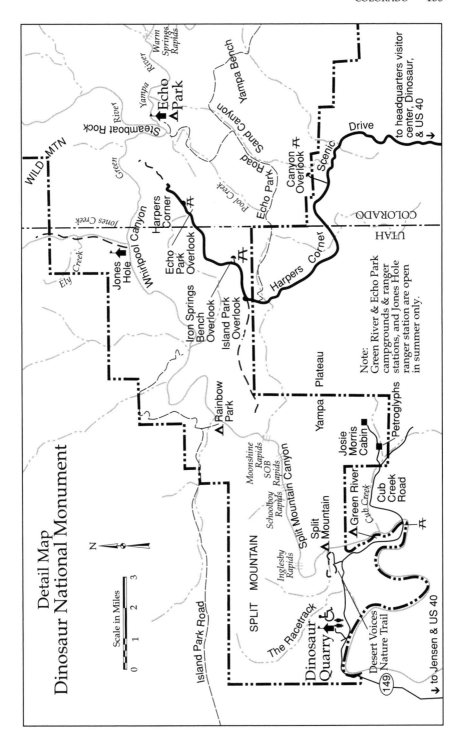

Detail Map
Dinosaur National Monument

N

Scale in Miles
0   1   2   3

Island Park Road

SPLIT   MOUNTAIN

The Racetrack

Dinosaur Quarry

Desert Voices Nature Trail

149

→ to Jensen & US 40

Inglesby Rapids

Schoolboy Rapids

SOB Rapids

Moonshine Rapids

Split Mountain Canyon

Split Mountain

Green River

Cub Creek

Cub Creek Road

Josie Morris Cabin

Petroglyphs

Yampa Plateau

Note:
Green River & Echo Park campgrounds & ranger stations, and Jones Hole ranger station are open in summer only.

Rainbow Park

Iron Springs Bench Overlook

Island Park Overlook

Harpers Corner

Echo Park Overlook

Harpers Corner

Whirlpool Canyon

Jones Hole

Ely Creek

Jones Creek

WILD MTN

Green River

Steamboat Rock

Echo Park

Yampa River

Warm Springs Rapids

Yampa Bench

Sand Canyon

Echo Park Road

Pool Creek

Canyon Overlook

Scenic Drive

COLORADO

UTAH

to headquarters visitor center, Dinosaur, & US 40 →

Horseback riding is permitted in many areas of the monument; check at either visitor center for details.

To many, the best way to see this rugged country is from the river, alternately crashing through churning white water and gliding over the smooth, silent stretches. Experienced whitewater boaters can experience the rivers on their own, and about a dozen outfitters are authorized to run the Yampa and Green Rivers through the monument, offering trips ranging from one to five days. The peak boating season is usually from mid-May through mid-September. A list of authorized river-running companies and information on running the river on your own can be obtained from monument headquarters.

Rangers warn that rivers are not safe for swimming or wading. The water is cold and the current is stronger than it may first appear.

Catfish and pike are caught in the Green and Yampa Rivers, and Jones Hole Creek has brown and rainbow trout. Four endangered species of fish—the Colorado pike minnow, humpback chub, bonytail chub, and razorback sucker—must be returned unharmed to the water if caught. Anglers need either or both Utah and Colorado fishing licenses, and special regulations apply to Jones Hole Creek, including the use of artificial flies and lures only.

The extremes of elevation and availability of water in different parts of the monument mean that there is a great variety of wildlife here. Large animals to watch for include mule deer, bighorn sheep, an occasional elk, and mountain lions. The monument is also home to coyotes, yellow-bellied marmots, mink, river otters, beavers, muskrats, porcupines, prairie dogs, ground squirrels, and chipmunks. There are also a variety of lizards, including the common tree lizard, eastern fence lizard, and side-blotched lizard, which are seen in rocky areas throughout the monument.

Among the monument's almost 200 species of birds is the sage grouse (the largest grouse in North America). Numerous raptors can be seen in the canyons, including peregrine falcons, red-tailed hawks, common nighthawks, northern harriers, and golden and bald eagles. Along the rivers, such as in the Canyon of Lodore, you're likely to see mallards, pintails, wigeons, green-winged teal, Canada geese, great blue herons, sandhill cranes, common loons, hummingbirds, and swallows.

Both sections of the monument have campgrounds, although there are far more sites in the Utah section. All the campgrounds have picnic tables and fireplaces. RVs more than 35 feet are prohibited, and the dirt roads to Echo Park and Rainbow Park campgrounds are not recommended for motor homes and trailers because of steep dips and sharp turns.

In the Utah section, the Green River Campground has eighty-eight mostly well-shaded RV and tent sites, flush toilets, drinking water, firewood for sale, and offers ranger talks at the campground campfire circle. It is usually open from April through October.

Nearby, the Split Mountain Campground, with four group sites, is open all year but in summer allows group camping only by reservation. It is shady, has drinking water and flush toilets, tables, fireplaces, and firewood for sale. The third Utah camping area is Rainbow Park Campground. It has only two sites, but it is open all year. Amenities include tables and fireplaces, vault toilets, but no drinking water. The dirt access road to the campground becomes impassable in wet weather.

In the monument's Colorado section, the Echo Park Campground has thirteen sites, vault toilets, drinking water, fireplaces and tables. The dirt access road becomes impassable when wet. It is open in summer only.

The Deerlodge Park Campground, open all year, is at the eastern edge of the monument in Colorado. It has eight shady sites, vault toilets, tables and fireplaces, but no drinking water. At the northern tip of the park, in Colorado, the Gates of Lodore Campground has seventeen tent and RV sites, some shaded, with drinking water, vault toilets, tables and fireplaces. It is open all year.

Backcountry camping is also permitted for both backpackers and horseback riders, but is recommended only for those skilled in map reading. Free

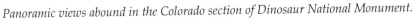

Panoramic views abound in the Colorado section of Dinosaur National Monument.

backcountry permits are required. One backcountry campground—Ely Creek Campground—has two sites that can accommodate ten people each. Fires are not permitted, and permits can be obtained at the Dinosaur Quarry Visitor Center. There are also river camps along the Green and Yampa Rivers that are available to backpackers in the slow river-use times, generally from mid-September through mid-May.

The monument offers a Junior Ranger program for kids from 5 to 12 years old that involves both children and parents completing activities in a workbook to earn rewards.

Because of the national monument's wide range in elevations, from 4,500 feet to 9,000 feet, the climate varies greatly depending on where you are. Generally, though, summers have hot days with temperatures in the 90s, and cool nights, when temperatures drop into the low 50s. Winters are cold and snowy, with daytime temperatures often in the upper 20s and 30s and nighttime temperatures in the single digits or below zero. January is the coldest and snowiest month. Fall is often the most pleasant time at the monument, with daytime highs in the 60s and 70s and nighttime temperatures in the 30s and 40s.

Nearby is the Flaming Gorge National Recreation Area, which is discussed elsewhere in this book.

FLORISSANT FOSSIL BEDS NATIONAL MONUMENT

HOURS/SEASONS:	8 A.M to 7 P.M. daily in summer; 8 A.M. to 4:30 P.M. daily the rest of the year. Closed Thanksgiving, Christmas, and New Year's Day
BEST TIME TO VISIT:	Summer through early fall
AREA:	5,998 acres
ELEVATION:	8,400 feet
FACILITIES:	Visitor center, interpretive exhibits, nature trails, picnic tables, restrooms, public telephone
ATTRACTIONS:	Hiking, wildlife viewing, bird-watching, wildflower viewing, interpretive programs, historical exhibits, cross-country skiing, snowshoeing
NEARBY:	Mueller State Park, Pike National Forest
ACCESS:	35 miles west of Colorado Springs via US 24 and Teller County Road 1

This beautiful high mountain landscape, set among colorful wildflower-studded meadows and forests of tall pines, firs, and aspens, contains one of the world's most spectacular fossil deposits. Here you can see incredibly detailed fossils of insects and plants that lived millions of years ago as well as huge petrified stumps from giant redwoods that grew here when this was a very different place indeed.

The fossils in this National Park Service property are preserved in the rocks of ancient Lake Florissant (the French word for "flowering"), which existed some 34 to 35 million years ago, when the climate here was much warmer and wetter than it is today. Volcanic eruptions that took place over the course of half a million years trapped plants and animals under layers of ash and dust and fossilized them as the sediment settled and became shale.

These detailed impressions offer the most extensive record of its kind in the world. Thousands of specimens have been removed by scientists, including 1,400 separate species of insects. Leaves and needles, many from extinct trees, have also been fossilized. They are very different from those found in the area today, showing how the climate has changed over the centuries. In addition to the incredibly delicate fossilized insects and plants, the volcanic eruptions also buried the forest here, beginning a process that turned the trees into stone where they stood.

Petrified redwood stumps and fossil-bearing shales can be seen on several of the monument's trails, and a number of exquisite fossils are displayed in the visitor center.

The monument also offers a look at the more recent past. The Hornbek Homestead is the preserved two-story log cabin that was home to Adeline Hornbek and her children, who established a farm and ranch here in 1878. Mrs. Hornbek, who is remembered for her striking red hair and independent spirit, had three husbands during her lifetime, but she was the sole supporter of her four children at the time she started this homestead. Building this homestead on her own was considered a very courageous act for a woman in the American West of the late 1800s.

The homestead includes the original cabin, which was quite large for its day with three rooms upstairs and three downstairs. Also at the site are a reconstructed root cellar, and a bunkhouse, carriage shed, and barn that have been moved in from other historic ranches in the area to replace outbuildings that had been torn down. The homestead can be seen from the outside whenever the monument is open, and the buildings are opened on a regular basis; check at the visitor center for the current schedule.

There are about 14 miles of hiking trails in the monument, including two easy self-guided walks and six moderate, relatively short hikes.

The 0.5-mile round-trip Walk Through Time Nature Trail provides an excellent introduction to Florissant Fossil Beds. A trail guide is available for this easy walk through the woods, where you see large petrified redwood stumps, a fossil-bearing shale outcropping, and views of 14,110-foot Pikes Peak, which was the inspiration for the song "America the Beautiful." A trail guide is also available for the easy, 1-mile Petrified Forest Loop Trail, which winds through the

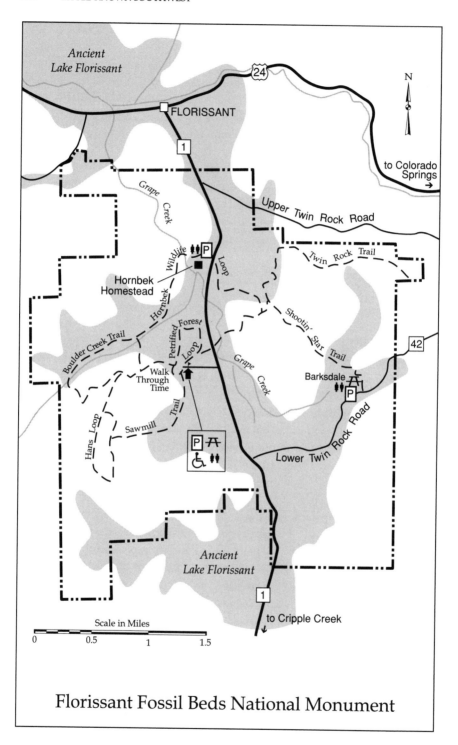

Florissant Fossil Beds National Monument

Visitors stop to ponder the Big Stump, all that remains of what must have been a huge sequoia, at Florissant Fossil Beds National Monument.

bed of the ancient lake, with good views of petrified redwood stumps, including one of the largest in the monument at 38 feet around.

The moderately rated 4-mile Hornbek Wildlife Loop is a good choice for those who hope to see some of the monument's larger animals. It follows meadows as it crosses the ancient lake bed, and goes by the historic Hornbek Homestead before returning to its starting point at the visitor center.

The 2.2-mile (round-trip) Sawmill Trail covers a wide variety of terrain on a moderate hike. It includes a walk along a shaded stream, distant views of Pikes Peak, lush meadows, and forests of spruce, pine, and fir. An extension of the Sawmill Trail is the moderate, 1-mile Hans Loop, which passes an historic homestead, a riparian area where you'll likely see birds and other wildlife, and provides additional views of Pikes Peak.

Boulder Creek Trail, at 3.2 miles round trip, is a moderate hike through wetlands and a forest of ponderosa pines, where you're likely to see a variety of birds. The moderate 1.4-mile one-way Shootin' Star Trail, named for a nearby ranch, follows an old logging road into a forest of ponderosas; and the 2.2-mile one-way Twin Rock Trail, also moderate, meanders through a wetlands offering views of aspen groves, willows, and a variety of rock formations.

During winter these trails are open to those on cross-country skis or snow-shoes; check at the visitor center for current conditions and any restrictions.

There is an abundance of wildlife to be seen among the ponderosa pine, fir, spruce, and aspen trees that cover these hills. Abert's squirrels and Richardson's ground squirrels are seen throughout the monument, and visitors should also be on the lookout for coyotes, red foxes, badgers, porcupines, mule deer, and pronghorn. The monument is also home to Rocky Mountain elk, which are some-times spotted in the meadows near groves of aspens; the Sawmill and Hans Loop Trails are usually good places to look, especially early and late in the day. Black bears and mountain lions also live in the area, but are only occasionally seen.

Birds to watch for include mountain bluebirds, western bluebirds, red-winged blackbirds, western meadowlarks, Brewer's blackbirds, evening grosbeaks, American robins, white-breasted nuthatches, gray and Steller's jays, violet-green swallows, yellow-rumped warblers, western tanagers, wild turkeys, dark-eyed juncos, and broad-tailed hummingbirds. Also sometimes seen soaring overhead are golden eagles, red-tailed hawks, American kestrels, and turkey vultures.

If winter snows have provided enough moisture, the monument bursts into color with a variety of wildflowers in late spring and through the summer. Among flowers you're likely to see are asters, harebells (also called bluebells of Scotland), Rocky Mountain iris, locoweed, wild geraniums, columbine, and pasque flowers.

The visitor center has a small museum and bookstore where you can see a number of magnificent fossils that have been recovered from the monument, as well as exhibits on how fossils form.

During the summer rangers give talks and lead hikes and walks; seminars are often scheduled on summer weekends. The monument's Junior Ranger pro-gram offers activities for kids from 5 to 12 years old on most summer week-ends, and at other times children can complete projects in an activity book to earn badges or patches. Each year in late July Hornbek Homestead Days is cel-ebrated with crafts demonstrations, 1880s games and foods, and special ranger-guided tours. In December, an old-fashioned Christmas is celebrated at the Hornbek Homestead.

Weather here has changed a bit in the past 35 million years. Then it was warm and humid, but now this area is cool and dry. The short summers see daytime temperatures in the 70s and low 80s, with nighttime temperatures dropping into the 30s and low 40s, sometimes below freezing. Thunderstorms are common in July and August. Winters, which usually last from late October into April, are snowy and cold, with daytime highs usually in the 30s and low 40s and night-time temperatures near or below zero.

There are no campgrounds at Florissant Fossil Beds National Monument, but you'll find camping, hiking trails, and numerous other outdoor recreation op-portunities nearby at Mueller State Park and in the Pike National Forest.

GREAT SAND DUNES NATIONAL PARK

HOURS/SEASONS: Overnight; year-round
BEST TIME TO VISIT: Summer through fall
AREA: 38,662 acres
ELEVATION: 8,175 feet
FACILITIES: Visitor center, exhibits, nature trails, picnic tables, group shelter, restrooms, 88 campsites (no showers or hookups), 3 group campsites, amphitheater, firewood sales, public telephone, RV dump station
ATTRACTIONS: Hiking, wildlife viewing, bird-watching, wildflower viewing, programs, fishing, archeological sites, historical exhibits, horseback riding
NEARBY: Rio Grande National Forest
ACCESS: 35 miles northeast of Alamosa via US 160 and CO 150

This 39-square-mile expanse of sand dunes, which seems strangely out of place in southern Colorado, became America's newest national park in November, 2000. Far from any sea or even a major desert, these sand dunes piled nearly

Shifting sands produce an ever-changing landscape at Great Sand Dunes National Park.

750 feet high—the tallest in North America—impatiently push against the western edge of the Rockies' Sangre de Cristo Mountain range.

The dune field was formed when streams of water from melting glaciers carried rocks, gravel, and silt down from the mountains. As the Rio Grande changed its course, it also left behind sand, silt, and debris. The dunes continue to be reshaped today. What are called "reversing winds" from the mountains pile the dunes back upon themselves, building them higher and higher.

Although sand never piles steeper than a 34-degree angle, these dunes often appear more steep due to deceptive shadowing, which changes with the light. As the sun moves over the shifting sand, the shadows appear tan, gold, pink, or sometimes even blue. Summer evenings after a storm often offer the most dramatic scenes, when sunlight streams almost horizontally across the dunes under brilliantly outlined clouds.

Hiking in the dunes is one of those delightful activities that seems to bring out the kid in all of us. But it's also tiring at this 8,200-foot altitude, and rangers warn against giving in to the temptation to go barefoot in summer, when the sand's surface temperature can reach 140 degrees.

There are no designated trails in the dunes, and you're free to hike anywhere you want. Those who make it all the way to the top are rewarded with spectacular views of the dunes and the surrounding mountains. It usually takes about 90 minutes to get to the crest of a 750-foot dune and back to the base. Hiking in the dunes is especially delightful on a moonlit night.

The park also has 18 miles of somewhat more conventional trails. These include the easy 0.5-mile round-trip Montville Nature Trail that runs along shady Mosca Creek and from several high points offers dramatic views of the dunes. A trail guide is available at the visitor center. Another easy 0.5-mile loop trail is the Visitor Center Trail, which has exhibits on the area's natural and human history.

The easy, 2-mile round-trip Wellington Ditch Trail offers good views of the dune field as it partly follows an irrigation ditch that was hand dug by a 1920s homesteader named Wellington. The Castle Creek Trail (rated moderate), which is 5 miles round trip, follows the creek upstream to a spot where the dunes avalanche into the creek.

Those looking for a challenge should pack a lunch for the 7-mile round-trip Mosca Pass Trail, which climbs 1,463 feet into the mountains. It traverses forests of piñon, juniper, aspen, spruce, and fir, and offers good chances of seeing quite a bit of wildlife. Rangers say that each year hikers report seeing bears and mountain lions on this trail.

The 11-mile round-trip Little Medano Creek Trail, rated easy to moderate, passes through grasslands and other environments and offers panoramic vistas. The moderate 12-mile round-trip Sand Creek Trail crosses Little Medano

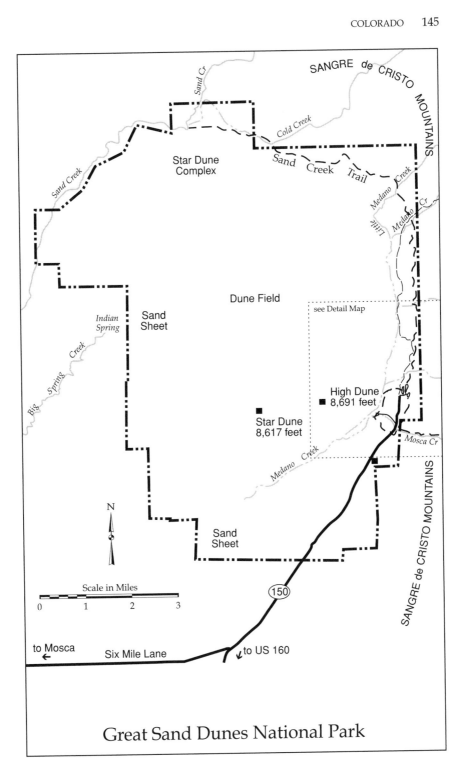

SANGRE de CRISTO MOUNTAINS

Sand Cr.

Cold Creek

Star Dune
Complex

Sand Creek Trail

Sand Creek

Medano Creek

Little

Medano

Medano Cr

Dune Field

see Detail Map

Indian
Spring

Sand
Sheet

Creek

Big Spring Creek

High Dune
■ 8,691 feet

■
Star Dune
8,617 feet

Mosca Cr

Medano Creek

SANGRE de CRISTO MOUNTAINS

N

Sand
Sheet

Scale in Miles

0   1   2   3

(150)

to Mosca
←

Six Mile Lane

↙to US 160

Great Sand Dunes National Park

Creek, Cold Creek, and a section of the Rio Grande National Forest as it crosses the northern edge of the dunes.

Backpacking is permitted throughout the park, and there are backcountry campsites along the Little Medano Creek and Sand Creek Trails. The required free backcountry permits are available at the visitor center. Horseback riding is also permitted in some areas of the park; contact the main office for information.

Although these barren, constantly shifting sand dunes may appear to be an inhospitable environment devoid of life, that is not the case. Among the specialized creatures that survive here are the Ord's kangaroo rat, which never drinks water, and four types of beetle, including the Great Sand Dunes tiger beetle, which is found nowhere else on earth.

Hikers going into the dunes early in the day will often see the tracks of animals that usually visit the dunes only in the cool of night. One of the best wildlife-viewing locations is along Medano Creek, which usually flows along the base of the dunes in spring and early summer. You're also likely to observe humans there, building castles in the wet sand.

Seen fairly regularly are pine squirrels, golden-mantled ground squirrels, Colorado and least chipmunks, desert cottontails, black-tailed and white-tailed jackrabbits, mule deer, and Rocky Mountain elk. There are also bighorn sheep, mountain lions, bobcats, and black bears at Great Sand Dunes, although most visitors do not see them. Pronghorns are sometimes observed just outside the park.

More than 150 species of birds have been sighted in the park, and a surprisingly large number of them are year-round residents. These include commonly seen mourning doves, downy woodpeckers, northern flickers, horned larks, Steller's and piñon jays, Clark's nutcrackers, black-billed magpies, common ravens, mountain chickadees, bushtits, mountain bluebirds, Townsend's solitaires, American robins, red-winged blackbirds, pine siskins, dark-eyed juncos, American kestrels, and red-tailed hawks.

Birds frequently seen in summer are common nighthawks, white-throated swifts, broad-tailed hummingbirds, Lewis' woodpeckers, Say's phoebes, violet-green swallows, yellow-rumped warblers, western tanagers, black-headed grosbeaks, and chipping sparrows. Prime bird-watching areas include the Montville and Wellington Ditch Trails.

Anglers can fish Sand Creek and Medano Creek. Medano is stocked with Rio Grande cutthroat trout, and is catch-and-release only. A Colorado fishing license is required.

The meadows and open piñon-juniper forests here often put on a good wildflower show if there's been enough precipitation at the right time. Look for the flowers of claret cup and prickly pear cactus in the Mosca Pass area in early June.

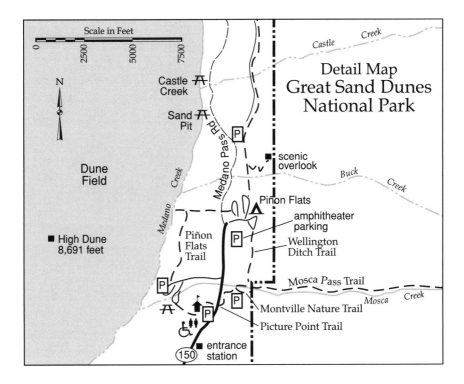

A variety of wildflowers burst into color in July. These include yarrow, pink pussy-toes, spreading fleabane, prairie sunflowers, hoary asters, western wallflowers, mouse-ears, white geraniums, wild iris, orange globemallow, sand verbena, stemless evening primrose, blue gilia, orange paintbrush, narrow-leaf penstemon, and blue violets.

Piñon Flats Campground, with lots of piñon and juniper trees, is open year-round. The tent sites are especially nice. The paved parking areas at the campsites are shallow but generally wide enough for a tow vehicle and trailer side-by-side. However, not many sites can accommodate long RVs. There are flush toilets, drinking water, picnic tables, and fire pits.

Eighty-seven percent of the park is designated wilderness, and off-road vehicular use is prohibited. The only place that four-wheel-drive vehicles may be used (off the park's regular established roadways) is on the Medano Pass Primitive Road, which begins in the park and follows the eastern edge of the dunes north into the Rio Grande National Forest. A park concessionaire operates tours on the Medano Pass Road in summer; contact park offices for current information.

The visitor center has exhibits on sand dune formation, a 15-minute video, and a small bookstore. During summer, rangers offer guided nature walks, short talks at the visitor center patio, and evening amphitheater programs, which are often slide shows. There is also a Junior Ranger program in which children complete various activities to earn badges.

The legislation giving Great Sand Dunes national park status also authorizes the government to purchase an adjacent ranch, which will greatly enlarge the park, and will also protect an underground aquifer that is a valuable source of water.

Cool, sunny days are the norm at Great Sand Dunes. Summer daytime temperatures rarely reach 90 degrees, with nighttime temperatures often dropping into the 40s. Thunderstorms are common in July and August, and hikers are advised to leave the dunes quickly when lightning threatens to avoid being struck. In winter, highs average in the 30s and 40s, with nighttime temperatures in the teens, single digits, or below zero. Snowfall averages a bit over 3 feet annually, with March being the snowiest month. Fall and spring are pleasant, although cool, with daytime temperatures often reaching the 60s and nighttime temperatures in the upper 20s and 30s. High winds (and blowing sand) should be expected at any time.

Nearby, the Rio Grande National Forest offers almost countless opportunities for hiking, mountain biking, horseback riding, camping, cross-country skiing, and snowshoeing.

Right: *A lone hiker (bottom center) rests among the towering rocks at Chaco Culture National Historic Park.*

NEW MEXICO

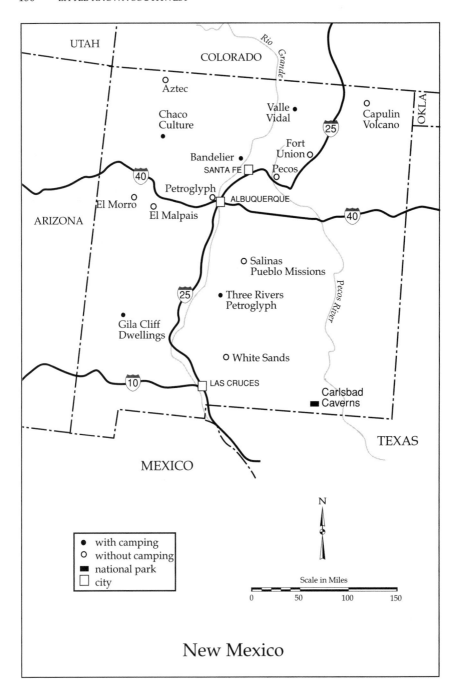

UTAH

COLORADO

Rio Grande

O Aztec

Chaco
Culture
•

Valle •
Vidal

O Capulin
Volcano

OKLA

25

Fort
Union O

Bandelier •
SANTA FE ☐

Pecos
O

Petroglyph
O

40

ARIZONA

O El Morro
O El Malpais

ALBUQUERQUE ☐

40

O Salinas
Pueblo Missions

• Three Rivers
Petroglyph

Pecos River

25

• Gila Cliff
Dwellings

O White Sands

10

LAS CRUCES ☐

Carlsbad
■ Caverns

TEXAS

MEXICO

N

•	with camping
O	without camping
■	national park
☐	city

Scale in Miles

0   50   100   150

New Mexico

A land of contrasts and contradictions, New Mexico has spectacular scenic
beauty, from the towering Rocky Mountains to pristine desert sands, and even
vast underground caverns. Covering 121,666 square miles, it is the meeting

ground for the Great Plains, the southern Rockies, and the Colorado Plateau, and its elevations range from 2,800 to more than 13,000 feet. New Mexico includes six of the United States' seven life zones; the only one missing is tropical.

A moderate climate—neither as hot as Arizona nor as cold as Colorado—helps make New Mexico an excellent destination for hiking, mountain biking, and camping, and the state has numerous public lands, from state parks to national forests, plus areas administered by the Bureau of Land Management.

The Rio Grande, the state's major river, offers whitewater boating and good fishing in the Bureau of Land Management's Wild Rivers Recreation Area. The finest beach in the West, with sparkling white sand but not a drop of water, is found at White Sands National Monument. Arguably the best overall, most easily accessible cave in the United States is found at Carlsbad Caverns National Park, which also offers rugged crawling-along-on-your-belly adventures for the experienced caver.

New Mexico's three dominant cultures—American Indian, Hispanic, and Anglo—are unique but intertwined, each retaining its individual identity while influencing the others in a sometimes uneasy alliance.

To many people, New Mexico conjures up an image of American Indians wrapped in blankets and going about life in their centuries-old adobe pueblos. You'll find Indian culture well represented in national monuments and historic sites such as Chaco Culture National Historical site, Aztec Ruins National Monument, and Three Rivers Petroglyph Site. Fort Union and Salinas Pueblo Missions National Monuments and the Valle Vidal Unit of the Carson National Forest tell of later times, of Spanish conquistadors who arrived in the 1500s and the Anglo pioneers that followed.

NEW MEXICO'S
NATIONAL PARK

New Mexico has an intriguing variety of public lands, but only one that the federal government labels a national park.

CARLSBAD CAVERNS NATIONAL PARK

Boasting one of the largest and most spectacular cave systems in the world, Carlsbad Caverns National Park includes about eighty-five known caves that snake through the porous limestone reef of the Guadalupe Mountains. Fantastic and sometimes bizarre formations fascinate visitors, who find practically every shape imaginable naturally sculpted in the underground, from frozen

This cave formation known as the Klansman is deep underground at Carlsbad Caverns National Park.

waterfalls to strands of pearls, soda straws to miniature castles, draperies to ice-cream cones.

The creation of these caverns goes back about 250 million years, to a time when an inland sea covered this area. When the sea eventually dried up, it left a reef buried beneath deposits of salt and gypsum. The natural forces of up-lifting and erosion brought the reef to the surface, at which point the actual cave-building began. Water seeped down through cracks in the earth's surface, dissolving the limestone and creating open spaces. Sulfuric acid, created by gases from underground oil and gas deposits, helped enlarge these cavities, some of which became large chambers.

The decorative work got underway as slowly dripping water, loaded with calcite and other minerals extracted from limestone, started its gravity-dictated journey. As each drop of water deposited its tiny load of calcite, the fanciful cave formations that we enjoy today began to build.

These formations include stalactites, pointed cones hanging from the ceilings; stalagmites, upside-down stalactites sitting on the floor pointing up; and columns, which are produced when stalactites and stalagmites meet. There are also wavy draperies, popcorn, and numerous other formations that stir the imagination and often remind us of sights from above ground. A particularly delightful example is the Bashful Elephant formation.

The caverns had been known to American Indians for centuries. Area ranchers then discovered them in the 1880s when they noticed sunset flights of bats emerging from the cave mouth. The first reported trip into the cave was in 1883, when a man supposedly lowered his 12-year-old son into the cave entrance. A cowboy named Jim White, who worked for mining companies that collected bat droppings for use as a fertilizer, began to explore the main cave in the early 1900s.

Carlsbad Cave National Monument was created in 1923, and the first electric lights were installed in 1926. In 1930 Carlsbad Caverns gained national park status.

Today's visitors see the various caves at Carlsbad on self-guided and guided tours over paved, relatively well-lighted trails, as well as through tight passages aided by the light of flashlights.

The famous Big Room in Carlsbad Cavern (the park's main cave), is one of the largest and most easily accessible of the caverns. The ceiling is 25 stories high and its floor could easily hold 14 football fields. Carlsbad Cavern even has elevators, a paved walkway, and an Underground Rest Area. Visitors can tour parts of it on their own, aided by a portable CD audio guide.

There are also other sections of the main cave to see, as well as several other caves open to the general public, depending on your time, interest, and physical abilities. Experienced cavers with professional-level equipment can request permission to explore ten of the park's other caves on their own.

Carlsbad Caverns is also a summer home to about a million Mexican free-tailed bats, which hang from the ceiling of Bat Cave during the day and put on a spectacular show each evening as they leave the cave in search of food and again in the morning when they return for a good day's sleep.

In addition to the underground world, the national park has a 9.5-mile scenic loop drive that offers dramatic views of the surrounding Chihuahuan

Desert, backcountry hiking trails for exploring that desert, and an interpretative nature trail. There are no campgrounds in the park, but camping is available nearby.

The park is busiest in summer and during school vacations year-round, but since the caverns are always a cool 56 degrees it doesn't matter when you visit.

NEW MEXICO'S NATIONAL MONUMENTS AND OTHER LESSER-KNOWN FEDERAL LANDS

The federally managed lands discussed in the following pages range from an extinct volcano to an expanse of shifting sand dunes and sites that represent practically every era in this region's history.

AZTEC RUINS NATIONAL MONUMENT

HOURS/SEASONS: 8 A.M. to 6 P.M. daily Memorial Day through Labor Day; 8 A.M. to 5 P.M. daily the rest of the year. Closed Thanksgiving, Christmas, and New Year's Day

BEST TIME TO VISIT: Summer through fall

AREA: 319 acres

ELEVATION: 5,644 feet

FACILITIES: Visitor center/museum/bookstore, interpretive exhibits, interpretive trail, restrooms, picnic tables

ATTRACTIONS: Archeological sites, interpretive programs, bird-watching

NEARBY: Salmon Ruin, Chaco Culture National Historical Park, Mesa Verde National Park, Navajo Lake State Park

ACCESS: 0.5 mile north of US 516 (formerly US 550) on Ruins Road (County Road 2900) on the north edge of the city of Aztec

These ruins, with a huge excavated pueblo and an impressive reconstructed Great Kiva (a large circular chamber traditionally used for religious ceremonies), date from the early twelfth century and show the influences of two distinct but related cultures. The name of this monument, however, is misleading. Early Anglo settlers, convinced that the ruins were of Aztec origin, named the site, but it's now known that the structures here were built long before the Aztecs of central Mexico lived.

Under the jurisdiction of the National Park Service, Aztec Ruins National Monument contains a number of ruins that apparently were part of a large complex, although only the West Ruin has been completely excavated and is open to the public. Nearby, the Hubbard Site is an unusual tri-wall circular structure, which consists of three concentric walls divided into twenty-two rooms around a kiva. Although it had been excavated, it has been backfilled to protect it from the elements, leaving only evidence of the upper walls visible.

Several other ruins are completely off limits to the public. These include the East Ruin, a large pueblo similar to the West Ruin, that has been only partially excavated; and another tri-walled circular building that is believed to be the largest of its kind in the Southwest.

Among the largest Ancestral Puebloan communities in the Southwest, this pueblo is particularly interesting because it appears that it was designed as a single unit, and didn't simply expand in response to a growing population, as is the case at many other prehistoric sites. This kind of planning obviously shows that the builders were part of a highly organized society.

T-shaped doorways at Aztec Ruins National Monument cause us to wonder if the builders had exceptionally wide shoulders, but there is likely a better reason.

There is evidence that two different groups of Ancestral Puebloans, or at least people with two different influences, lived here. The fine stone masonry, open plaza, and other features indicate that the site was built and initially used either by people from Chaco, 55 miles to the south, or by a group strongly influenced by the Chacoans. These people built the West Ruin and some of the other structures, but apparently only lived in them for a few generations in the 1100s. A later occupation, however, occurred from about 1200 to 1275. It shows signs of influence from Mesa Verde, about 40 miles northwest. This second group, who may have been a new people or simply descendents of the first group with strong influence from Mesa Verde, remodeled the old pueblo and built others nearby, using techniques less elaborate and decorative than the Chacoans.

One early archeologist confirmed this theory of two distinctive occupations by digging in the courtyard. At lower levels he found pieces of Chaco-style pottery, while closer to the ground surface were found pieces of broken Mesa Verde pottery.

By 1300 Aztec was deserted, and, as at most other prehistoric ruins, archeologists are not certain why the people left or where they went. Tree rings show that there was a drought in the late 1200s, and their farmland and other natural resources may have been depleted. Another theory is that the people here were driven out by some enemy. Hopis and other modern tribes, however, say that their oral traditions tell that these prehistoric people periodically embarked on mass migrations for spiritual reasons, and their departure from Aztec may have simply meant that it was time for them to move on. It is likely that some of the people of Aztec moved southeast and may have established or joined existing pueblos along the Rio Grande, while others went to what is now Zuni Pueblo to the south, or possibly to the Hopi villages to the west.

Following the 0.25-mile trail through the West Ruin gives modern visitors a unique perspective on the people who lived here centuries ago, providing a peek into their daily lives. The trail is easy and partly paved, but there are some stairs and low doorways. A trail guide is available at the visitor center/museum.

The structures here are built primarily of sandstone, which was hauled from at least a mile away and squared off and finished using stone tools. Ceiling beams of spruce, fir, and pine were brought from mountains at least 20 miles away. They were covered with posts of local cottonwood and juniper, then grasses, and, finally, a coating of mud.

Rooms in the West Ruin are small and often dark, and some contain wood from the original ceilings. Some rooms were entered through openings in the roof, which also let light in; others had traditional doorways that were covered with mats, animals skins, or blankets. Covering one doorway is an original mat made of willows stitched together with strands of yucca.

The rooms surround a courtyard that contains a Great Kiva, the only completely reconstructed one in existence. The Great Kiva measures about 50 feet in diameter and its main floor is 8 feet below the outside ground level. Four huge columns support the roof and there is a raised fireplace in the center. What may have been an altar stands in an alcove. The kiva is surrounded at ground level by fifteen rooms, which open into the courtyard.

Because of the tremendous size of the West Ruin, archeologists at first believed that it may have been home to 1,000 people. However, some archeologists now theorize that only 200 to 300 people actually resided in the pueblo at any given time, with the pueblo's main function being a ceremonial center, where people might have stayed only during events, while they actually lived elsewhere. Excavations have shown that many of the pueblo's 450 rooms were not living quarters, per se, but were used for trash dumps, storage, toilets, work areas, and burial chambers.

Because of its location along the Animas River, with a pond just outside the national monument boundaries, Aztec is a good spot for bird-watching.

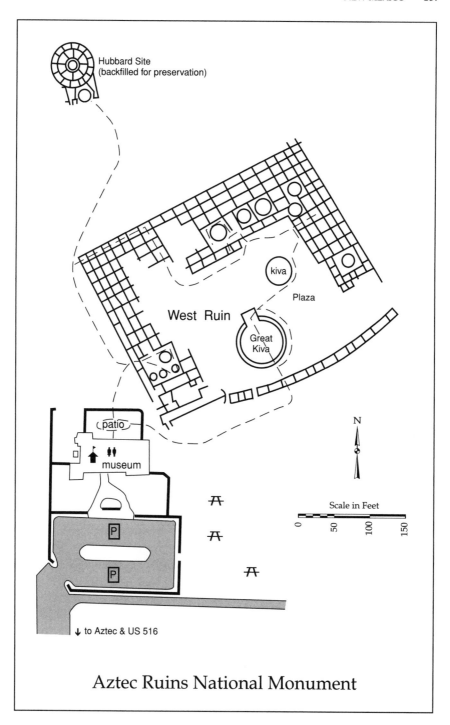

Hubbard Site
(backfilled for preservation)

kiva

Plaza

West Ruin

Great
Kiva

patio

museum

N

Scale in Feet

0   50   100   150

P

P

↓ to Aztec & US 516

Aztec Ruins National Monument

Year-round, be on the lookout for Gambel's quail, ring-necked pheasants, mourning doves, horned larks, black-billed magpies, piñon jays, American robins, starlings, house sparrows, red-winged blackbirds, and western mead-owlarks. In addition, in winter and spring watch for dark-eyed juncos, white-crowned sparrows, mountain bluebirds, and mallards. In summer you're likely to see black-chinned hummingbirds and western kingbirds.

The visitor center displays outstanding examples of Ancestral Puebloan pots and baskets, with exhibits that show the differences in styles among various groups as well as such finds as an intact Ancestral Puebloan ladder. A 25-minute video documents the history of prehistoric cultures in the area, and rangers occasionally present talks during the summer. The monument also offers a Junior Ranger program in which kids complete workbook projects.

Summers here are warm, with daytime temperatures usually in the upper 80s and low 90s, and afternoon thunderstorms are common during July and August. Daytime temperatures in the winter range from the 20s to the 50s, with measurable snowfall expected by late November. Spring weather varies, and is often windy. Fall is generally the most pleasant time of year, with daytime temperatures commonly in the 60s and 70s.

Nearby attractions include Chaco Culture National Historical Park and Mesa Verde National Park, which are discussed elsewhere in this book. Also in the vicinity is Salmon Ruin, near Bloomfield, which is a fairly large Chacoan Pueblo built in the late eleventh century. Scenic Navajo Lake State Park, also close by, offers camping, hiking, boating, and fishing.

BANDELIER NATIONAL MONUMENT

HOURS/SEASONS:	Trails are open dawn to dusk; campground and backcountry are open overnight in season
BEST TIME TO VISIT:	Fall
AREA:	32,737 acres
ELEVATION:	6,066 feet
FACILITIES:	Visitor center/museum, interpretive exhibits, gift shop/snack bar, nature trail, picnic tables, restrooms, 94 campsites (no showers or hookups), group campground, public telephone, RV dump station
ATTRACTIONS:	Archeological sites, hiking, bird-watching, wildlife viewing, interpretive programs
NEARBY:	City of Los Alamos, several American Indian pueblos
ACCESS:	48 miles northwest of Santa Fe via US 285/84 and NM highways 502 and 4

This is one of those delightful parks that has something for practically every-one. There are easily accessible prehistoric American Indian ruins, a nature trail, a hiking trail to two picturesque waterfalls, miles of backcountry trails, a developed campground, and almost unlimited backcountry camping opportunities.

The monument, which is operated by the National Park Service, was named for Adolph Bandelier, a self-taught anthropologist-historian who left his native Switzerland in 1880 to study the early peoples of the American Southwest. He was enthralled with the ruins that would someday bear his name, and used them and the canyon in which they were built as the setting for a novel, *The Delight Makers*, a story of American Indian life before the arrival of Spanish explorers in the 1500s.

The monument's main claim to fame is its numerous thirteenth-century Ancestral Puebloan ruins, ranging from a variety of cliff dwellings to a large pueblo, plus a variety of petroglyphs and pictographs.

The Main Loop Trail begins just outside the visitor center/museum and leads through the ruins of Tyuonyi Pueblo to a series of cliff dwellings. The paved 1.2-mile loop is relatively level and easy and takes you to Tyuonyi Pueblo, the fascinating ruins of an almost perfectly round pueblo that once had about 400 rooms and housed about 100 people.

It is likely that Tyuonyi had a combination of one-, two-, and three-story structures that were built around a large central plaza in which there were three small kivas (circular chambers traditionally used by Southwestern tribes for religious rites). There were probably no windows on the compound's exterior walls, and

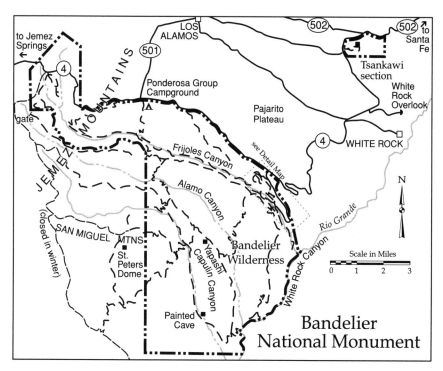

Hikers stop to examine a reconstructed talus house along the Tyuonyi Trail at Bandelier National Monument.

only one ground-level exterior entrance. The pueblo was built in the 1300s, and was likely occupied into the early 1500s, but by the time Spanish explorers arrived later that century it was deserted.

From Tyuonyi Pueblo the trail continues to a series of cliff dwellings, cleverly built into a south-facing canyon wall that caught the warming winter sun. Here you have a choice of taking a level, easy walk with views up at the cliff dwellings, or following a paved but somewhat steep and narrow route along the cliff side, with ladders providing access to some of the dwellings.

The canyon walls are composed of tuff, a soft, pinkish volcanic rock that weathers easily, producing holes that the prehistoric residents enlarged for storage and living quarters. These caves were often used as back rooms of more formal houses, which were constructed on the cliff face from talus, the broken chunks of rock deposited at the cliff base. One talus home has been reconstructed.

Further along the trail is Long House, a condominium-style community. Extending for about 800 feet along the side of the cliff, there are rows of holes dug into the rock to support roof beams, called vigas, which show clearly the outline of the multistoried cliff dwelling. Also along the cliff side here are a number of petroglyphs and a large pictograph, likely created by people standing on roofs. Petroglyphs are designs chipped or pecked into a rock surface, while pictographs are images painted onto a rock surface. Above the pictograph is a tall, narrow cave which is the summer home to a colony of bats.

From the Long House cliff dwellings the path turns to return to the visitor center via a shady nature trail that has signs describing the area's plant and animal life. A side trail leads to another cliff dwelling called Ceremonial Cave, a natural cave that was enlarged by the prehistoric residents, who constructed clusters of rooms and a small kiva. Located about 150 feet above the canyon floor, it is accessed by a level dirt trail plus a steep 140-foot climb up a series of ladders and steps. This side trip adds about 1 mile round trip to the Main Loop Trail.

Those looking for an easy to moderate hike of a few hours, with wonderful scenery and possible wildlife sightings, can't do better than Bandelier National Monument's Falls Trail. This hike follows the Frijole Canyon (named for the beans Ancestral Puebloans grew here) to two picturesque waterfalls, passing through a lush forest of juniper, ponderosa pine, and cottonwoods before dropping to the falls area, where yucca, cactus, and sagebrush predominate.

The trail begins near the visitor center and crosses Frijoles Creek on wooden bridges several times. The dramatic Upper Falls plunges 80 feet; the smaller Lower Falls is more subdued. It is an easy 1.5 miles with a 400-foot elevation drop from the visitor center parking area to the Upper Falls viewing area. Then the trail becomes somewhat rocky as it continues another 0.25 mile to the Lower Falls, where most people turn around and head back. For those who feel the need to work harder, from the Lower Falls it is 0.75 mile down a steep, rocky trail to the creek's confluence with the Rio Grande.

In the Tsankawi section of the monument (about 11 miles north of the main entrance), the Tsankawi Trail is a 1.5-mile loop that is generally easy and fairly level, but does include some narrow passages between rocks and a 12-foot ladder climb. The trail passes among juniper, piñon, rabbitbrush, and yucca and provides good views of a variety of petroglyphs, including images of birds, humans, and four-pointed stars. You will also see the mounds of dirt and rock that mark the unexcavated ruins of a pueblo, probably built in the 1400s, that contained about 350 rooms.

The Lower Falls at Bandelier National Monument

Trail guides for the three trails described above are available in the visitor center.

In addition to the park's main trails there are about 70 miles of backcountry trails, most of which are in the Bandelier Wilderness, a designated wilderness area that comprises more than 70 percent of the monument's 32,737 acres. The terrain is rugged, with steep canyons, and the trails take hikers to relatively secluded sections of the monument where there are additional archeological sites and excellent chances of seeing wildlife. Detailed maps, additional information, and the required free permits for overnight trips can be obtained at the visitor center.

Birds and a variety of other animals are seen throughout the monument. Species of squirrels you're likely to see in the picnic area, campgrounds, and other wooded areas include Abert's, rock, golden-mantled ground, and red. You will probably also see their cousins, the least and Colorado chipmunks. Also seen are coyotes, raccoons, porcupines, mule deer, and elk. Numerous lizards inhabit the drier areas, as do a few snakes, including the poisonous western diamondback rattler.

Among birds seen year-round are Steller's jays, western scrub jays, northern flickers, common ravens, canyon wrens, pygmy nuthatches, and rufous-sided and canyon towhees. In the warmer months, look for western bluebirds, violet-green swallows, white-throated swifts, broad-tailed hummingbirds, and turkey vultures.

The visitor center/museum, several adjacent buildings, the main road, and some of the monument's trails were built in the 1930s by the Civilian Conservation Corps (CCC). In the museum are exhibits on both the prehistoric and more recent peoples who have lived here. There is a series of sculptures of those that inhabited the monument, in authentic dress, that shows the continuity of the Puebloan culture from the mid-1100s to the early 1900s.

During the summer there are regularly scheduled guided walks, and rangers present talks and other programs in various locations, including nightly programs in the campground amphitheater. On summer weekends there are often crafts demonstrations by members of local pueblos who trace their heritage to the people who lived at Bandelier more than 500 years ago.

Parking is limited and there can be waits of up to an hour for a parking space on summer weekends, with the busiest times from late morning through early afternoon. Holiday weekends get so packed that visitors may be turned away and told to come back later. Parking for RVs and other large vehicles is extremely limited. Trailers and towed vehicles are prohibited from the visitor center area, but can be left in the amphitheater parking lot near Juniper Campground. In addition to the main parking lot, there is space for visitors to park in the nearby picnic area. A separate parking area is provided for backpackers.

Bandelier's delightful Juniper Campground is in a forest of junipers with nicely spaced campsites, each with a picnic table and fireplace. There is a relatively easy trail that connects the campground with Frey Trail, which leads to the visitor center. The distance from the campground to the visitor center is 2 miles. The campground is open year-round, weather permitting, on a first-come, first-served basis. Backcountry camping is also permitted.

Because of the high elevation, summer temperatures are pleasant, with highs often in the 80s and 90s, while nighttime lows drop into the 50s and 60s. Afternoon thunderstorms are common in July and August. Winters here are cold and snowy, but offer a lot more solitude than summer. Spring is fickle, changing unexpectedly from beautiful to horrible, and spring winds are common. Perhaps the best time to visit Bandelier is in the fall, after the summer crowds have gone home, when skies are often blue and clear, daytime temperatures are in the 70s and low 80s, and nights are frosty.

Among nearby attractions is the city of Los Alamos, considered the birthplace of the atomic bomb, which has two museums—a science museum with exhibits

A tree lizard along the Falls Trail soaks up the sun's warmth at Bandelier National Monument.

on the development of the bomb and other scientific research at Los Alamos National Laboratory, and an historical museum that looks more at the human side of the area's history. There are also several local Indian pueblos that are open to the public; ask at the national monument's visitor center for current information.

CAPULIN VOLCANO NATIONAL MONUMENT

HOURS/SEASONS: 7:30 A.M. to 6:30 P.M. daily Memorial Day through Labor Day; 8 A.M. to 4 P.M. daily the rest of the year. Closed Thanksgiving, Christmas, and New Year's Day

BEST TIME TO VISIT: Late spring through fall

AREA: 793 acres

ELEVATION: 7,242 feet

FACILITIES: Visitor center/museum, interpretive exhibits, nature trail, picnic tables, restrooms, public telephone

ATTRACTIONS: Geologic formations, hiking, bird-watching, wildlife viewing, wildflower viewing, interpretive programs

NEARBY: Sugarite Canyon State Park

ACCESS: 33 miles east of Raton via US 64/87

This is the spot for anyone who has ever had the urge to walk into a volcano, but Capulin Volcano National Monument offers more than that. In addition to a close-up view of the volcanic crater and a chance to walk around the rim as well as down into its depths, this monument provides opportunities to see plenty of birds and animals and a variety of colorful wildflowers.

An almost perfectly shaped cinder cone, Capulin Volcano has been a landmark for centuries—first for American Indians, then for Spanish explorers, who named it *capulin* for the wild chokecherries that grow on its slopes, and then for white settlers and others traveling the Cimarron Cutoff of the Santa Fe Trail.

The volcano was born some 60,000 years ago, near the end of a long period of volcanic activity. Had we been there we would have felt the grassy plain start to shake, then, assuming we were brave enough to stay, we could have watched as the earth split open, emitting black smoke. Soon glowing cinders and ash shot high into the sky, and the volcano released its river of lava, covering almost 16 square miles. By the time the earthquakes and eruptions finally came to an end, a new mountain had been created—a cinder cone rising more than 1,200 feet above the surrounding plains.

The first thing we notice about Capulin Volcano is its shape. It is beautifully symmetrical, largely because most of the lava did not flow out the main crater and down the side, but instead escaped through a mouth along the cone's western base.

As with all dramatic episodes of natural history, as soon as the ground had ceased shaking and the volcanic rocks had cooled, the forces of nature went to work to bring this newcomer into line with its surroundings. Water and wind began eroding the tough volcanic rock to create soil, giving lichen and then small plants a chance to grow, which helped further the breakdown of rock into soil. Gradually grasses, bushes, and finally trees moved in, creating the velvety appearance of the cone that we see as we approach it today.

The monument, operated by the National Park Service, is extremely easy to explore. The 2-mile Volcano Road leads to a parking lot at the Volcano's rim, where an overlook with interpretive signs offers good views into the crater as well as out over the surrounding countryside. This road is narrow, with no shoulders, and trailers, towed vehicles, bikes, and pedestrians are prohibited.

From the rim parking area the self-guided Crater Rim Trail loops around the rim of the crater, passing volcanic boulders spotted with lichen as well as Gambel oak and a variety of bushes and low plants. In a few areas you'll also see ponderosa pines, the monument's tallest living thing, towering above everything else. Although paved and mostly easy, the trail has a few steep grades near the beginning as it climbs about 300 feet to the monument's highest point of 8,182 feet, and an equal descent at the end.

There are splendid views both into the crater and out across the plains, where dozens of other extinct volcanoes are visible. On a clear day, you can see Colorado to the north, Oklahoma and Texas to the east, and New Mexico's rugged Sangre de Cristo Mountains to the west. The trail has benches and

The volcanic crater at Capulin Volcano National Monument.

overlooks with signs that help hikers identify the distant landmarks. In summer, thousands of small orange ladybugs are often seen blanketing rocks and bushes.

Also from the rim parking area, the 0.2-mile (one-way) Crater Vent Trail drops into the crater. It leads to the vent—the spot on the earth's surface from which the cinders, ash, and lava erupted. The paved trail drops a bit over 100 feet.

Near the picnic area, off Volcano Road, the 1-mile Lava Flow Trail loops through a piñon-juniper forest at the base of the volcano. This easy walk is on a surface of reddish-brown crushed lava rock.

Along all three trails, as well as in the visitor center area, watch for a variety of birds, many attracted by the numerous chokecherry bushes here. Among species seen year-round are rufous-sided towhees, canyon towhees, scrub jays, common ravens, mountain chickadees, American robins, and red-tailed hawks. Mountain bluebirds are year-round residents as well, but are especially prevalent in early fall. Common in summer are wild turkeys, turkey vultures, blue-gray gnatcatchers, mourning doves, black-chinned and broad-tailed hummingbirds, house wrens, Virginia's warblers, western meadowlarks, and black-headed grosbeaks. Birds that drop by in winter include dark-eyed juncos and Townsend's solitaires.

Year-round there's a good chance of seeing mule deer, especially early and late in the day along the wooded edges of meadows. Also watch for porcupines, chipmunks, rock squirrels, bobcats, and coyotes. Occasionally black bears are seen. There are several species of lizards, including eastern fence and short-horned lizards. Among the monument's snakes the only poisonous one is the western prairie rattlesnake.

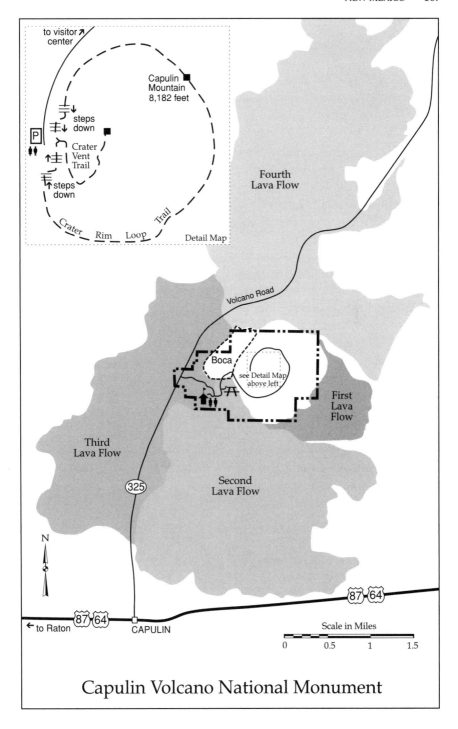

to visitor center

Capulin Mountain
8,182 feet

steps down

Crater Vent Trail

P

steps down

Crater Rim Loop Trail

Detail Map

Fourth Lava Flow

Volcano Road

Boca

see Detail Map above left

First Lava Flow

Third Lava Flow

Second Lava Flow

325

N

87 64

87 64

← to Raton   CAPULIN

Scale in Miles

0   0.5   1   1.5

Capulin Volcano National Monument

Wildflowers come to life from late June through July, assuming there has been sufficient winter moisture. These include delicate red Indian paintbrush, big yellow sunflowers, bluebells, lupines, daisies, and verbena.

The visitor center/museum has exhibits on the creation of Capulin Volcano and other aspects of the area's geology, as well as the human history and plants and animals of the area. A 10-minute video on the volcano's creation is shown, as is a film of a volcanic eruption in Mexico in 1943 that is believed to be similar to the one that created Capulin. Outside the visitor center is a short, easy nature trail.

During the summer months 15-minute ranger talks on volcanos are offered several times each day. Children's programs include the Junior Ranger Program, for those aged 6 to 12; kids complete projects in an activity book to earn certificates and badges. For children under 6, the Lady Bug Hunt is a self-guided project in which kids locate a variety of park features to earn ladybug stickers and certificates.

Because of its high elevation, summers here are very pleasant, with highs often in the mid-80s, although early mornings and late afternoons can be chilly. Afternoon thunderstorms are common in July and August. Winters are cold, and snow sometimes temporarily closes Volcano Road. Fall is usually moderate, with daytime temperatures in the 60s and 70s, but nights are cold. Springtime temperatures vary considerably, and high winds are frequent.

The monument is very busy on summer weekends, especially near the middle of the day, so it is best to visit on weekdays or early or late in the day on weekends in the summer.

There is no camping at the monument, but nearby Sugarite Canyon State Park

Mule deer are among the wildlife you may see at Capulin Volcano National Monument. (photo by Don MacCarter, courtesy New Mexico Department of Game and Fish)

has two attractive campgrounds as well as hiking trails, lakes, an abundance of wildlife, and the ruins of an early-twentieth-century coal camp.

CHACO CULTURE NATIONAL HISTORICAL PARK

HOURS/SEASONS: Trails and sites are open daily sunrise to sunset year-round; campground is open overnight year-round

BEST TIME TO VISIT: April, May, September, October

AREA: 33,974 acres

ELEVATION: 6,200 feet

FACILITIES: Visitor center, interpretive exhibits and trails, picnic tables, restrooms, 48 campsites (no showers or hookups), group campground, dump station, public telephone

ATTRACTIONS: Archeological sites, hiking, biking, wildlife viewing, bird-watching, interpretive programs

NEARBY: Aztec Ruins, El Malpais, and El Morro National Monuments

ACCESS: South of Farmington via US 550 (formerly NM 44) about 55 miles, then follow signs the remaining 21 miles (5 miles paved, 16 miles graded dirt)

For those who want to peek into the prehistoric world of the Ancestral Puebloans, the people who dominated the Four Corners area 1,000 years ago, there are a variety of fascinating archeological sites available, a number of which are described in this book. But to get a close-up view of some of these prehistoric people's finest masonry work, and to appreciate their planning and engineering skills, a trip to Chaco Culture National Historical Park is mandatory.

This is not simply an opportunity to see another ruin. What one experiences at this park, managed by the National Park Service, is a sense of the immensity of what we now call the Chacoan Culture. The park is a link with a distant past that provides an awe-inspiring look into the very center of a remarkable civilization.

A paved loop road through Chaco Canyon provides access to pullouts and parking areas from which you can see many of the sites, but to fully appreciate Chaco it's best to hike some of its mostly easy trails that lead into the ruins. In addition, the park has two trails that are open to bikes and which offer opportunities to see a variety of wildlife.

Although nomadic Paleo-Indians were in this area some 10,000 years ago, and there is evidence that prehistoric people lived in Chaco Canyon 3,000 to 4,000 years ago, it was not until about 1,200 years ago that this stone city began to evolve.

Construction in prehistoric times generally used whatever materials were on hand, and here that meant rock. Over the centuries techniques had evolved

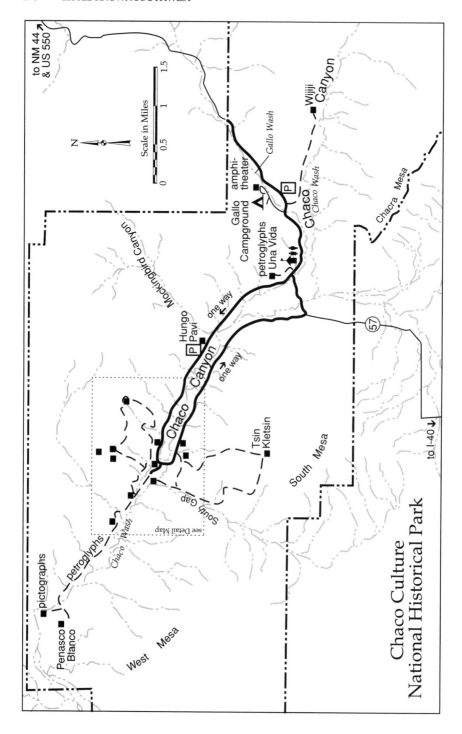

Chaco Culture
National Historical Park

Chaco Culture National Historical Park preserves the remains of what was once the center of a large and sophisticated society.

in which builders created walls one stone thick, held together with generous portions of mud. Then in the mid-800s the Ancestral Puebloans of Chaco started building on a larger scale. Instead of simply building a few small rooms and adding additional rooms as the need arose, as had been the practice, they constructed stone public buildings of multiple stories with large rooms. Perhaps most significant, though, their buildings began to show evidence of skillful planning. Obviously, a central government was in charge.

Within a century, six large, pre-planned public buildings, or "great houses," were under construction. New communities, each consisting of a large central building surrounded by smaller villages, sprang up. Established villages followed the trend by adding large public and ceremonial buildings. Eventually there were more than 150 such communities, most of them closely tied to Chaco by an extensive system of roads and shared culture.

By A.D. 1000, Chaco had become the center of commerce, ceremony, and culture for the area, with as many as 5,000 people living in some 400 settlements. As masonry techniques advanced, walls rose more than four stories high. Some of these are still standing today.

Aerial photos show hundreds of miles of roads connecting these outlying towns with the large buildings at Chaco. Settlements were spaced along the roads at travel intervals of one day. These were not simply trails worn into the stone by foot travel but were carefully engineered roadways 30 feet wide with a berm of rock to contain the fill. Where the roads went over flat rock, walls were built along the edges. It is this road network that leads some scholars to believe Chaco was the center of a widespread but unified society.

Artifacts found at Chaco, including shell necklaces, turquoise, copper bells, and the remains of Mexican parrots called macaws, indicate that their trade network stretched from the California coast to Texas and south into Mexico.

Chaco's decline in the twelfth century coincided with a drought in the area, although archeologists are not certain that this was the only or even the major reason that the site was eventually abandoned. Some argue that an influx of outsiders may have brought new rituals to the region, causing a schism among tribal members. A recent controversial theory maintains that cannibalism existed at Chaco, practiced either by the Ancestral Puebloans themselves or by invaders, such as the Toltecs of Mexico.

Even though archeologists do not agree on why Chaco Canyon was abandoned, they generally concur that the Chacoans' descendants live among today's Pueblo people of the Four Corners region, who today consider Chaco a sacred area.

A paved one-way road of about 9 miles loops from the visitor center through Chaco Canyon, providing access to five self-guided trails that lead into Chaco's major sites, plus one trail from the visitor center. Allow about an hour for each of these walks. Trail guides are available at the visitor center and at the sites. The park also has four longer backcountry trails.

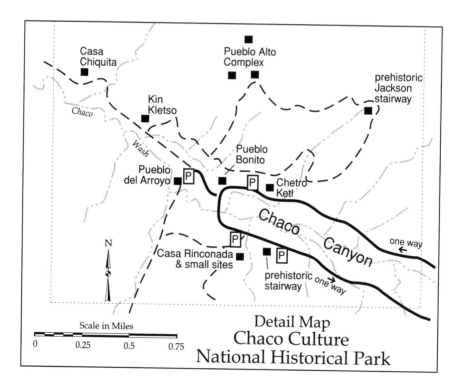

Scale in Miles

0   0.25   0.5   0.75

Detail Map
Chaco Culture
National Historical Park

While some would lend a hand to a fellow hiker, others would rather take a picture, as seen here at Chaco Culture National Historical Park.

Impressive Pueblo Bonito (Spanish for "Beautiful Town") is believed to have been the largest structure in the Chacoan system, and is also the largest prehistoric dwelling ever excavated in the Southwest. Covering more than 3 acres, it contains some 800 rooms surrounding two plazas in which there were more than two dozen kivas, some quite large. The easy trail through Pueblo Bonito is 0.6 mile round trip.

Other ruin sites accessible directly from the loop road include Chetro Ketl, which had about 500 rooms, 16 kivas, and an impressive enclosed plaza. It is accessed via an easy 0.6-mile round-trip trail with a few steep portions. Pueblo del Arroyo was a four-story, D-shaped structure with about 280 rooms and 20 kivas, which is seen on an easy 0.25-mile round-trip walk.

Casa Rinconada is reached on a 0.5-mile round-trip trail that has loose gravel and some steep sections. The largest Great Kiva in the park, Casa Rinconada is astronomically aligned to the four compass points and the summer solstice. It may have been a center for the community at large and used for major religious observances.

Una Vida, a short walk from the visitor center, was one of the first of the Chacoan buildings to be constructed and has been only partially excavated. Considered a "great house," it had 150 rooms and five kivas, including a Great Kiva. A 1-mile round-trip walk, rocky with steep sections, includes a stop at Una Vida and a side trip to some petroglyphs.

Hungo Pavi, which is just off the roadway via a short walk, is another of Chaco's "great houses." It contained about 150 rooms and rose up three stories in places.

Backcountry trails, for which free permits are required, lead to a number of additional archeological sites. Those hiking into the backcountry should carry raingear to avoid the chance of hypothermia. Hikers are also advised to wear good hiking boots and take drinking water.

The 5.4-mile round-trip Pueblo Alto Trail climbs up the canyon rim and offers panoramic views of Pueblo Bonito and other sites as it leads to several prehistoric structures. This moderate trail gains about 350 feet. The easy to moderate Penasco Blanco Trail gains 150 feet elevation in its 6.4 miles round trip. It leads to some of the oldest structures at Chaco, and also affords views of a large number of petroglyphs, with a side trail to a pictograph.

South Mesa Trail, which leads to Tsin Kletsin, is moderate to difficult, climbing 450 feet over its 4.1-mile loop. With the highest elevation of any Chaco Canyon trail, it provides panoramic vistas as well as views of myriad wildflowers in spring and summer.

Wijiji, which is open to both hikers and bikers, is fairly easy, with virtually no elevation change over its 3 miles round trip. This route follows an old ranch road to ruins of a pueblo built about A.D. 1100 and a small pictograph panel. A longer excursion for those with bikes is the Kin Klizhin Trail, a 23.8-mile round-trip ride that follows a dirt road (occasionally used by motor vehicles) to the ruins of one of Chaco's outlying sites. The name is Navajo for "Black House," so-called because of the dark stones that were used in this building's construction.

Although not a prime wildlife viewing area, there is a surprising amount of wildlife here. The most commonly seen animals in the park are white-tailed antelope squirrels and several species of mice. Also be on the lookout for desert cottontails, black-tailed jackrabbits, prairie dogs, porcupines, gray foxes, deer, badgers, coyotes, and bobcats.

The plains spadefoot toad is often seen along arroyos after early summer rains, and those visiting Pueblo Alto and Chetro Ketl have a good chance of spying collared lizards, which can grow to over a foot long and are named for the black-and-white collars over their mostly yellowish or yellow-green bodies. Harmless bullsnakes are commonly seen in and near the ruins, and hikers should watch out for the poisonous prairie rattlesnake, which frequents the backcountry.

Among birds to watch for are killdeer, scaled quail, western meadowlark, mountain chickadee, western bluebird, white-crowned sparrow, loggerhead shrikes, American robins, canyon towhees, rock and canyon wrens, Say's phoebe, turkey vultures, common ravens, and golden eagles.

The visitor center has a museum with exhibits on the Chacoan Culture, the construction of this prehistoric metropolis, and some of the artifacts discovered here during excavations. A video program tells about the Ancestral Puebloans. The visitor center also has a small bookstore and a gift shop, and is the only place in the park where you can get drinking water. During the summer rangers lead guided hikes and walks and also present evening campfire programs. In addition, rangers present evening astronomy programs four times weekly during the summer.

Gallo Campground, like most of the rest of the park, is out in the open with little shade, but provides great views of the surrounding countryside. Sites have fire grates (bring your own wood or charcoal) and tables. Central toilets are available, but there is no drinking water. Most sites have tent pads, and tents must be placed on pads where available. The campground cannot accommodate trailers over 30 feet long.

The one constant in Chaco's weather is its unpredictability, and park rangers warn that visitors should be prepared for practically anything at any time. Temperature variations of more than 60 degrees in a 24-hour period are not uncommon. Generally, summer days are hot, with highs in the upper 80s and 90s, while nighttime temperatures are pleasantly cool, dropping into the 50s and low 60s. Thunderstorms, sometimes torrential, are common from July through September. Winter days are cool, with highs from the 30s to the 50s and lows below freezing. There are occasional snowstorms.

This is an isolated area, and there are no services available within or close to the park.

Relatively nearby are Aztec Ruins, El Malpais, and El Morro National Monuments, which are discussed elsewhere in this book.

EL MALPAIS NATIONAL MONUMENT AND NATIONAL CONSERVATION AREA

HOURS/SEASONS:	Overnight; year-round
BEST TIME TO VISIT:	Spring and fall
AREA:	376,000 acres
ELEVATION:	6,500 to 8,300 feet
FACILITIES:	Visitor center, interpretive exhibits, nature trail, picnic tables, restrooms
ATTRACTIONS:	Hiking, caving, backpacking, wildlife viewing, bird-watching, interpretive programs
NEARBY:	Cibola National Forest, El Morro National Monument
ACCESS:	South of Grants (I-40 exit 81) via NM 53; or from I-40 exit 89 south on NM 117

Its name is Spanish for "badlands," and this arid region of sharp volcanic rocks and towering sandstone formations must have seemed a very bad land indeed for early explorers. In fact, there is no evidence that Spanish settlers saw any value in this land, and after New Mexico became a U.S. territory in 1848 the area was almost completely ignored. It was not until the Great Depression in the 1930s that people were so desperate to make a living that homesteaders and sheepherders moved in.

However, El Malpais (pronounced el mal-pie-EES) had not always been devoid of humanity. There is evidence that prehistoric peoples as early as 10,000 years ago spent time here, and from about A.D. 950 to 1350 El Malpais was an

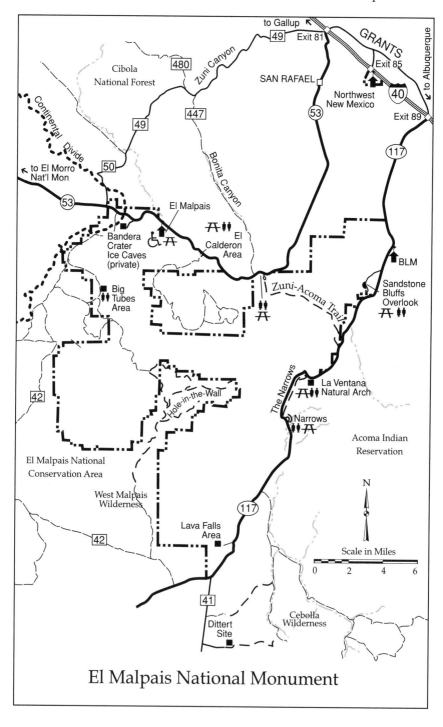

El Malpais National Monument

outlying community of the vast Chacoan Culture, which was centered some 80 miles to the north (see the section on Chaco Culture National Historical Park, above). Then, in the mid-1300s, following a period of drought, these Ancestral Puebloans left El Malpais, and are believed to have established the pueblos of Acoma to the east and Zuni to the west, where their descendents live today.

El Malpais was created by volcanic eruptions from as recent as 2,000 to 3,000 years ago and has an eerie beauty with its lava flows, cinder cones, and sandstone cliffs and arches. It also enchants visitors with its strange lava tubes, oases of green among the barren, black landscape, and the ruins left by prehistoric American Indians and twentieth-century homesteaders. There are scenic drives, opportunities for hiking, backpacking, and caving, and a surprising amount of wildlife. Partly a national monument and partly a national conservation area, El Malpais is managed jointly by the National Park Service and the Bureau of Land Management.

It is easy to see many of the main attractions at El Malpais from roadside viewpoints, and those who want to venture off the main routes will be well rewarded. However, conditions in the backcountry can be brutal, with burning sun, no shade, flesh-ripping lava rocks, hard-to-follow trails, and dirt roads that become mud bogs when it rains, leaving motorists, even those with high-clearance four-wheel-drives, stranded miles from paving.

Therefore, it is strongly recommended that those planning to hike or drive into the backcountry check first with the Bureau of Land Mangement's ranger station or the National Park Service's information center. Rangers will have current trail and road conditions and can provide detailed topographic maps and help you decide what areas of El Malpais to explore, based on your desires, abilities, and equipment.

Among the most popular hikes in El Malpais is the relatively level but still challenging Zuni-Acoma Trail, which runs 7.5 miles one way and follows an historic trade route between Zuni and Acoma Pueblos. The trail is a strenuous hike that crosses four of the area's five lava flows over jagged chunks of unstable lava. Although it is marked by cairns and trail posts, it is difficult to follow. Arranging a shuttle and hiking from west to east is recommended, and sturdy hiking boots with good ankle support are mandatory. In addition, hikers should carry plenty of drinking water. Heavy leather gloves will protect your hands from sharp rocks and cactus spines.

For those who want to combine hiking and caving, Big Tubes trailhead offers a relatively easy way to see a variety of volcanic features up close, including a system of fascinating lava tubes. Lava tubes are formed from a river of molten lava when the surface cools faster than the core. The outer edges harden into solid rock and the molten lava pours out, leaving a tunnel. At 17 miles long, this is one of the largest lava tube systems in North America.

The trail itself is easy, but the dirt road to it, County Road 42, is rough and rutted when dry and completely impassable when wet. The trail follows rock

La Ventana Natural Arch at El Malpais National Monument

cairns about 0.5 mile to a junction, where it branches into three sections that lead to a variety of lava tubes and collapsed tubes, including 1,200-foot-long Four Windows Cave.

Many of the lava tubes have holes, called skylights if they're large and windows if they're small. Lava tubes that have caved in are called collapses. This excursion can easily total several miles, depending on how much lava tube exploration you do. Those planning to enter the tubes are advised to carry three separate sources of light, and to check with El Malpais rangers on current conditions before setting out. A trail guide is available at the information center and at the trailhead.

A section of the national Continental Divide Trail crosses El Malpais. Check at the information center or ranger station for specific directions and current conditions. Backcountry hiking and camping are permitted, although all overnight trips require a free backcountry permit, which is available at the information center.

La Ventana Natural Arch can be seen from a viewpoint along NM 117 or from an easy ⅛-mile (one-way) hike into the Cebolla Wilderness. *La Ventana* is Spanish for "The Window." This spectacular arch, among the largest in New Mexico, was sculpted by the forces of erosion from sandstone deposited during the time of the dinosaurs.

Nearby, NM 117 passes through The Narrows, which marks the boundary between jet-black lava rocks deposited about 3,000 years ago, and 500-foot-high light tan sandstone cliffs, the same rock from which La Ventana Natural Arch was created. From a picnic area near the south end of The Narrows, The Narrows Rim Trail heads north along the top of the cliffs. There are no trail signs, so check with rangers before setting out.

Other highlights of El Malpais include the rugged West Malpais Wilderness, which includes an island of ponderosa pine in a sea of lava, and the Chain of Craters Backcountry Byway, a 36-mile section of County Road 42 that is suitable for high-clearance vehicles in dry weather and which provides delightful views of lava rocks with a backdrop of sandstone bluffs.

Those interested in the people who lived at El Malpais sometime between A.D. 1000 and 1300 can see the remains of a pueblo at the Dittert Site, Armijo Canyon, on the edge of the Cebolla Wilderness off County Road 41. This L-shaped sandstone structure was originally two stories high and had thirty to thirty-five large rooms. The site was named for Alfred "Ed" Dittert Jr., one of the archeologists who excavated the site in the late 1940s. Nine rooms and a kiva have been excavated.

Located on private land within the national monument boundaries is the Bandera Crater Ice Caves, a lava tube that contains ice year-round. A separate fee is charged for entrance.

This rugged and seemingly desolate land supports a surprising amount of wildlife, some of which has adapted its colors to blend in with the dark volcanic rocks. Among the lava flows watch for species such as lizards, rodents, and rabbits. Mule deer, coyotes, bobcats, and black bear are more commonly seen in the sandstone bluffs and forested areas. Watch for pronghorn in the West Malpais Wilderness.

Almost 200 bird species frequent the monument, with The Narrows picnic area an especially good bird-watching location. Resident species include northern harriers, killdeer, western bluebirds, mountain bluebirds, red-tailed hawks, American kestrels, common ravens, horned larks, mountain chickadees, bushtits, white-breasted nuthatches, dark-eyed juncos, red-winged blackbirds, western meadowlarks, rock wrens, canyon wrens, mourning doves, northern flickers, Steller's jays, western scrub jays, and piñon jays.

In summer, watch in open woodlands for rufous, broad-tailed, and black-chinned hummingbirds; Cassin's kingbirds; spotted and canyon towhees; and chipping sparrows. In the summer white-throated swifts, cliff swallows, and an occasional violet-green swallow are seen along the sandstone cliffs, and turkey vultures can often be spotted soaring overhead.

The El Malpais Visitor Center on NM 53, operated by the National Park Service, contains exhibits on volcanos and the flora, fauna, and human history of the monument and conservation area. The Bureau of Land Management operates a ranger station along NM 117 where you can also learn about El Malpais. In addition, information can be obtained at the Northwest New Mexico Visitor Center, just south of I-40 exit 85 in Grants.

On summer weekends, rangers lead hikes and cave trips and offer evening bat flight programs and other activities.

Summer days are warm to hot, with highs in the 80s and 90s and lows in the 50s. Afternoon thunderstorms are common in July and August. Winters are brisk, with daytime highs in the 40s and 50s and nighttime temperatures in the teens. September and October are usually quite pleasant, with days in the 60s and 70s and nighttime temperatures in the 30s and 40s.

Nearby, there are hiking and camping opportunities in the Cibola National Forest. Also nearby is El Morro National Monument, which is discussed below.

EL MORRO NATIONAL MONUMENT

HOURS/SEASONS:	Trails open 9 A.M. to 6 P.M. in summer and 9 A.M. to 4 P.M. in winter; campground open overnight, year-round
BEST TIME TO VISIT:	Late spring through fall
AREA:	1,279 acres
ELEVATION:	7,218 feet
FACILITIES:	Visitor center/museum, interpretive exhibits, interpretive trail, picnic tables, restrooms, 9 campsites (no showers or hookups)
ATTRACTIONS:	Hiking, archeological sites, historical exhibits, interpretive programs
NEARBY:	El Malpais National Monument and National Conservation Area
ACCESS:	42 miles southwest of Grants via NM 53

Long a stopping point for weary and thirsty travelers, Inscription Rock at El Morro National Monument is literally a page in the history of this region—one that has been signed personally by some of the people who made that history happen. This National Park Service property also includes pre-Columbian American Indian ruins and a variety of petroglyphs, all of which can be see via two interconnecting trails.

It is believed that prehistoric hunter-gatherers visited this area to take advantage of a permanent waterhole that lay at the base of a 200-foot sandstone bluff. Then, about 1275, Ancestral Puebloans (also called Anasazi) constructed two multistoried stone villages on the mesa above the bluff. The larger of the pueblos was excavated in the 1950s and has been stabilized. The smaller pueblo remains unexcavated and is seen only as a mound of dirt covered with desert plants.

The excavated pueblo contained almost 900 living, work, and storage rooms surrounding an open courtyard, and probably housed from 1,000 to 1,500 people. There were also several kivas (circular rooms used for ceremonies and religious rites), grinding bins, and fire pits. Rainwater was captured in cisterns. A series of hand and toe steps led from the mesa top down to the waterhole at the base of the bluff. By about 1350 the pueblos' residents were gone, and it is believed that the people of nearby Zuni Pueblo are their descendents.

While no one actually lived here after the Ancestral Puebloans left, this is not to say that El Morro received no visitors. Its reliable year-round water source guaranteed that this would be a popular spot.

An excavated kiva at El Morro National Monument

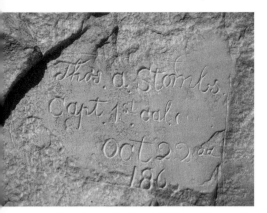

Inscription Rock at El Morro National Monument

Spanish explorers made their first treks into this region in 1540, and during the sixteenth century at least some conquistadors stopped at the base of this bluff for water and a night's rest.

However, it was not until 1605 that Don Juan de Oñate, who established the first Spanish colony in what is now New Mexico, made his visit official. Perhaps inspired by petroglyphs left by American Indians, he became the first European to etch his name in the soft sandstone. The Spanish inscription reads, *"Paso por aqui el adelantado Don Juan de Oñate del descubrimiento de la mar del sur 16 de Abril de 1605.,"* This translates to: "Here passed the governor Don Juan de Oñate from the discovery of the Sea of the South April 16, 1605." The Sea of the South refers to the Gulf of California.

Numerous subsequent Spanish travelers left their names on the rock. They include Diego de Vargas, who stopped by in 1692 during his mission to retake New Mexico for Spain following an Indian revolt in 1680.

After New Mexico became a territory of the United States in 1848, English-speaking people continued the tradition. The first white Americans to add their signatures were U.S. Army cartographer Lieutenant J. H. Simpson and artist R. H. Kern, who did so on September 18, 1849. Kern made drawings of the inscriptions, and Simpson is credited with coining the name "Inscription Rock."

Travelers on their way to California stopped at El Morro, adding their names. Several inscriptions from the late 1850s were left by members of a unique U.S. Army caravan—a short-lived experiment in using camels imported from Egypt and Turkey to travel through the Southwest's deserts. The Union Pacific Railroad surveyed the area in 1868, and many of its workers added their names, usually followed by the initials U.P.R. The use of the El Morro waterhole, and Inscription Rock, essentially ended when the Santa Fe Railroad laid its tracks 11 miles to the north.

Today's travelers are prohibited from adding their names to Inscription Rock, of course, but two self-guided trails, with trail guides available at the visitor center, provide easy access to both Inscription Rock and the Ancestral Puebloan ruins.

The easy, paved Inscription Rock Trail Loop leads from the visitor center past the waterhole to Inscription Rock, and then loops back to the visitor center, a total distance of 0.5 mile.

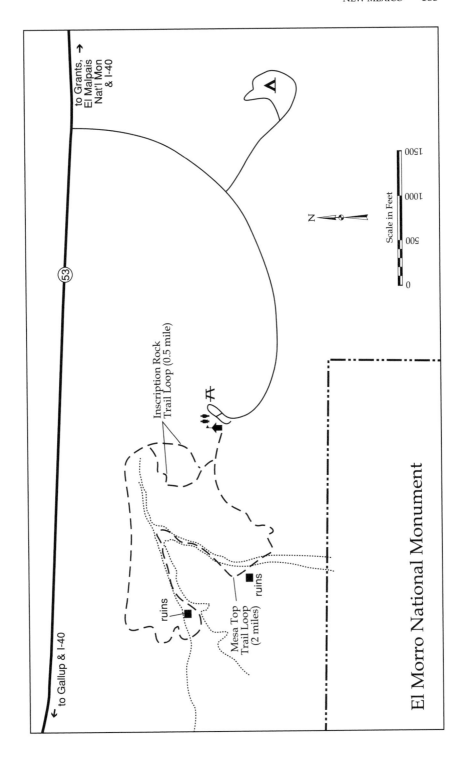

to Grants,
El Malpais
Nat'l Mon
& I-40

53

to Gallup & I-40

Inscription Rock
Trail Loop (0.5 mile)

Mesa Top
Trail Loop
(2 miles)

ruins

ruins

N

Scale in Feet

0   500   1000   1500

El Morro National Monument

Hikers pause along the barren rock that serves as a trail at El Morro National Monument.

However, instead of heading back from Inscription Rock, most visitors continue from here onto the 2-mile round-trip Mesa Top Trail Loop, which follows the base of the cliff through an open wood of ponderosa pines before climbing about 200 feet to the top of the bluff. There it leads past the unexcavated pueblo site to the excavated pueblo. The mesa top also provides panoramic views of the surrounding mountains and canyons. The trail then climbs back down from the mesa, among juniper and piñon trees, and ends back at the visitor center. Because of the climb up onto the mesa and the uneven sandstone surface, this trail is considered moderate. Total distance for both trails is about 2.3 miles.

The monument's visitor center/museum has exhibits on the various people who have lived here or visited El Morro, a 15-minute introductory video program, and a small bookstore. Information on the monument can also be obtained at the Northwest New Mexico Visitor Center, just south of I-40 exit 85 in Grants.

Rangers offer talks and other programs during the summer, and arts and crafts demonstrations are occasionally scheduled at the visitor center during summer months.

The weather here is hot in summer and cold in winter, but with plenty of sunshine year-round. High temperatures in summer often reach the 90s, with lows in the 50s, and summer thunderstorms are common. Winters may see daytime highs in the 40s and 50s, and nighttime temperatures in the teens. Winds, particularly in late winter and spring, make it feel colder. Winters can also be snowy, sometimes closing Mesa Top Trail Loop. September and October are usually quite pleasant, with daytime temperatures in the 60s and 70s and nighttime temperatures in the 30s and 40s.

Nearby are the badlands of El Malpais National Monument and National Conservation Area, discussed elsewhere in this book.

FORT UNION NATIONAL MONUMENT

HOURS/SEASONS: 8 A.M. to 6 P.M. daily Memorial Day through Labor Day; 8 A.M. to 5 P.M. daily the rest of the year. Closed Christmas and New Year's Day

BEST TIME TO VISIT: Summer through fall

AREA: 720 acres

ELEVATION: 6,760 feet

FACILITIES: Visitor center/museum, interpretive exhibits and trail, picnic tables, restrooms, public telephone

ATTRACTIONS: Historic sites and exhibits, interpretive programs

NEARBY: Pecos National Historical Park and Capulin Volcano National Monument

ACCESS: 28 miles north of Las Vegas, NM via I-25 (exit 366) and NM 161

The remains of what was once the Southwest's largest frontier fort are the focus of this national monument. It also includes a section of the Santa Fe Trail, which is evidenced by the large number of ruts left by the wagons traveling through some 150 years ago. This National Park Service–operated monument has a self-guided interpretive trail, a museum that helps explain the real West of the 1800s, and a variety of summer programs.

Commissioned in 1851, Fort Union's major function was to protect settlers and traders using the Santa Fe Trail, as well as local residents, from attacks by American Indians. The Santa Fe Trail was the main wagon route from the Missouri River, which was then the western edge of the United States' railroad network, to the Wild West of New Mexico. The trail had opened in 1821, but it was not until the Mexican-American War ended in 1848 and New Mexico was ceded to the United States, that the U.S. had any jurisdiction here.

At first, army troops were stationed in Santa Fe, but Col. Edwin Sumner, whose job it was to protect the citizens of what was now the United States, opted to move army headquarters from Santa Fe, which he called "that sink of vice and extravagance," to a lonely spot near where two branches of the Santa Fe Trail met and where his men would be much closer to the trouble spots.

The first fort, which was used for 10 years, consisted of makeshift log and dirt cabins that were, by all accounts, pretty awful.

As the Civil War began, the army built a new, star-shaped partly underground fort that was designed to repel a Confederate attack. It was never tested in battle, but soldiers from Fort Union traveled to Glorieta Pass, southeast of Santa Fe, to meet the Confederates, who were advancing from Texas. The Fort Union soldiers sent the Confederates retreating back to Texas, essentially ending the Civil War in the New Mexico Territory.

Soon after the Battle of Glorieta Pass, construction of the third and final Fort Union began. The second Fort Union, in large part because of its sunken-earth

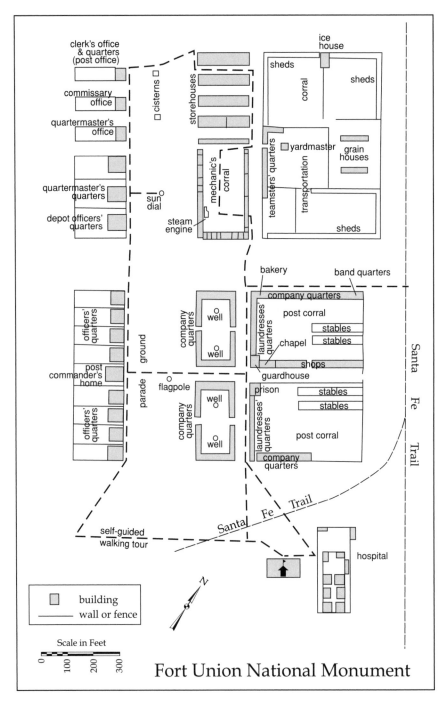

Fort Union National Monument

construction, was damp and apparently less livable than the first fort, as many of the soldiers opted to sleep outside in tents.

This third fort, which constitutes the majority of the ruins preserved at the national monument, was a handsome structure that took 6 years to complete. Constructed of adobe bricks on a foundation of stone, it was neatly plastered and included large glass windows, porches, fences, and even street lights.

The fort was built at a cost of more than 1 million dollars and included all the usual military facilities—numerous offices, barracks, workshops, a prison, guardhouse, and of course a parade ground. In addition, in part because of its role as the Southwest's primary military supply depot, the fort had large storehouses, corrals, and the region's largest hospital.

Despite continuing problems with leaking roofs, Fort Union was considered state of the art for its time and place, and an army inspector who visited in 1867 wrote that the officers' quarters were "far better than any officers' quarters that I have seen at any other frontier post."

However, the end was in sight for this and many other frontier forts. By the mid-1870s the Indians had been conquered, and in 1879 the Santa Fe Railroad arrived at nearby Las Vegas, New Mexico, replacing the Santa Fe Trail as the primary trade route. With less need for a military presence, the federal government began to consolidate its western military posts, and in 1891 Fort Union was abandoned.

Today visitors view the stabilized ruins of the third Fort Union, as well as some of the remains from the second fort, from a 1.6-mile self-guided walking trail. There are also good views of wagon ruts from the Santa Fe Trail along the east edge of the fort.

The visitor center/museum has exhibits on the construction of all three forts, life at Fort Union, the Civil War in New Mexico, and the Santa Fe Trail. There is

Fort Union National Monument Superintendent Harry Myers talks to some visiting photographers in front of the ruins of the historic fort.

an audiovisual program, and the visitor center boasts a well-stocked bookstore with titles on the history of New Mexico and the Southwest.

Living history talks and demonstrations are presented on summer weekends. Special events include one guided tour each year (in June) to the site of the first fort. Cultural Encounters on the Santa Fe Trail, scheduled in July, is a living history camp with talks and demonstrations presented in period dress. An evening walk through the ruins, with scenes re-created from the past, is presented in August (reservations are required). Contact monument offices for specific dates and times.

Summer daytime temperatures at Fort Union are pleasant, with highs usually in the 80s, while nighttime temperatures drop into the 50s. Winters are cool but sunny, with highs commonly in the 40s and low 50s and lows often in the teens. Light snow is fairly common, and late winter and spring winds can be annoying. Fall is often beautiful, with warm days, cool nights, and clear skies.

Nearby attractions include Pecos National Historical Park and Capulin Volcano National Monument, each of which is described elsewhere in this book.

GILA CLIFF DWELLINGS NATIONAL MONUMENT

HOURS/SEASONS:	Cliff dwelling trail open 8 A.M. to 6 P.M. daily Memorial Day through Labor Day; 9 A.M. to 4 P.M. daily the rest of the year. Closed Christmas and New Year's Day. Trail to the Past and campgrounds open daily, overnight, year-round
BEST TIME TO VISIT:	Spring through fall
AREA:	533 acres (national monument only)
ELEVATION:	5,700 feet
FACILITIES:	(in national monument and national forest) Visitor center, visitor contact station, interpretive exhibits and trails, restrooms, amphitheater, self-serve dog kennels, picnic tables, 17 campsites (no showers or hookups), dump station, horse corrals
ATTRACTIONS:	Archeological sites, hiking, wildlife viewing, bird-watching, interpretive programs
NEARBY:	Gila National Forest and Gila Wilderness
ACCESS:	44 miles north of Silver City via NM 15 (narrow, winding mountain road; allow 2 hours)

This national monument takes visitors back some 700 years to the time when this was the home of the Mogollon (MUGGY-own), who hunted and gathered wild plants and planted corn, squash, and beans on the mesa tops and along the rivers. The Mogollon also built homes—first simple pit houses dug into the earth, then rectangular above-ground buildings of stone or interwoven twigs.

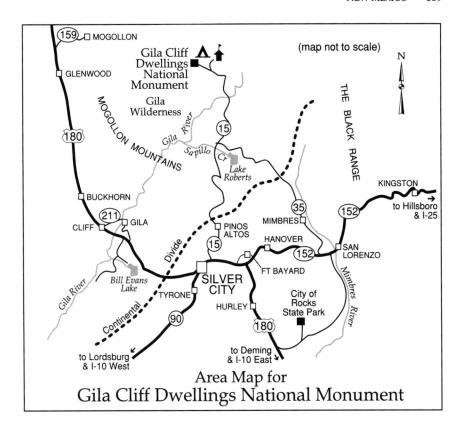

Area Map for
Gila Cliff Dwellings National Monument

Finally, the well-protected cliff dwellings that are the national monument's main attraction appeared.

Archeologists say there may have been two groups of Mogollon people here at different times, as evidenced by differences in pottery found during excavations. There are numerous ruins of Mimbres Mogollon pit houses dating to between A.D. 200 and 550, as well as later above-ground structures. However, the cliff dwellings, which are simply homes built into natural caves, were constructed by a different group of Mogollon, the Tularosa, who relocated from an area about 75 miles to the northwest.

This later group built their cave houses in the late 1270s and 1280s, as determined by tree-ring dating. There are about forty stone rooms spread among five caves along a southeast-facing cliff, and archeologists believe that forty to sixty people lived there. In addition to what they could grow or catch, the Mogollon traded with other tribes for cotton, shells, and obsidian (used for arrow points). They also weaved and produced striking white pottery with black designs.

Although it appears that these cliff dwellers thrived for a while, in about one generation, by 1300, they had abandoned their homes. Why they left and where they went remains a mystery, although there is speculation that they joined other Indian pueblos to the north and east.

Impressive cliff dwellings at Gila Cliff Dwellings National Monument

The ruins are accessible via the unpaved Gila Cliff Dwellings Trail, a somewhat rocky 1-mile round-trip loop. This easy to moderate interpretive trail has a few steep sections, stairs, and ladders, as it leads visitors about 180 feet up the side of the cliff and into the cliff dwellings. Many of the rooms can be entered, although some are off limits because of their fragile condition. The trail becomes muddy when it rains and slick in freezing or snowy conditions, so good traction footwear is recommended. A trail guide is available at the trailhead, and rangers are stationed at the ruins to provide additional information. A daily guided tour is offered at 1 P.M.

The cliff dwellings that comprise the national monument are under the jurisdiction of the National Park Service but managed on a day-to-day basis by the U.S. Forest Service, which also manages the surrounding Gila National Forest and adjacent Gila Wilderness.

Near the cliff dwellings, but officially in the national forest, are two small campgrounds and the Trail to the Past. This easy 0.25-mile round-trip walk provides access to a small two-room cliff dwelling, which was occupied about 700 years ago. There is also a Mogollon pictograph panel—a series of rock art designs created with a paint made from water and powdered hematite. You can also see what appears to have been a Mogollon work area—a boulder worn smooth from what may have been the sharpening of stone tools.

Among the 1,500 miles of trails open to hikers and horseback riders in the Gila National Forest and Gila Wilderness, one of the most easily accessible is

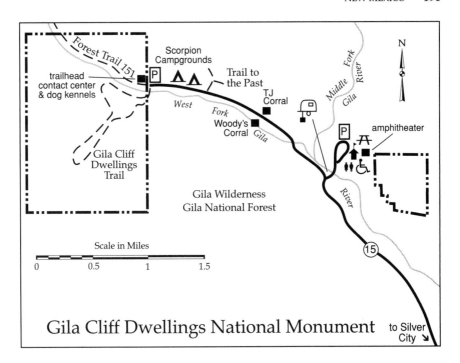

Gila Cliff Dwellings National Monument   to Silver City ↘

Forest Trail 151, a moderate hike that begins at the Gila Cliff Dwellings parking lot and follows the West Fork of the Gila River into the Gila Wilderness, crossing the river a number of times. A popular turn-around point is a small cliff dwelling ruin located 3 miles up the trail. To that point there is an elevation gain of just over 400 feet as the trail follows the river through an open forest, past the ruins of a log cabin and the grave of a nineteenth-century murder victim, and to the cliff dwelling.

Several trails into the wilderness area also take off from the TJ Corral Trailhead along NM 15 between the visitor center and the Gila Cliff Dwellings site. A handout on the trails is available at the visitor center and visitor contact station.

Wildlife viewing and bird-watching opportunities are abundant in and near the national monument, as well as throughout the national forest and wilderness area. Some of the best viewing spots are along the West Fork of the Gila River. Birds frequently seen include great blue herons, red-tailed hawks, turkey vultures, American kestrels, canyon wrens, red-faced warblers, hooded orioles, Steller's and scrub jays, and Bell's vireos. Bald eagles are occasionally seen in winter. Mammals to watch for include mule deer, Abert's squirrels, raccoons, and the occasional elk. Black bear and mountain lions also live in the area, but are seldom seen.

The Upper and Lower Scorpion Campgrounds are little more than parking lots for RVs, but offer pleasant tent sites that are nicely spaced among the trees and which have grills and picnic tables. The campgrounds have restrooms with cold running water in the sinks. Only trailers under 17 feet are permitted.

The visitor center, operated jointly by the U.S. Forest Service and National Park Service, has a museum with exhibits on the Mogollon culture and a small bookstore. There is also a visitor contact station at the Gila Cliff Dwellings trailhead, which also has exhibits and a small bookstore.

Summer activities may include evening campfire programs at the amphitheater near the visitor center. The monument offers a Junior Ranger program, in which kids complete projects in an activity guide to earn badges.

Summers days here are usually warm to hot, with highs in the 80s and 90s, and nighttime temperatures dropping into the 40s and 50s. Thunderstorms are common in July and August. Winters are sunny but cool, with highs in the 40s and 50s and lows in the teens and 20s. Trails and the entry road are occasionally closed temporarily by snow. Spring and fall offer pleasantly warm days, with highs often in the 70s and low 80s and nighttime temperatures near or below freezing. Spring tends to be windy.

There are numerous opportunities for backpacking, horseback riding, and fishing in the national forest and wilderness area, and for mountain biking in the national forest (but not in the wilderness area). In addition, there are several hot springs nearby. Check at the visitor center or visitor contact station for maps and recommendations.

PECOS NATIONAL HISTORICAL PARK

HOURS/SEASONS:	8 A.M. to 6 P.M. daily Memorial Day through Labor Day; 8 A.M. to 5 P.M. daily the rest of the year. Closed Christmas and New Year's Day
BEST TIME TO VISIT:	Summer through fall
AREA:	6,671 acres
ELEVATION:	7,000 feet
FACILITIES:	Visitor center/museum, interpretive exhibits and trail, picnic tables, restrooms, public telephone
ATTRACTIONS:	Archeological and historical sites and exhibits, interpretive programs, guided tours
NEARBY:	Fort Union National Monument and Santa Fe National Forest
ACCESS:	25 miles southeast of Santa Fe via I-25 and NM 63 and/or NM 50

Preserving well over 1,000 years of human history, Pecos National Historical Park takes us from prehistoric times through Spanish colonization up to the early twentieth century. Here, the National Park Service protects and interprets prehistoric American Indian ruins, a mission church built by Spanish

The ruins of a mission church, built by the Franciscans in 1717, are among the highlights of Pecos National Monument.

conquistadors, a Santa Fe Trail trading post, the site of New Mexico's most decisive Civil War battle, and an early-twentieth-century cattle ranch.

Although not all of these sites are fully open to the public on a daily basis as of this writing, a new park management plan is being prepared that is expected to change that within the next few years. In the meantime, guided tours are offered by reservation to many of the park's remote sites.

There is also plenty to see for those who drop in without calling for tour reservations. The park's main activities are exploring the ruins of Pecos Pueblo and the Spanish mission and seeing the excellent museum exhibits.

Nomadic hunter-gatherers had been attracted to this area for thousands of years before pit houses began to appear in the ninth century. Then in the twelfth century, the pueblo of Pecos began taking shape. Although it started as one small village among about two dozen small villages in the Pecos Valley, protection and other issues initiated a move to create Pecos Pueblo by consolidating the smaller villages into a single large one. By 1450, Pecos had become one of the largest and most important Southwestern pueblos, a walled compound standing five stories high that housed some 2,000 persons.

The people of Pecos grew corn, beans, squash, and cotton, and traded with Apaches and other Plains tribes, as well as other pueblos. By the late 1500s they were also trading with the Spanish, who visited Pecos in 1540 on their very first foray into New Mexico in search of the fabled cities of gold.

Although the Spanish conquistadors did not find gold, they did discover what they believed were souls that needed saving, and by the late 1500s began setting up missions to convert the Pueblo people to Christianity. In all, four mission churches were built at Pecos, including the last one, built in 1717, whose ruins remain today.

The people of Pecos and other New Mexico pueblos did not appreciate being told by the Franciscan missionaries that their religious views and ceremonies, which they had practiced for centuries, were wrong. That, combined with the demand that they pay tribute to this new religion, the introduction of European diseases, a drought and the resultant famine, led to the Pueblo Revolt of 1680, in which the scattered pueblos joined together to force the Spanish back to Mexico.

At Pecos, the priest was killed and the mission church, which had been the most impressive in the region, was destroyed. On the site of the mission's living quarters the Pecos people built a kiva, their own traditional ceremonial chamber, that had been forbidden under Spanish rule.

The Spaniards returned 12 years later to retake New Mexico. Although their reconquest required bloodshed at some pueblos, the takeover of Pecos Pueblo was peaceful, and a new Pecos mission, built on the ruins of the old one, was the first mission reestablished after the revolt.

Although the Franciscans now treated the Indians better, disease, raids by other Indian tribes, and additional problems led to the decline of Pecos, and its few final tribal members abandoned Pecos to join Jemez Pueblo, about 80 miles to the west, in 1838. Pecos Pueblo and its mission then fell into ruin.

Today, a 1.25-mile round-trip self-guided trail leads from the visitor center through the ruins of Pecos Pueblo and the Spanish mission church. The two reconstructed kivas in the pueblo may also be entered. A trail guide is available at the visitor center.

In addition to the ruins of the pueblo and mission, the park has a number of nearby sites that presently can be seen only on guided tours. The free tours are offered year-round, but fill quickly in summer. Calling for reservations at least two weeks in advance is recommended.

These nearby sites include several early Puebloan ruins, the remains of a nineteenth-century Spanish settlement, a section of the Santa Fe Trail (complete with wagon wheel ruts), and a stage station along the trail. The Forked Lightning Ranch, a working cattle ranch in the early 1900s that became known as a dude ranch and tourist attraction, has a main ranch house designed by famed architect John Gaw Meem. Nearby are two sites from the Battle of Glorieta Pass, which occurred in March of 1862. That battle was considered the decisive contest of the Civil War for New Mexico, in that it prevented the Confederates from overrunning the Southwest.

The visitor center's museum contains exhibits on the pueblo, missions, and other aspects of the park, including a number of prehistoric Indian and Spanish colonial artifacts discovered during excavations. A 10-minute introductory video program is shown, and there is also a bookstore. During the summer, crafts demonstrations by local American Indian and Hispanic artisans are presented several weekends each month. There are also full moon tours, a traditional Feast Day Mass in the mission church the first Sunday in August, and other activities, in addition to the guided tours discussed above.

Sunny days are the norm in this part of New Mexico. Daytime temperatures during summer are mild, with highs usually in the 80s, while nighttime temperatures drop into the 50s. Winters are cold and there is often snow on the ground, with highs in the 40s and low 50s and lows in the teens or below. Fall is often beautiful, with warm days and cool nights. Spring tends to be windy.

Nearby is Fort Union National Monument, discussed elsewhere in this book, and the Santa Fe National Forest, which offers camping, hiking, mountain biking, cross-country skiing, fishing, and a variety of other activities.

PETROGLYPH NATIONAL MONUMENT

HOURS/SEASONS:	8 A.M. to 5 P.M. daily; closed Thanksgiving, Christmas, and New Year's Day
BEST TIME TO VISIT:	Year-round
AREA:	7,236 acres
ELEVATION:	5,000 feet
FACILITIES:	Visitor center/museum, interpretive exhibits and trails, picnic tables, restrooms
ATTRACTIONS:	Petroglyph viewing, archeological sites, hiking, interpretive programs
NEARBY:	Coronado State Monument, Rio Grande Nature Center State Park
ACCESS:	Visitor center is 3 miles north of I-40 via Unser Boulevard

Situated in the northern reaches of the Chihuahuan Desert on the site of Albuquerque's West Mesa, Petroglyph National Monument guards some 20,000 petroglyphs, most believed to have been created by the ancestors of today's

Pueblo Indians. These petroglyphs, the creations of prehistoric and later residents of this area, were carved into black lava rocks deposited here some 130,000 years ago by a series of volcanic eruptions.

The monument, managed by the National Park Service and the City of Albuquerque, offers several hiking trails that

The namesake of the Macaw Trail at Petroglyph National Monument

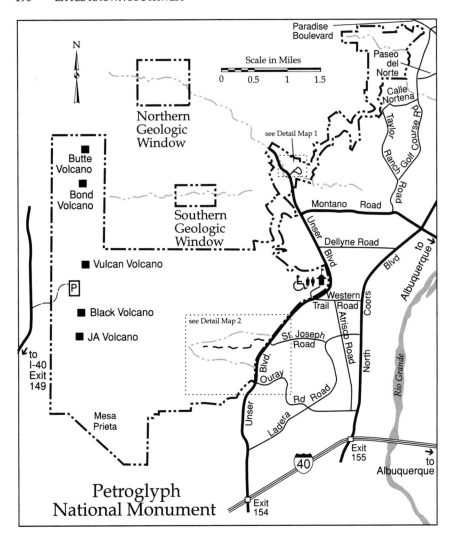

provide easy access to the petroglyphs, a look at the volcanos that created this rugged badlands, and opportunities for wildlife viewing and bird-watching.

Petroglyphs, from the Greek words *petra* (rock) and *glyph* (carving) are simply images carved or chipped into the surfaces of rocks, in this case scratching away the black desert varnish to expose the light gray below. As in many other areas of the Southwest, most of the monument's petroglyphs are on east and south-facing slopes.

Although the bulk of the petroglyphs here were created between A.D. 1300 and 1600, there are some abstract images that are believed to have been made by nomadic hunter-gatherers at least 2,000 years ago. Later, as farming became more important, the petroglyphs became a little less abstract, with circles that

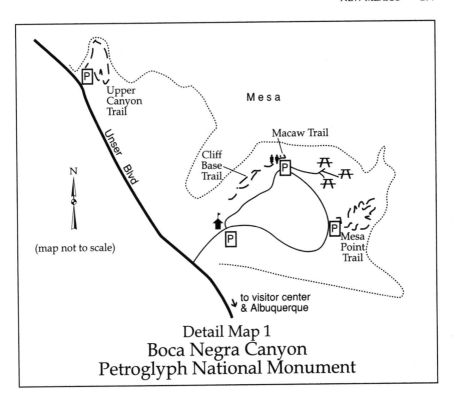

Detail Map 1
Boca Negra Canyon
Petroglyph National Monument

perhaps symbolized the sun or moon, and "rake" designs that may have represented rain or the rays of the sun. Then, beginning in about A.D. 900, people began creating images of wolves, mountain lions, and other animals as well as humans, masks, and some curious animal bodies with human heads. There are also animal tracks, occasionally animals with arrows or spears in them, handprints, and what appear to be clouds.

In addition to the images created by prehistoric American Indians, there are also petroglyphs here from Spanish settlers, created in the seventeenth and eighteenth centuries, that often show images of livestock brands and Christian crosses. There are also later images, usually initials, left by settlers in the late nineteenth and early twentieth centuries.

The Boca Negra Canyon has a fantastic variety of images that are easily seen along three short, paved trails, each with interpretive signs. In addition, a guide to the three trails is available at the visitor center.

The Mesa Point Trail, although only 0.75-mile round trip, is considered moderately strenuous because it gains about 200 feet elevation in a steep climb to the top of the escarpment. Along the route are petroglyphs of four-pointed stars, animals, handprints, and a human-like mask on the corner of a rock that

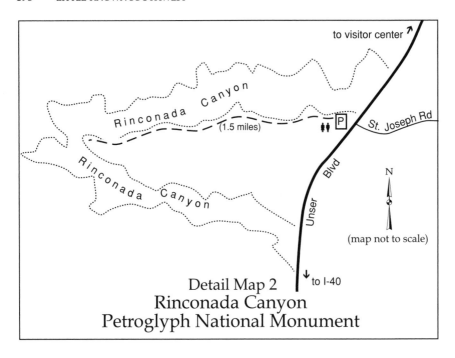

Detail Map 2
Rinconada Canyon
Petroglyph National Monument

"looks" in two directions. Visible from the top of the escarpment are the Sandia Mountains to the east, with the city of Albuquerque spread out below them, and the volcanic cinder cones that created this escarpment to the west.

The two other Boca Negra Canyon trails are easy. The 0.25-mile Macaw Trail, named for a wonderful image of this Mexican parrot, also has petroglyphs depicting what appear to be yucca seed pods. The 0.5-mile Cliff Base Trail offers a variety of petroglyphs, including four-pointed stars, circles, spirals, birds, serpents, and masked figures.

Hundreds of petroglyphs can also be seen along the 3-mile round-trip Rinconada Trail in Rinconada Canyon. The moderately rated hiking trail follows a path created by wildlife and used by Spanish sheepherders. Petroglyphs here include roadrunners and lizards, handprints, and human and godlike figures. There are also images of livestock brands, crosses, and sheep left by Spanish settlers, and the names of two young Anglo men—Milton Thorpe and Victor Buday—who were hunting rabbits and rattlesnakes in the canyon on February 22, 1919.

Hikers also discover a variety of petroglyphs along the Piedras Marcada Canyon trail at the north edge of the monument. The sandy, 3-mile round-trip hike is considered easy, and in addition to being a good place from which to view petroglyphs, is a good setting for observing wildlife.

For those who want to get a close-up view of the five volcanos that created this harsh terrain, an unpaved road along the west edge of the monument leads to a parking area, from which hikers can follow various routes among the volcanic cones.

Throughout the monument visitors can see a variety of wildlife adapted to the desert environment, including desert cottontail and black-tailed jackrabbits, white-tailed antelope squirrels, rock squirrels, coyotes, and various lizards, including the colorful collared lizard. There are also snakes, including the poisonous western diamondback and the western prairie rattlesnake.

Birds frequently seen in the monument include horned larks, rock and canyon wrens, northern mockingbirds, canyon towhees, white-crowned and sage sparrows, western meadowlarks, house finches, Say's phoebes, loggerhead shrikes, barn swallows, mourning doves, scaled quail, American kestrels, turkey vultures, and great horned owls.

The monument's visitor center has exhibits on the petroglyphs and the people who created them. There is also a small bookstore. Outside the visitor center a short paved nature trail with identifying signs leads past a variety of desert plants such as prickly pear cactus, soapweed yucca, snakeweed, lemonade bush, winter fat, and four-winged saltbush. There is also an information booth adjacent to the Boca Negra Canyon trailheads. During the summer and early fall rangers give occasional talks and guided hikes and walks, including excursions into undeveloped areas of the monument.

Summer days are warm to hot, with daytime temperatures often in the 90s or above and afternoon thunderstorms being fairly common. Spring and fall

Hikers watch for petroglyphs etched into the rocks along the Macaw Trail at Petroglyph National Monument.

are very pleasant, although spring winds can be ferocious. Winter days are often comfortable, with temperatures in the 50s, although below freezing temperatures and biting winter winds are not uncommon. There are few trees and little shade in the monument, so sun protection is recommended, even for short walks.

Nearby attractions include Coronado State Monument, which preserves the ruins of a prehistoric pueblo and has a reconstruction of a rare square kiva. Also nearby is Rio Grande Nature Center State Park, an environmental education center along the Rio Grande that offers nature trails, demonstration gardens, and the opportunity to see numerous birds and other wildlife.

SALINAS PUEBLO MISSIONS NATIONAL MONUMENT

HOURS/SEASONS:	9 A.M. to 6 P.M. Memorial day to Labor Day; 9 A.M. to 5 P.M. the rest of the year
BEST TIME TO VISIT:	Summer through fall
AREA:	1,100 acres
ELEVATION:	6,520 feet
FACILITIES:	Visitor center, interpretive exhibits and trails, picnic tables, restrooms, public telephone
ATTRACTIONS:	Archeological and historical sites, bird-watching
NEARBY:	Manzano Mountains State Park and Cibola National Forest
ACCESS:	Monument headquarters and the visitor center are in Mountainair. From Mountainair: Abó is 9 miles west on US 60 and 0.5 mile north on NM 513, Gran Quivira is 25 miles south on NM 55, and Quarai is 8 miles north on NM 55 and 1 mile west on the Quarai access road

This national monument is actually made up of three separate sites that preserve the ruins of three large Indian pueblos and what are considered the best remaining seventeenth-century Franciscan mission churches in the United States. Each of the sites can be explored via easy walking paths. There is a centrally located visitor center, and the monument also offers good bird-watching opportunities.

Although each site offers a slightly different perspective on the history of this region, they all tell the story of the conflict of cultures that occurred between the native Pueblo people and the Spanish colonists who arrived in the 1500s.

The pueblos of Abó, Gran Quivira (also called Las Humanas), and Quarai were constructed by people of the Ancestral Puebloan (also called Anasazi) and Mogollon cultures beginning in the 1300s. They were impressive and thriving

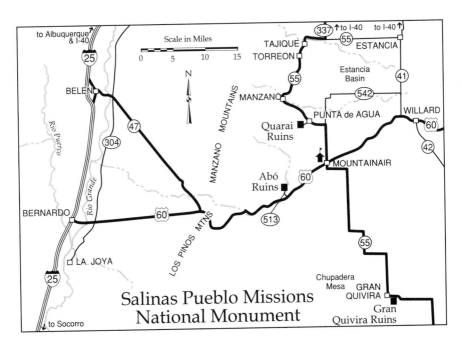

Salinas Pueblo Missions National Monument

communities when Spanish conquistadors first saw them in the late 1500s. The pueblos were ideally situated for trade, and their residents were the merchants of their day, trading with the Plains tribes to the east as well as the peoples of the Rio Grande pueblos to the west and north. Collectively, these pueblos are known as the *Salinas*, the Spanish word for "salt," which was abundant in the area and an important trading commodity.

Spain had begun its explorations of New Mexico in hopes of finding vast amounts of gold, and when that did not occur Spanish authorities were ready to forget about the region. However, the pope wanted Spain to convert the native people of the New World to Christianity, so Spanish King Phillip II sent missionaries and settlers to the colony in an effort to bring Roman Catholicism and the Spanish way of life to the Indians. That effort was at least partly successful, but along with God, European traditions, and technology they also brought a great deal of bitterness as well as European diseases to which the Indians had little immunity.

The Pueblo people practiced a religion in which dances and other rituals were intended to take the people's prayers to the gods in hopes of ensuring sufficient rain, good harvests and hunting, and universal harmony.

The Franciscan missionaries considered this polytheistic religion to be idolatry and tried to prevent the Pueblo people from practicing their dances and other rituals. At first the Pueblo religious leaders thought they could incorporate this new Christian god into their rituals, but after some of the Franciscans destroyed

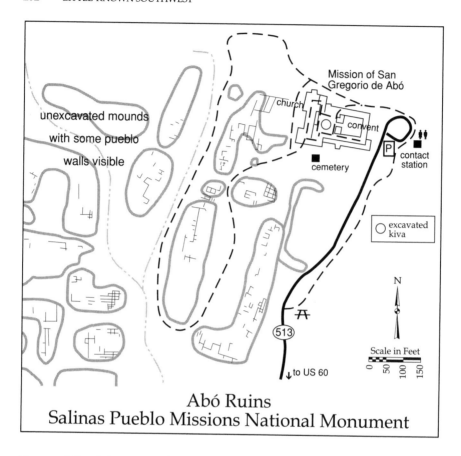

Mission of San Gregorio de Abó

church

convent

unexcavated mounds with some pueblo walls visible

P

contact station

cemetery

excavated kiva

N

Scale in Feet

0 50 100 150

513

to US 60

Abó Ruins
Salinas Pueblo Missions National Monument

kivas and the elaborate masks worn during the dances, it became obvious that there could be no middle ground.

Some Spanish colonists were permitted to demand tribute from the Indians, often in the form of grain or cloth, in exchange for teaching them European ways, protecting them, and helping to provide military assistance for the Spanish colonial government. This state of affairs contributed further to the ill feelings of the Pueblo people toward the Spanish.

A drought and famine in the 1660s and 1670s, along with epidemics of European diseases, finally did these Pueblos in, and the remaining residents abandoned their villages in the 1670s, most of them joining other pueblos in the middle Rio Grande area. Within a few years the pueblos to the north revolted against the Spanish colonizers, driving them back into Mexico, where they stayed until the reconquest of New Mexico in 1692.

The best place to begin a visit to these sites is the park headquarters' visitor center in Mountainair, which has exhibits on the three pueblos and the missions. A film explains this clash of cultures and helps visitors see it in its historical context. From the visitor center, head out to the individual sites. Each has impressive ruins that can be seen on short, easy paths; a visitor contact station with

The impressive Nuestra Señora de la Purísima Concepción de Cuarac Church, at the Quarai section of Salinas Pueblo Missions National Monument

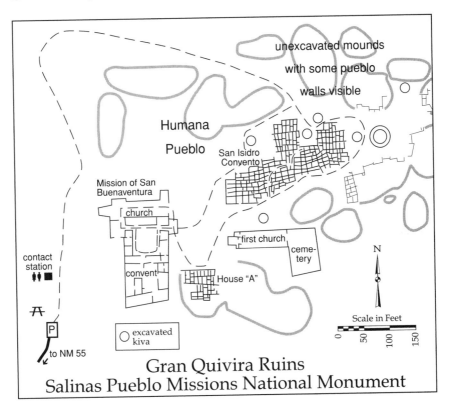

unexcavated mounds
with some pueblo
walls visible

Humana
Pueblo

San Isidro
Convento

Mission of San
Buenaventura

church

first church

cemetery

contact
station

convent

House "A"

N

excavated
kiva

Scale in Feet

0   50   100   150

to NM 55

**Gran Quivira Ruins
Salinas Pueblo Missions National Monument**

exhibits, restrooms, and a bookstore; and rangers to answer questions.

At Abó, a paved 0.25-mile trail leads to the towering walls of San Gregorio de Abó Church and continues for another 0.5 mile among the unexcavated ruins, which have a number of visible walls. Gran Quivira's 0.5-mile gravel trail winds among the ruins of two churches—both called San Buenaventura—plus the

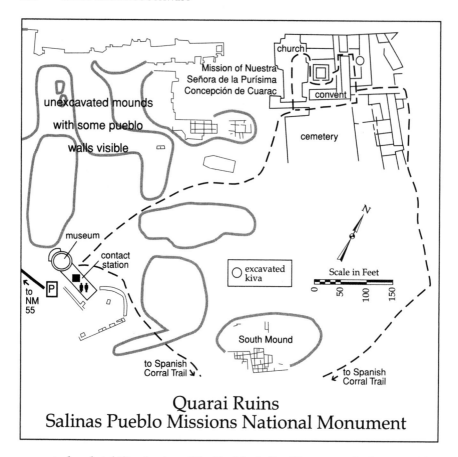

church
Mission of Nuestra
Señora de la Purísima
Concepción de Cuarac

convent

unexcavated mounds
with some pueblo
walls visible

cemetery

museum

contact
station

excavated
kiva

N

Scale in Feet

0   50   100   150

to
NM
55

P

South Mound

to Spanish
Corral Trail

to Spanish
Corral Trail

Quarai Ruins
Salinas Pueblo Missions National Monument

excavated and stabilized ruins of the Pueblo de Las Humanas, the largest of the Salinas pueblos. Also at the Gran Quivira site visitors can see a 1-hour video on the excavation of a section of the pueblo.

Quarai has perhaps the most impressive mission, the Nuestra Señora de la Purísima Concepción de Cuarac Church, whose red rock walls stand tall in a field of grasses. A 0.5-mile gravel loop leads from the contact station, where there is a museum, into the church and past some partially excavated pueblo ruins.

An easy side trip off the main Quarai trail takes you onto the 1-mile round-trip Spanish Corral Trail, which follows a hillside through a woodland of piñon, juniper, willow, and cottonwood with a stream and a variety of shrubs and other plants. This is a good spot for bird-watching. From here you'll also see the remains of the stone walls of what historians believe was a pen for sheep used by Hispanic settlers in the nineteenth century. Also from this trail are views east into the Estancia Valley and its salt lakes, from which people since prehistoric times have obtained salt for their own use as well as for trade.

More than 100 species of birds frequent the three units of Salinas Pueblo Missions National Monument, with the most variety and an especially colorful assortment in the riparian area along the Spanish Corral Trail at Quarai. Some species, such as Say's phoebes, nest in the ruins themselves.

In warmer weather watch for mourning doves, cliff swallows, northern mockingbirds, lesser goldfinches, house finches, black-headed grosbeaks, rock wrens, bushtits, violet-green swallows, Say's phoebes, and common nighthawks. Species more often seen from late fall through early spring include northern flickers, piñon jays, mountain bluebirds, Townsend's solitaires, American robins, song sparrows, and dark-eyed juncos. Year-round, watch for scrub jays, common ravens, and red-tailed hawks.

The monument has a Junior Ranger Program in which kids earn certificates by completing various projects. Heritage Preservation Week, held for one week each May, offers visitors a hands-on experience at stabilizing ruins. Fiestas and Holy Mass are periodically scheduled, and in recent years International Migratory Bird Day, held in May, has been celebrated with guided walks at the Quarai site. Check with monument offices for specific times and dates.

Weather here is fairly mild, with summer daytime temperatures usually in the 80s and low 90s and nighttime temperatures dropping into the 50s. Winters are cool, with highs in the 40s and 50s and lows in the teens and 20s; there is occasional snow. Spring tends to be windy, while September and October are often delightful. More than one-third of the area's precipitation occurs in July and August.

Nearby one has opportunities for camping, hiking, wildlife viewing, and other activities at Manzano Mountains State Park and in the Cibola National Forest.

THREE RIVERS PETROGLYPH SITE

HOURS/SEASONS: Overnight; year-round
BEST TIME TO VISIT: Spring and fall
AREA: 1,036 acres
ELEVATION: 5,000 feet
FACILITIES: Visitor contact station, interpretive exhibits, nature trail, picnic tables, restrooms, 8 campsites (no showers; 2 sites with electric and water hookups)
ATTRACTIONS: Petroglyph viewing, archeological sites, hiking
NEARBY: Lincoln National Forest, White Sands National Monument
ACCESS: 25 miles north of Tularosa via US 54 and County Road B30

It might be a bit out of the way but it is well worth the trip; Three Rivers Petroglyph Site is one of the best places in the Southwest to see prehistoric rock art. The site, operated by the Bureau of Land Management, offers hiking among the petroglyphs plus the opportunity to visit a partially excavated prehistoric village.

Petroglyphs are pictures on rocks that are created by scratching or chipping designs into the rock's weathered surface. Those designs that were simply scratched into the rock are generally the simplest and most primitive. Those made by striking the rock surface with a pointed stone created somewhat more sophisticated designs. The best petroglyphs, however, are believed to have been created by hitting a chisel-like piece of stone with another rock, which resulted in more control by the artist. It is believed that in some of the more complex petroglyphs, designs were painted on the rock before the chipping process began.

Three Rivers Petroglyph Site is located at the foot of the Sacramento Mountains, along the eastern edge of lands occupied by the Mogollon (MUGGY-own) people. The site contains more than 21,000 individual petroglyphs in one

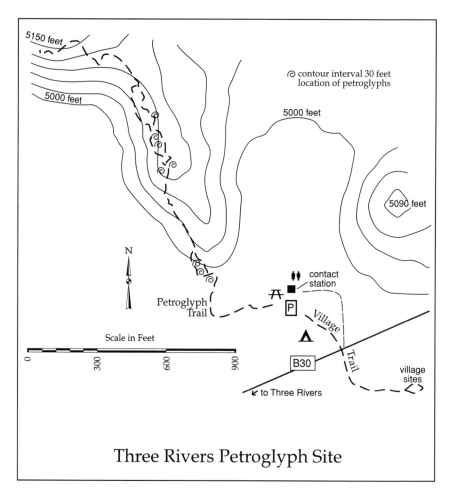

Three Rivers Petroglyph Site

of the greatest concentrations to be found anywhere. Archeologists believe that these images were etched into the black lava rock at least 1,000 years ago, and some theorize that at least some of the petroglyphs were created by lookouts who were posted on the rocky hillside.

The inhabitants of the Three Rivers area hunted, as is evident by their many depictions of game animals. They also apparently planted corn, beans, and squash. As with many of the prehistoric cultures of the Southwest, archeologists

Numerous petroglyphs can be seen at Three Rivers Petroglyph Site.

are at a loss as to why they abandoned the area by the early fifteenth century. Some theorize that climate changes made farming unproductive or that there were conflicts with other prehistoric groups. It is also not known where they went, although one theory is that they joined existing pueblos in northern New Mexico.

Petroglyph images here range from handprints to geometric patterns, including a large number of circles surrounded by dots. There are also animal tracks, usually identified as either turkey or roadrunner tracks. The more complex designs include fairly detailed images of bighorn sheep and stylized images of birds, which may have had religious meanings. There are also images of fish, lizards, mountain lions, and bears, and some stylized animals that have not been identified. Some animal images are pierced by arrows or spears, which may have been a report of a successful hunt or a plea to the gods for a good hunt.

There are also images of faces and masks, sometimes positioned on a rock in such a way as to give it a three-dimensional effect. Human faces are usually round with almond-shaped eyes, and heads are often shown somewhat flattened on top. Archeologists say that the Mogollon carried infants on cradleboards that flattened the babies' developing skulls.

The petroglyphs are easily seen along a 1-mile round-trip hike on a well-marked trail. Although it is short and considered easy, the trail does have some steep inclines and is rocky, so good hiking boots are recommended. There is little shade along the trail, except at one shelter located on a knoll. This is also a good vantage point for viewing the towering mountains to the east and the shimmering white gypsum sands and black lava flows to the west. From the shelter the main petroglyph trail loops back down the hillside, or hikers can continue on for a ways before turning around. A free brochure includes a trail guide keyed to numbers along the route.

A covered visitor contact station at the base of the hill is usually staffed by volunteers, and when someone is on duty a spotting scope aimed up at the hillside enables those not taking the hike to see some of the petroglyphs.

Another short trail leads from the picnic/camping area to the partially excavated remains of a prehistoric village, which includes the foundations of a pit house, a multiroom adobe building, and a rock structure.

The campground, which also serves as the picnic area, includes six primitive sites with shelters, tables, and barbecue grills. There are also two sites for recreational vehicles and one group site. A few trees are found at the campground.

Summers here are hot, with temperatures often in the 90s and above during the day but dropping into the 60s at night. Winters are cool, but not usually bitter cold, and spring is often windy. Rattlesnakes are fairly common, so hikers are advised to watch where they put their feet and hands.

Nearby attractions include the Lincoln National Forest, which has hiking and camping; and stunning White Sands National Monument, which is discussed in its own section in this book.

VALLE VIDAL UNIT OF THE CARSON NATIONAL FOREST

HOURS/SEASONS:	Overnight; year-round
BEST TIME TO VISIT:	Summer through fall
AREA:	100,000 acres
ELEVATION:	8,100 feet
FACILITIES:	Visitor center, interpretive exhibits, picnic tables, restrooms, 92 campsites (no hookups or showers)
ATTRACTIONS:	Hiking, historical sites, wildlife viewing, bird-watching, fishing
NEARBY:	Wild Rivers Recreation Area
ACCESS:	Via US 64 and the communities of Eagle Nest and Cimarron to the east, and from NM 522 and the towns of Questa and Costilla to the west

Wide open spaces dotted with sparkling lakes, tall pines, and snowcapped peaks highlight this beautiful outdoor playground, which offers hiking, camping, fishing, hunting, and some of the best wildlife viewing in the region. Once the site of pioneer logging and ranching communities and then the exclusive domain of the rich and famous, Valle Vidal has numerous historic ruins ranging from cattle ranches to railroad trestles to cemeteries dating back more than 100 years.

Valle Vidal is part of the Maxwell Land Grant, a parcel of land about the size of Rhode Island that in 1841 was deeded by the Mexican government to French

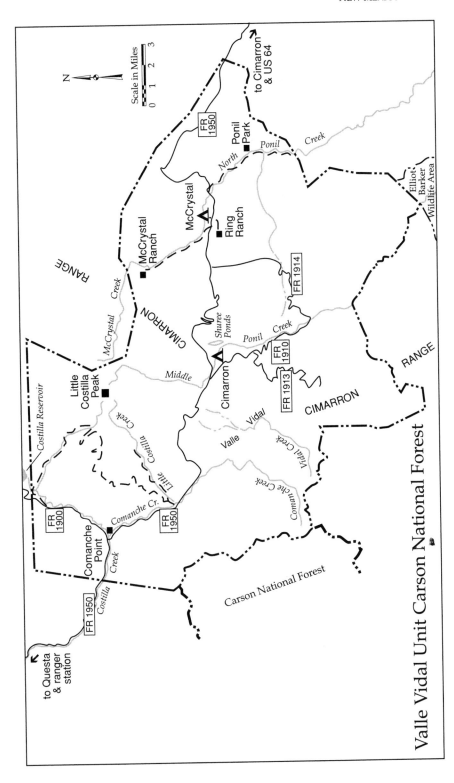

Valle Vidal Unit Carson National Forest

A father and daughter test their fishing skills in the Shuree Ponds in the Valle Vidal Unit of the Carson National Forest.

Canadian Carlos Beaubien and Mexican citizen Guadalupe Miranda. By the late 1840s it became the property of Beaubien's daughter Luz and her husband Lucien Maxwell, who sold it about 20 years later to an English company, which then sold it to a Dutch firm.

That's when the trouble began.

Under the Maxwell's ownership, settlers had been allowed to move into the grant, usually with a verbal agreement. But the new owners considered them squatters, and ordered them out.

What resulted was the Colfax County War, in which a number of settlers—fighting for what they believed was theirs—were killed. In 1887 the U.S. Supreme

The Valle Vidal has numerous reminders of New Mexico's pioneer days, including these ruins of the McCrystal Place.

Court ruled in favor of the Dutch Company, and the settlers either left or purchased their homesteads from the legal owners. The rest of the grant was sold for ranching, farming, and logging.

However, in 1926 one 200,000-acre tract became an exclusive hunting, fishing, and recreational retreat for the VIPs of the day. Accepting only "men worth knowing" for a one-time fee of $5,000, the Vermejo Park Club included as its members Herbert Hoover, Andrew Mellon, Douglas Fairbanks, Cecil B. DeMille, Harvey Firestone, and at least one woman: actress Mary Pickford.

Ranching returned after the club disbanded during the depression, and in the late 1940s Fort Worth industrialist W.J. Gourley bought the club property and about 300,000 adjoining acres and enlarged the elk herd by buying several hundred head from Yellowstone National Park at a cost of $5 each. After Gourley died the property was purchased by Pennzoil Company, which donated 100,000 acres of it to the U.S. Forest Service in 1982. Today Valle Vidal is managed as a unit of the Carson National Forest.

Although far from pristine after years of ranching and logging, Valle Vidal offers a rugged beauty, with its broad valleys, meadows of prairie grasses and wildflowers, bubbling streams, and stunning mountain peaks. There is a feeling here, enhanced by the remains of pioneer ranch houses and railroad beds, that this is the genuine Old West. The eastern side of the unit consists mostly of grasslands and rolling hills. The western section is more mountainous and contains dramatic rock formations such as Comanche Point, which stands near

The Wild Rivers Recreation Area, near the Valle Vidal, lives up to its name with a raft trip down the Rio Grande.

the confluence of Comanche and Costilla Creeks. Roads through Valle Vidal are gravel, but generally well-maintained, although they can become washboards at times.

Although the scenery is spectacular—it's sometimes compared to Yellowstone National Park—what really sets the Valle Vidal apart is the richness and diversity of its wildlife. There are 1,700 to 2,000 elk, several hundred mule deer, wild turkeys, hawks, bobcats, cougars, beavers, coyotes, and black bears. Abert's squirrels are often seen on the east side of the unit, and bald eagles are occasionally spotted passing through.

The best times to see elk and other wildlife are just after sunrise and before sunset, and elk and deer are often observed along the edges of open meadows. Visitors are urged to view wildlife from a distance, both for their own protection and to avoid causing the animals unnecessary stress.

Because protection of wildlife is a top management priority, off-road motor vehicle use is forbidden, and even foot travel is prohibited off the main road in sections of the unit's west side during elk calving season in May and June.

In addition to wildlife, Valle Vidal contains one of the largest pure stands of bristlecone pine trees in the Southwest, a species considered to be the world's oldest living tree. The stand, located northwest of Clayton Corral about a half mile off the roadway, includes what is believed to be the world's largest bristlecone, a healthy 76-footer with a trunk almost 4 feet across.

Northern New Mexico's pioneer days are in evidence throughout Valle Vidal, and especially at the imposing Ring Ranch House, which is listed on the National

Register of Historic Places. In the 1890s, this two-story log building was head-quarters for a 320-acre ranch and home to Irish immigrant Timothy Ring, his wife Catherine, and seven daughters—Margaret, Mabel, Mary, Maud, Myrtle, Amy, and Anna. Ring had come to the United States just in time for the Civil War. He fought on the Union side, was injured, and after the war married Irish-born Catherine before heading west.

An interpretive trail leads about 0.5 mile from McCrystal Campground to the Ring place, with photo exhibits that describe the history of the ranch. Daily from mid-June through mid-August, youths from nearby Philmont Scout Ranch give short talks at the ranch house on the Ring family and the log house. The scouts also lead nature walks and present star-watching sessions each evening, in which participants use telescopes to see the rings of Saturn, constellations, and other heavenly objects.

There are few developed and marked trails in Valle Vidal, but numerous old logging roads lead to pioneer homesteads, railroad buildings, and cemeteries. In fact, of the roughly 350 miles of dirt roads open when Valle Vidal was donated to the U.S. Forest Service, all but 42 miles are now closed to motor vehicles and avail-able for hiking, mountain biking, and horseback riding.

A hike of several miles south from McCrystal Campground, over an abandoned dirt road and rail bed, leads to the weathered remains of Ponil Park. Dating back to at least the 1870s, the town was a major logging center of several hundred resi-dents by 1908, when the railroad arrived. The trail follows North Ponil Creek along a delightful meadow where you'll likely see colorful lavender and red penste-mon in summer. Ruins include several log buildings, a railroad trestle, and the town cemetery.

You can also step back in time on a walk to the McCrystal Ranch, a large two-story log cabin built in the late 1800s by rancher Jon McCrystal. The trail is an old dirt road that leaves the main road about 0.25 mile west of the McCrystal Camp-ground entrance. It heads northwest, eventually following McCrystal Creek to the ranch. The relatively flat and easy hike is about 3.5 miles each way.

Those seeking panoramic views can follow an old logging road from near the confluence of Comanche and Little Costilla Creeks for about 8 miles to 12,584-foot Little Costilla Peak. The trail is closed during spring elk-calving, but is usu-ally open by early July.

Rio Grande cutthroat trout are found in the unit's 67 miles of streams; you'll probably have the best luck in Costilla Creek and Middle Ponil Creek or the Shuree Ponds, which also contain rainbow trout. All are catch-and-release streams, and a number of other special regulations apply. One of the two Shuree Ponds is open for fishing only by children under 12. Valle Vidal is also a popular hunting desti-nation during the fall elk season.

Much of Valle Vidal's mountainous west side is open to cross-country skiing and snowshoeing, and some areas are open to snowmobiling, once the elk have moved to their winter range on the east side. Check with the U.S. Forest Service office in Questa for current information.

The unit has two shady campgrounds, both with grills, picnic tables, vault toilets, and horse corrals. Cimarron Campground, at an elevation of 9,400 feet, has drinking water available; 8,100-foot McCrystal Campground does not. The U.S. Forest Service maintains a ranger station with a visitor center in the community of Questa.

Summer and fall are the best and busiest times at Valle Vidal, with cool nights and daytime temperatures in the 70s and 80s. Afternoon thunderstorms are common from mid-July through August. Winter can be cold, although sunny winter days are quite pleasant. Snow sometimes closes the one road through the unit. Spring is often windy, with occasional snow.

West and south of Valle Vidal is the Wild Rivers Recreation Area, operated by the Bureau of Land Management. It offers a visitor center, camping, spectacularly scenic views, and hiking into the 800-foot deep Rio Grande Gorge, where you'll find prehistoric rock art and the Rio Grande Wild and Scenic River.

WHITE SANDS NATIONAL MONUMENT

HOURS/SEASONS:	Memorial Day through mid-August: Dunes Drive 7 A.M. to 9 P.M., visitor center 8 A.M. to 7 P.M.; mid-August until Memorial Day: Dunes Drive 7 A.M. to sunset, visitor center 8 A.M. to 4:30 P.M. Open later during full moon in summer; closed Christmas
BEST TIME TO VISIT:	June through October
AREA:	144,000 acres
ELEVATION:	3,900 feet
FACILITIES:	Visitor center, interpretive exhibits, nature trail, picnic tables, amphitheater, restrooms, 10 primitive backcountry hike-in campsites, public telephone
ATTRACTIONS:	Hiking, wildlife viewing, bird-watching, photography, interpretive programs
NEARBY:	Oliver Lee Memorial State Park
ACCESS:	15 miles southwest of Alamogordo via US 70/82

This awe-inspiring public sandbox stops you in your tracks at the first sight of its stark beauty. The picture-perfect sand dunes glistening in the light of sun or moon bring out the kid in all of us, and it's hard to resist shedding shoes and socks to run barefoot through the dunes.

Many visitors feel that they must get out in the dunes (with or without shoes) to fully appreciate them, that they must experience this wonderland of sand from

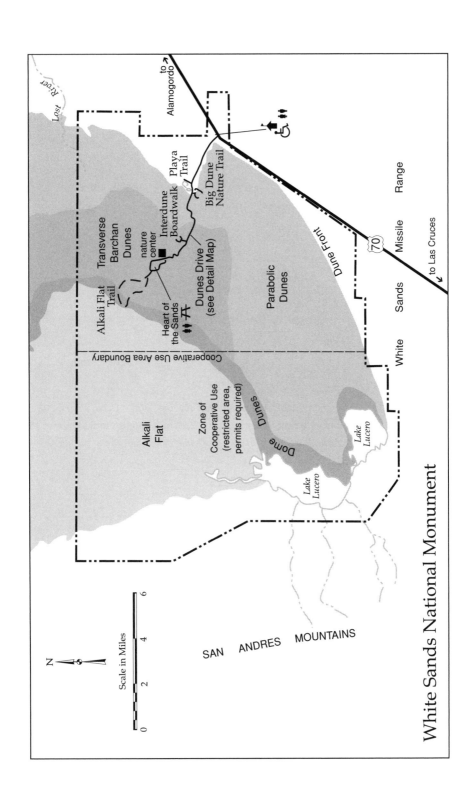

White Sands National Monument

The Southwest's largest public beach, White Sands National Monument, is hundreds of miles from the nearest ocean.

an aesthetic rather than geologic perspective. However, discovering something about the geology and plant and animal life also provides a fascinating perspective on what's going on here.

The sparkling white dunes that comprise this National Park Service property are part of the world's largest gypsum sand dune field, which has been formed over thousands of years as rain and snow brought minerals down from the surrounding mountains. The water evaporated, gypsum crystallized into minute grains of sand, and the prevailing southwest winds piled the white granules into row upon row of intricately shaped and constantly shifting dunes. The process continues to this day.

The easiest way to see the dunes is on the 16-mile round-trip Dunes Drive, which leads from the visitor center into the dunes. Pullouts along the route have exhibits that help to explain the monument's geology and ecology. The road, which is paved for 5 miles and packed with gypsum for the last 3 miles, also provides access to the monument's four designated hiking trails and parking areas where you can leave your vehicle to take off on foot among the dunes.

The best times to go are early or late in the day, when the dunes display mysterious shadows.

The first trail along the Dunes Drive, and the monument's shortest, is the Playa Trail. This is an easy (1,000 feet round trip) walk to a small playa—a shallow basin in the desert floor that becomes a temporary pond after a rain.

Shortly after the Playa Trail is the Big Dune Nature Trail, an easy to moderate 1-mile loop through the dunes that includes one steep section. The trail, located along the edge of the dune field, is marked by brown posts sticking out of the sand. With more vegetation than other sections of the monument, this is a good choice for those who want to examine the various plants—such as soaptree yucca, Indian ricegrass, and hoary rosemarymint—that manage to survive among the dunes. A guide keyed to numbers along the trail is available at the trailhead.

The next trailhead along the Dunes Drive is the Interdune Boardwalk, an elevated boardwalk that has benches and informational signs along its route and that is accessible to both wheelchairs and strollers. It loops less than 2,000 feet through a low-lying area between dunes covered by cryptobiotic crust, a fragile, dark surface on the sand made up of microscopic organisms that provide the stability and nutrients needed by young plants to survive in the constantly shifting sands.

The boardwalk provides the best way to see the monument's wildflowers, which include the pink trumpet-shaped centaury, the bright yellow paperflower, the delicate pink flowers of sand verbena, and the yellow evening primrose. A 450-foot (one-way) side trail leads to an overlook with views of several plant pedestals—parts of dunes held in place by the roots of plants.

The monument's longest hike is at the end of the Dunes Drive in the Heart of the Sands. The moderately rated Alkali Flat Trail is 4.6-miles round trip, but it isn't necessary to hike the whole thing to appreciate the wide panoramic views across a seemingly endless ocean of sand with practically no vegetation in sight. The trail, which gains about 100 feet elevation, leads to the edge of Alkali Flat, a dry lakebed that during the last Ice Age was part of a 1,600-square-mile lake.

The Alkali Flat Trail is marked by white posts topped with orange reflective tape, and hikers are warned to turn back if blowing sand obscures the posts. Because it is easy to get lost in the shifting dunes, hikers on this trail are required to sign in and out at the register at the trailhead.

The Heart of the Sands is the monument's playground. Here you can run up and down huge piles of sand or lie in the warm sun with your toes buried in the cool subsurface sand. Although hiking is permitted anywhere in the monument, rangers warn that it is easy to become lost among the constantly changing dunes, where the wind sometimes sweeps away footprints in a matter of minutes. Therefore, before hikers set out they should orient themselves to the

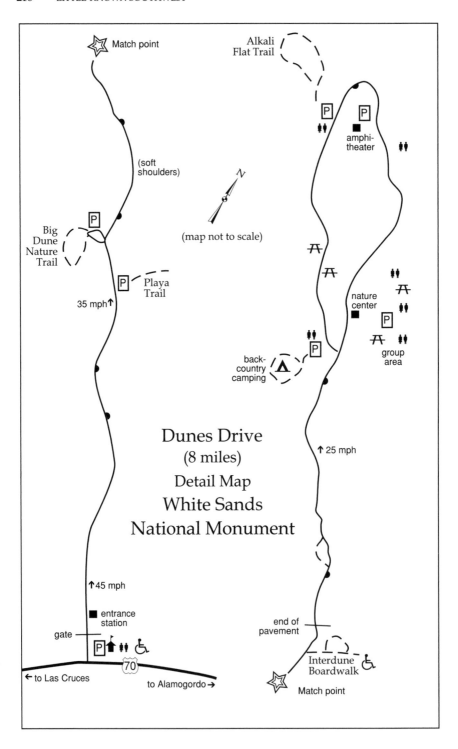

Match point

Alkali
Flat Trail

P   P

amphi-
theater

(soft
shoulders)

N

(map not to scale)

Big
Dune
Nature
Trail

P

P   Playa
Trail

35 mph↑

nature
center

P

group
area

back-
country
camping

P

Dunes Drive
(8 miles)
Detail Map
White Sands
National Monument

↑ 25 mph

↑45 mph

■ entrance
station

gate

P

70

← to Las Cruces

to Alamogordo →

end of
pavement

Interdune
Boardwalk

Match point

more permanent landmarks, such as mountain ranges and water towers.

A visitor center has exhibits explaining the formation of the dunes, and a 17-minute orientation video is shown in the auditorium. There is also a bookstore and gift shop. The visitor center has the only source of drinking water in the monument.

In the Heart of the Sands, near the end of the Dunes Drive, a nature center has exhibits on the monument's plant and animal life, including a hands-on demonstration that shows the distinguishing variations among animal tracks.

Guided walks and a variety of interpretive programs are offered, with the greatest number and variety during the summer. Especially popular are the Sunset Stroll Nature Walks, leisurely 1-hour guided walks in which rangers discuss the monument's plants and animals as the sun is setting.

From May through September, the monument holds Full Moon Programs on or near the evenings when there is a full moon. These events include talks on subjects such as bats, the biological diversity of the Chihuahuan Desert, and local historical points of interest. Also in the warmer months, evening stargazing programs are scheduled several times each month, usually on Friday evenings. Other special activities, scheduled periodically, include moonlight bicycle tours and photography workshops.

Once each month year-round, usually on a Saturday, rangers give tours of Lake Lucero, the lowest point in the Tularosa Basin, where sand dunes begin to form. Because access to Lake Lucero crosses White Sands Missile Range, it is open to the public only during these monthly tours, in which rangers lead an auto caravan to the lake. The tours take about 3 hours, including the drive, and also involve a fairly easy 1.5-mile round-trip hike. Advance registration is required; contact monument offices for details.

More than 200 species of birds have been observed at White Sands. Commonly seen year-round throughout the monument are greater roadrunners (the New Mexico state bird), mourning doves, cactus wrens, loggerhead shrikes, and Chihuahuan ravens. Also seen year-round, mostly in the vicinity of the visitor center, are American kestrels, red-shafted flickers, ladder-backed woodpeckers, house finches, and great-tailed grackles. Permanent residents more likely to be seen in and near the dunes are horned larks, black-throated sparrows, and great-horned owls.

In summer look in the visitor center area for Swainson's hawks, lesser nighthawks, and black-chinned hummingbirds. Summer residents seen throughout the monument include western kingbirds and northern mockingbirds. Species often seen in winter include red-tailed hawks and lark buntings in the dunes, dark-eyed juncos and Brewer's blackbirds near the visitor center, and northern harriers and white-crowned sparrows throughout the monument.

Many of the mammals that inhabit the monument are nocturnal, and rather than actual sightings of the animals themselves you're more likely to see their tracks in the sand, especially along the Big Dune Nature Trail. In the early morning or late evening you might see desert cottontails, black-tailed jackrabbits, coyotes, or kit foxes.

Among the numerous lizards to watch for are the desert side-blotched lizard, the Cowles prairie lizard, the round-tailed horned lizard, the New Mexican whiptail, the bleached earless lizard, and the collared lizard. There are also a number of snakes, including the poisonous western diamondback and prairie rattlesnakes.

The monument does not have a drive-in campground, but backcountry hikers can make in-person requests for permits to camp in a small backcountry camping area, located about a mile into the dunes from a parking area along the Dunes Drive. The camping area has no drinking water or toilets, and ground fires are not permitted.

Summers here are hot, with daytime highs often climbing to the mid-90s or over 100 degrees. Summer nighttime temperatures usually drop to very mild 50s and 60s. Thunderstorms, often accompanied by hail, are common from July through August. Winter days are often in the 50s, but nighttime temperatures usually fall below freezing and there is occasional snow. Fall is especially pleasant, with daytime temperatures commonly in the 80s. Spring has moderate temperatures, but also has high, sometimes gale-force, winds that are common from February through May.

Occasionally the Dunes Drive, as well as US 70/82, is closed for an hour or two during missile testing on the adjacent White Sands Missile Range, at which times you must stay put until the testing is completed. Those on a particularly tight schedule can check with monument offices a day in advance for information on possible closures.

Nearby attractions include Oliver Lee Memorial State Park, a scenic park with hiking trails, camping, an abundance of plant and animal life, and historic sites from New Mexico's Wild West days.

Right: *Delightful rock formations fill the natural amphitheater at Cedar Breaks National Monument.*

UTAH

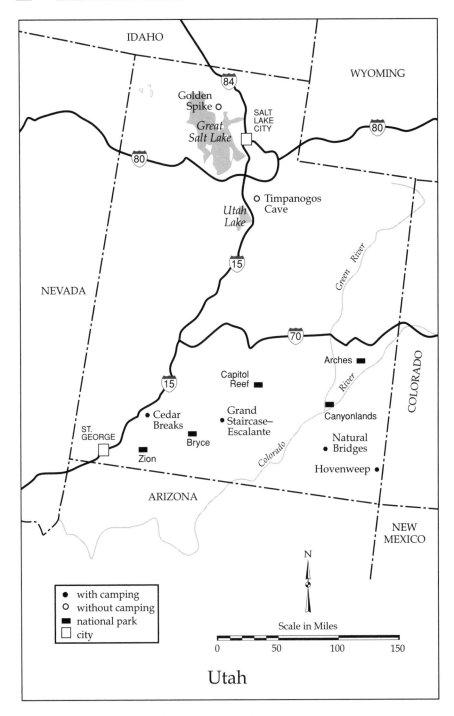

Stunning scenery, ranging from rugged wilderness and spectacular red rocks to deep green forests and sparkling blue lakes, plus numerous outdoor recreation

Mule deer, like this one spotted at Arches National Park, are seen throughout the Four Corners states.

opportunities make Utah an almost ideal vacation destination. Its 84,990 square miles contain some of America's most magnificent national parks and other public lands, and here modern-day explorers see the West in much the same way as the pioneers did some 150 years ago.

Utah's wonderful red rock country, for which it is internationally famous, is the result of millions of years of uplifting and erosion. Here is the over-simplified story: Different types of rocks combined to form layers of varying densities. As wind and water began the inevitable process of erosion, softer rock wore down faster than harder rock, and the intricate and sometimes bizarre shapes prevalent throughout southern Utah were created. The shades of red, orange, and tan come from minerals, mostly iron.

In many ways, a walk through Utah is a walk through the Old West, where you can see the land through the eyes of the pioneers, miners, outlaws, and missionaries who built the Utah we see today. Settled by members of the Church of Jesus Christ of Latter-day Saints (LDS), also known as Mormons, Utah continues to be strongly influenced by the LDS church, with its emphasis on work, strong family ties, and abstinence from tobacco and alcoholic beverages.

The state's five national parks are dominated by red rock country that remains almost as untamed as it was a hundred years ago, when famed outlaw Butch Cassidy hid out there after many a successful bank or train robbery. Considering that this is primarily a desert state, there are plenty of opportunities for water sports. You can raft the rapids of the Colorado and Green Rivers and lounge on the deck of a houseboat on Lake Flaming Gorge or Lake Powell, which Utah shares with Arizona (see the section on Glen Canyon National Recreation Area in this book's section on Arizona).

Some of Utah's best adventures are found in its lesser-known federal properties such as Cedar Breaks National Monument, a small, high-altitude version of Bryce Canyon National Park that receives only a fraction of the number of people who visit Bryce, and Timpanogos Cave, a delightful cave with a variety of formations that is reached by a steep hike up the side of a mountain. Fans of historic steam trains won't want to leave Utah without seeing Golden Spike National Historic Site, which marks the location of the completion of the first continental railroad. One of the world's most impressive dinosaur quarries is found in Dinosaur National Monument, which straddles the Utah–Colorado border (see the description in the section on Colorado).

UTAH'S
NATIONAL PARKS AND RECREATION AREAS

Utah's five national parks and one national recreation area are known primarily for their colorful rocks. However, it would be mistake to say that this is the only reason to visit them. They also offer historic sites, numerous hiking opportunities, and excellent camping possibilities.

ZION NATIONAL PARK

Sheer multicolored walls of sandstone, delicately carved canyons, and the roar of the churning, tumbling Virgin River are but a part of the fascination of this multifaceted park. Zion, which received its name from early Mormon settlers because it conjured up an image of heaven on earth, is a collage of sights, experiences, and even smells, from its massive stone sculptures and monuments to its lush forests and rushing rivers.

Top attractions include the park's towering Great White Throne, the deep Narrows Canyon, cascading waterfalls, and emerald green pools. There are viewpoints along park roads (some accessible via tram tours), and there is one paved trail open to bikes (an unusual feature for a national park). A concessionaire offers guided horseback rides, and the park's sheer cliffs tempt skilled rock climbers. Hiking trails range from flat and easy walks to extremely difficult treks along knife-edge ridges.

One of the park's most famous hikes is actually mostly wading; its "trail" is the Virgin River as it flows through The Narrows, a spectacular 1,000-foot-deep canyon that is only a few dozen feet wide in spots. Passing fancifully sculptured sandstone arches, hanging gardens, and waterfalls, this moderately strenuous hike can be completed in less than a day or in several days, depending on how much effort you want to expend.

Zion harbors a vast array of plants and animals. There are almost 800 native species of plants, ranging from cacti and yucca in the desert areas to ponderosa pines on the high plateaus and cottonwoods and box elders along the rivers. Wildflowers seen in the park include the manzanita, with its tiny pink blossoms; the bright red hummingbird trumpet; and the white funnel-shaped sacred datura, which is known as the "Zion Lily" because of its abundance in the park.

Fascinating are Zion's "spring lines" and their hanging gardens, which cling to the sides of cliffs. Because sandstone is porous, water percolates down through it until it is stopped by a layer of harder rock, at which point the water changes direction, moving horizontally to the rock face, where it oozes out, offering moisture to whatever plants are tenacious enough to hang onto the wall.

Wildlife here includes the commonly seen mule deer, numerous squirrels, coyotes, ringtails, beavers, porcupines, skunks, and mountain lions. There are

A hiker ascends the Emerald Pools Trail at Zion National Park.

Massive rock formations are one of the trademarks of Zion National Park.

also lizards of various shapes and sizes and more than 250 species of birds, including golden eagles and numerous piñon jays.

Zion National Park ranges from 3,700 feet to almost 9,000 feet in elevation, which has helped produce an extreme climate where summer temperatures can soar to over 100 degrees and winter temperatures in the higher elevations can drop well below freezing. In the winter, snow and ice make some of the trails impassable.

There are several sections to the park, including the main Zion Canyon and the detached Kolob Canyons, each with their own visitor centers. Rangers offer guided hikes and a variety of other programs. In Zion Canyon there is a concessionaire-operated lodge and two developed campgrounds, one with electric hookups for RVs.

BRYCE CANYON NATIONAL PARK

Unsurpassed for its fanciful formations and sheer beauty of design, Bryce Canyon National Park offers magic, inspiration, and spectacular colors among thousands of intricately shaped hoodoos—those silent sentinels that stand watch in these colorful amphitheaters. Hoodoos are rock pinnacles that have been left after millions of years of water and wind erosion has worn away the surrounding softer rock. These intricate and often whimsical formations, colored in shades of red, brown, orange, yellow, and white, give the park a somewhat unreal, fantasyland appearance.

What makes Bryce Canyon National Park extra special is that it is relatively easy to explore and offers splendid vistas from the viewpoints, paved Rim Trail, and its numerous moderately rated trails that also take day hikers down into the horseshoe-shaped amphitheaters to see the hoodoos up close. In all, the park has more than 50 miles of trails with a range of distances and difficulty levels.

Bryce Canyon was likely first seen by the Paiutes, and it's possible that trappers, prospectors, and early Mormon scouts may have visited in the early to mid-1800s, before Major John Wesley Powell conducted the first thorough survey of the region in the early 1870s. Soon after Powell's exploration, Mormon pioneer Ebenezer Bryce and his wife Mary moved to the area to raise cattle. They stayed only a few years, but Bryce left his name and his oft-quoted description of the canyon as "a helluva place to lose a cow."

While the colorful hoodoos and the trails that wander among them are the main attractions here, the park also contains three separate life zones, each with its own unique vegetation. This has resulted in a great variety of wildlife, from the busy chipmunks and ground squirrels to the stately mule deer and their archenemy, the mountain lion.

The park's 18-mile main road, which can be traversed by private vehicle or shuttle bus (in summer), leads to viewpoints and trailheads. Bryce Canyon has two campgrounds, a concessionaire-operated historic lodge, and a visitor center with exhibits and a video program. Rangers offer guided hikes and patio and campground talks, and a concessionaire offers guided horseback rides.

The park is busiest in summer, and although some trails may be icy and snowpacked in winter, visitors can tour the park on cross-country skis or

Majestic Queen Victoria is the centerpiece of a group of hoodoos called the Queen's Garden at Bryce Canyon National Park.

snowshoes. The red, orange, and brown hoodoos look spectacular when covered in a blanket of white snow.

CANYONLANDS NATIONAL PARK

Utah's largest national park is not for the casual sightseer out for a Sunday afternoon drive, but it is a delight for those willing to spend time and energy to explore the rugged backcountry. Sliced into districts by the park's primary architects, the Colorado and Green Rivers, this is a land of extremes, with vast panoramas, deep canyons, dramatically steep cliffs, expansive mesas, and towering red spires.

The most accessible part of Canyonlands is the Island in the Sky District, in the northern part of the park, where a paved road leads to sites such as Grand View Point, which overlooks some 10,000 square miles of rugged wilderness. Island in the Sky also has several easy to moderate trails offering sweeping vistas.

The Needles District, in the park's southeast corner, offers only a few viewpoints along the paved road, but there are numerous possibilities for hikers, backpackers, and those with high-clearance four-wheel-drive vehicles. Named for its tall, slim, red-and-white-striped rock pinnacles, this diverse district is home to impressive arches, grassy meadows, and the confluence of the Green and Colorado Rivers. Backcountry visitors to the Needles District will also find ruins and rock art left by the Ancestral Puebloans some 800 years ago.

Most park visitors don't venture into the Maze District, but they get a distant glimpse from Grand View Point at Island in the Sky or Confluence Overlook in the Needles District. This inhospitable and practically inaccessible area requires plenty of endurance and at least several days to see even a few of its sites. Hardy hikers can visit Horseshoe Canyon in one day, where they can see the Great Gallery, an 80-foot-long rock art panel.

The park is also accessible by boat, which is how explorer Major John Wesley Powell first saw the canyons in 1869, when he made his first trip down the Green to its confluence with the Colorado and then continued even farther downstream, eventually reaching the Grand Canyon.

Among the cottonwoods and willows along the rivers is Canyonlands' greatest variety of wildlife. Watch for deer, beaver, an occasional bobcat, and various migratory birds. Elsewhere in the park, you're likely to see red-tailed hawks in search of tasty rodents, as well as bighorn sheep, coyotes, Colorado chipmunks, and white-tailed antelope squirrels.

There are visitor centers in the Island in the Sky and Needles Districts but not in the Maze. Both have exhibits and sell maps and books, some of which are also available at the ranger station in the Maze. Evening programs and overlook talks are offered spring through fall. The Needles and Island in the Sky

Districts each have a campground with limited facilities. Backcountry camping is available but requires a permit.

ARCHES NATIONAL PARK

Natural stone arches and fanciful rock formations, sculpted as though by an artist's hand, are the defining features of this park, and they exist in remarkable numbers and variety. It seems that each one is more beautiful, colorful, or gigantic than the last, and it would take forever to see them all, especially since 1,700 are officially listed and more are discovered practically every day. Arches is an especially visitor-friendly park, with relatively short, well-maintained trails leading to most major attractions, including such formations as Delicate Arch, Landscape Arch, the Spectacles, and the Eye of the Whale.

The formations called arches resemble natural bridges, but geologically there's a big difference. Bridges are formed when a river slowly bores through solid rock. Arches, however, result from the erosive force of rain and snow and the freezing and thawing that dissolve the cement that holds sand grains together.

Although arches usually grow *very* slowly, something dramatic happens occasionally, such as on one quiet day in 1940 when a thundering crash doubled the size of the opening of Skyline Arch, leaving a huge boulder lying in its shadow. Luckily, no one was underneath it at the time. The same thing happened to the magnificently delicate Landscape Arch in 1991, when a slab of rock about 60 feet long, 11 feet wide, and 4.5 feet thick fell from the underside of the arch, leaving such a thin ribbon of stone that it's hard to believe it continues hanging on at all.

Landscape Arch is one of the highlights of Arches National Park.

Exploring the park is a fun and fairly easy adventure, making Arches a perfect family destination. Walk the terrain and watch the rainbow of colors deepen and explode with the long rays of the setting sun, or see the moonlight glisten on ribbons of desert varnish on tall sandstone cliffs. Watch for mule deer, cottontail rabbits, and bright green collared lizards as they go about the difficult task of desert living.

The visitor center, which houses a museum and bookstore, offers a short orientation program. The 48-mile round-trip paved park road leads to numerous hiking trails and eventually to the park campground. From spring through fall rangers offer walks, guided hikes, and evening campfire programs.

CAPITOL REEF NATIONAL PARK

Visitors to Capitol Reef National Park will find more of that spectacular southern Utah scenery, but here it has a unique twist and a personality all its own. These geologic formations are downright peculiar. Those able to give in to their imaginations see Hamburger Rocks sitting atop a white sandstone table; the silent and eerie Temple of the Moon; and the tall, rust-red Chimney Rock. The colors of Capitol Reef's canyon walls are taken from an astonishingly diverse palette, which is why the Navajos called the area "The Land of the Sleeping Rainbow."

More than just brilliant rocks and barren desert, though, Capitol Reef includes a delightful oasis of cottonwoods and willows along the Fremont River. Nineteenth-century pioneers found the land so inviting and the soil so fertile that they established the community of Fruita, planting orchards that have been continued by the National Park Service.

The park's unique topography owes its existence to a buckling of the earth. When the earth's crust uplifted some 60 million years ago, creating the Rocky Mountains and Colorado Plateau, most of the process was relatively even. But here, through a quirk of nature, the crust wrinkled into a huge fold. This strange formation, running for 100 miles (almost all within the national park) is known as the Waterpocket Fold.

Because of differences in geologic strata, elevation, and availability of water, the park has an assortment of ecosystems and terrain, and offers a variety of activities. There are hiking trails as well as mountain-biking and four-wheeling roads. The park has deep green forests, rocky desert canyons, and a surprising amount of wildlife, from lizards and snakes to an abundance of songbirds.

The early Fremont and Ancestral Puebloan peoples left petroglyphs to mark their passing. More recent peoples have left traces also, including the Utes and Southern Paiutes, Wild West outlaws (Cassidy Arch is named for Butch Cassidy), and of course the industrious Mormon pioneers, whose one-room Fruita Schoolhouse has been restored by the National Park Service.

The name Capitol Reef, which conjures up an image of a tropical shoreline, seems odd for a park composed of cliffs and canyons and situated in landlocked Utah. But many of the pioneers who settled the West were former seafaring men, and they extended the traditional meaning of the word "reef" to include these seemingly impassable rock barriers. The huge round white sandstone formations reminded them of the domes of capitol buildings, and so this area became known as Capitol Reef.

The park has a visitor center with interpretive exhibits and programs, an introductory slide show, and a bookstore. The Scenic Drive follows the western edge of the Waterpocket Fold and leads to several hiking trailheads. In summer there are walks, talks, and evening campfire programs. A Family Fun Pack is available to entertain the kids while they explore the park. The seventy-site campground, which is open year-round, has seven sites for tents only and no RV hook-ups.

FLAMING GORGE NATIONAL RECREATION AREA

As with most of the West's large lakes, Lake Flaming Gorge was born when a dam was built on the Green River for flood control, water storage, and the generation of electricity. The lake is about 91 miles long, with more than 350 miles of coastline. The recreation area, which covers parts of northern Utah and southern Wyoming, is operated by the U.S. Forest Service as part of the Ashley National Forest.

Named by Major John Wesley Powell during his exploration of the Green and Colorado Rivers in 1869, Flaming Gorge has a rugged, wild beauty that comes alive when the rising or setting sun paints the red rocks surrounding the lake with a fiery, brilliant palette.

Boaters enjoy a unique perspective of this wonderful scenery; magnificent red canyons surround the lake in the Utah section and the wide-open Wyoming badlands farther north. On the water are practically every type of craft imaginable, from kayaks and canoes to personal watercraft, ski and fishing boats, and comfortable houseboats. There are three marinas on the lake, which offer boat rentals, fuel, launching ramps, and boating and fishing supplies.

Lake Flaming Gorge offers some of the best fishing in the West, and is the place to come to catch record-breaking trout, such as the 51-pound, 8-ounce lake trout caught in 1988. Anglers also catch rainbow and brown trout, smallmouth bass, and kokanee salmon. Trout fishing on the Green River below the dam is also outstanding.

There are numerous roadside viewpoints, such as the dramatic Red Canyon Overlook, where a rainbow of colors adorns 1,000-foot-tall cliffs. Many of the more than 100 miles of trails offer spectacular views of the reservoir and its colorful canyons. Most trails are open to both hikers and mountain bikers, and some are also open to horses and four-wheel-drive vehicles.

This is also an excellent wildlife-viewing area. Boaters should watch for osprey, peregrine falcons, swifts, and swallows along the cliffs. Bighorn sheep are sometimes spotted on the rocky cliffs on the lake's north side in spring and early summer.

U.S. Forest Service campgrounds are located throughout the recreation area. These range from primitive sites to modern facilities with showers and flush toilets, but none have RV hookups.

UTAH'S NATIONAL MONUMENTS AND OTHER LESSER-KNOWN FEDERAL LANDS

Utah's lesser-known federal lands receive far fewer visitors than the state's national parks while offering a variety of scenic wonders, historic and prehistoric sites, and myriad recreation opportunities.

CEDAR BREAKS NATIONAL MONUMENT

HOURS/SEASON:	Overnight; year-round, although the entry road, visitor center, and other facilities are usually closed from mid-October through late May
BEST TIME TO VISIT:	Summer
AREA:	6,155 acres
ELEVATION:	10,350 feet
FACILITIES:	Visitor center, interpretive exhibits, picnic tables, restrooms, 30 campsites (no showers or hookups), public telephone
ATTRACTIONS:	Hiking, wildlife viewing, bird-watching, photography, guided hikes and walks, geology talks, campfire programs, cross-country skiing, snowshoeing
NEARBY:	Bryce Canyon and Zion National Parks
ACCESS:	21 miles east of Cedar City via UT 14 and UT 148. From points east, the monument is accessible through the town of Panguitch via UT 143. From the north, take the Parowan exit off I-15 and head south on UT 143

This serenely beautiful little park is a delightful escape. You can gaze down from the rim into an incredible natural amphitheater, hike through fields of

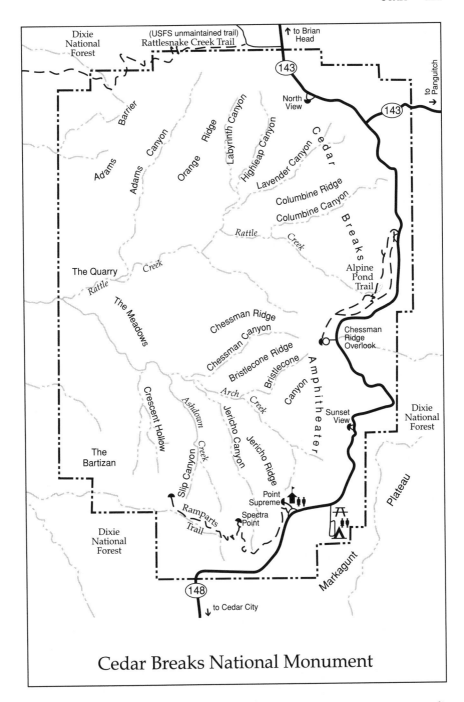

Cedar Breaks National Monument

wildflowers, and camp in a forest of spruce and firs. The focal point is a coliseum resembling Bryce Canyon, which is more than 2,000 feet deep and over 3 miles across and filled with stone spires, arches, and columns shaped by the forces of erosion and painted in ever-changing hues of red, purple, orange, and brown.

The monument, which is operated by the National Park Service, is fully open only from late May through mid-October, and covered by a thick blanket of snow the rest of the year. But during its short season Cedar Breaks is a wonderful destination park where you can easily spend two or three days.

Start at the visitor center and nearby Point Supreme for a panoramic view of the amphitheater. Then head out on the 5-mile scenic drive, which offers easy access to overlooks and trailheads. From the visitor center, drive north to Sunset View for a closer look at the amphitheater and its colorful canyons. Continue north to Chessman Ridge Overlook, so named because the hoodoos directly below the rim look like massive stone chess pieces. Then head north to Alpine Pond, the beginning of a self-guided nature trail. Finally, you'll reach North View, which offers perhaps the best look into the amphitheater, with its stately stone statues frozen in time. From each of these overlooks you'll be able to look west across Cedar Valley, over the Antelope and Black Mountains, and into the Escalante Desert.

There are no hiking trails from within the monument to the bottom of the

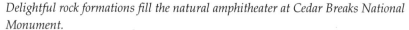

Delightful rock formations fill the natural amphitheater at Cedar Breaks National Monument.

amphitheater, but Cedar Breaks has two high country trails. The fairly easy 2-mile Alpine Pond Trail self-guided loop leads to a picturesque forest glade and pond surrounded by a sea of wildflowers, past quaking aspens, and through a grove of bristlecone pines, offering panoramic views of the amphitheater along the way. A trail guide is available at the trailhead.

A somewhat more challenging hike, the 4-mile round-trip Spectra Point Trail (also called the Ramparts Trail) follows the rim more closely than the Alpine Pond Trail, offering changing views of the colorful rock formations. It also takes you through fields of wildflowers and by bristlecone pines more than 1,500 years old. You'll need to be especially careful of your footing along the exposed cliff edges, and allow some time to rest, as the trail has numerous inclines.

Those who want to hike into the amphitheater will have to leave the monument to get to the trailhead for Rattlesnake Creek Trail, which is just north of the monument boundary off UT 143 in the Dixie National Forest. You can hike part of the trail as a day hike, hiking in for a few hours and then returning on the same route, but the entire trail entails a backpacking trip of several days. This trail drops 3,400 feet in 9 miles, and is recommended only for hikers in top physical condition and with good map-reading skills. Hikers also need to be aware of flash flood dangers. Information is available from national monument rangers and the U.S. Forest Service.

During its brief summer, Cedar Breaks makes the most of the warmth and moisture with a spectacular wildflower display as the rim comes alive in a blaze of color. The show begins almost as soon as the snow melts and reaches its peak in late July and August. It's as though the flowers are trying to outshine the colorful rocks below. In the meadows watch for mountain bluebells, spring beauty, beard tongue, and fleabane early in the season; those beauties then make way for columbine, larkspur, asters, Indian paintbrush, wild roses, and lupine. You'll probably see the pink flowers of fireweed and the yellow evening primrose along roadsides.

Because of its relative remoteness, Cedar Breaks is a good place for viewing wildlife. You're likely to see mule deer grazing in the meadows along the road early and late in the day. Yellow-bellied marmots make their dens near the rim, and are often seen along the Spectra Point Trail and sometimes along the road. You'll spot golden-mantled ground squirrels, red squirrels, and chipmunks everywhere. The monument is also home to coyotes, gray foxes, and white-tailed jackrabbits; pikas, which are related to rabbits, are here, too, but it's unlikely you'll see one. They're small, with short ears and stubby tails, and prefer the high, rocky slopes.

In the campground you'll almost certainly see the bold and sometimes food-stealing Clark's nutcrackers, identified by their gray torsos and black-and-white wings and tails. Other birds commonly observed at Cedar Breaks include

American kestrels, rufous and broad-tailed hummingbirds, mountain chicka-dees, mountain bluebirds, yellow-rumped warblers, dark-eyed juncos, violet-green swallows, white-throated swifts, blue grouse, hairy woodpeckers, and golden eagles.

Point Supreme Campground, just north of the visitor center, is open from June to mid-September. Situated in a beautiful high-mountain setting among tall spruce and firs, it's similar to many of the better western national park campgrounds, and has an amphitheater for the ranger's nightly campfire pro-grams.

One mile into the monument from the south entrance is a visitor center, usually open daily from late May through mid-October, with a bookstore and exhibits on the geology, flora, and fauna of Cedar Breaks. During the sum-mer, rangers offer talks on the area's geology at Point Supreme, a viewpoint near the visitor center. Also in summer, guided hikes are usually scheduled on Saturday and Sunday mornings. A complete schedule is posted at the visitor center and the campground.

At over 10,000 feet in elevation, it's always pleasantly cool at Cedar Breaks. In fact, it gets downright cold at night, so take a jacket or sweater, even at the height of summer. July and August, the busiest months, see daytime tempera-tures in the 60s and nighttime temperatures in the upper 30s and 40s. Although you can enter the monument year-round, roads are blocked by snow and the

Replicas of the steam locomotives that met here in 1869 recreate the moment for nostalgic visitors at Golden Spike National Historic Site.

facilities are shut down from late October through mid-May. Mid-winter temperatures often drop well below zero.

Although snow-blocked roads keep cars out of the monument during the long winter, these same roads are perfect for snowshoers and cross-country skiers, who usually come over from nearby Brian Head Ski Area. Keep in mind, though, that the only human you're likely to see will be an occasional park ranger.

The high elevation here is likely to cause shortness of breath and tiredness, and those with heart or respiratory conditions should probably consult their doctors before making the trip to Cedar Breaks. You should avoid overlooks and other high, exposed areas during thunderstorms, as they're often targets for lightning.

Incidentally, the name "Cedar Breaks" was bestowed by pioneers who arrived in the 1800s. They frequently called badlands such as these "breaks," and they mistook the juniper trees along the cliff bases for cedars.

Among nearby attractions are Bryce Canyon National Park, about 56 miles to the east, and Zion National Park, whose main section is about 85 miles to the south. Both are discussed elsewhere in this book.

GOLDEN SPIKE NATIONAL HISTORIC SITE

HOURS/SEASONS: 8 A.M. to 6 P.M. daily Memorial Day to Labor Day; 8 A.M. to 4:30 P.M. the remainder of the year. Closed Thanksgiving, Christmas, and New Year's Day

BEST TIME TO VISIT: May through mid-October

AREA: 2,735 acres

ELEVATION: 4,905 feet

FACILITIES: Visitor center/bookstore, interpretive exhibits, picnic tables, restrooms, public telephone

ATTRACTIONS: Historic exhibits, interpretive programs, hiking, wildlife viewing, bird-watching, steam locomotives, films, auto tours

ACCESS: From I-15 exit 368, go west on UT 13 and 83 about 21 miles to Golden Spike Drive, then turn south and continue for 8 miles

Golden Spike National Historic Site offers a driving tour, a hiking trail, and a visitor center with historic exhibits and films, but there's no denying that the stars of this show are the "Jupiter" and number "119." These are the full-size, completely functional replicas of the two steam engines that met here more than 130 years ago, as the United States celebrated the linking of its East and West coasts by the world's first transcontinental railroad.

After the laying of 1,776 miles of track over desert, rivers, and mountains, the Central Pacific's "Jupiter" and Union Pacific's "119," met here at Promontory Summit on May 10, 1869. However, within 8 months the railroads moved their terminal operations to Ogden, and in 1904, the Lucin Cutoff bypassed Promontory altogether. The final blow to the site came in 1942 when the rails were torn up for use in military depots.

Now, however, about 1.7 miles of track have been re-laid on the original roadbed and visitors can watch as these replica steam engines act out the drama, as well as a bit of comedy, from that historic meeting so many years ago.

Americans had been talking about a transcontinental railroad—although in that era it was referred to as a "Pacific Railroad"—since the country's first trains began operating in the 1830s. However, the problems involved with building such a system were tremendous. By the time of the Civil War the country had numerous rail lines in the East, but there were few west of the Missouri River, and none linking East to West. Congress chose two companies, one to start in Omaha, Nebraska, and head west, the other to start in Sacramento, California, and go east. The companies received loans and land for each mile of track laid.

Central Pacific crews, heading east from Sacramento, had the burden of crossing the Sierra Nevada Mountains. They also needed to bring all their equipment, including locomotives, by ship some 15,000 miles around Cape Horn. Working west from Omaha, the Union Pacific had the advantage of existing rail connections to the manufacturing centers of the East, plus somewhat easier terrain. They did, however, have to contend with hostile American Indians, who likely understood that the railroad would mean an end to their traditional way of life.

Because the companies received land for each mile of track laid, each wanted to put down as much track as possible, and their race took on absurd dimensions when their crews actually passed each other, furiously building parallel road beds, in sight of each other, in opposite directions! Finally, Congress approved Promontory, Utah, as the meeting spot.

The nation's second transcontinental telegraph had been strung along the track as it was laid, and the country was kept informed of the progress up to the moment the final spike was driven home. An hour-long ceremony, with speeches and prayers, accompanied the actual connecting of the lines, and at one point the telegraph operator sent this message: "We have got done praying. The spike is about to be presented."

Two symbolic golden spikes were driven in with a silver-plated spike maul (railroad hammer). Then the final iron spike was hammered down, the telegraph operator notified the country, and the two engines edged toward each other as if to kiss. Everyone had their photos taken, toasted each other with champagne, and celebrated into the night. The country had been united by rail.

Golden Spike, which is operated by the National Park Service, has a visitor center and bookstore that offers slide programs, films, and museum exhibits detailing the construction of the nation's first transcontinental railroad. From spring through fall, the magnificent steam engines are on display and make short runs about six times daily. In addition, presentations are given trackside, sometimes in period dress, and reenactments of the meeting of the rails take place most Saturdays and holidays in summer.

During the winter, when the locomotives are not operating, self-guided tours of the engine house are available most weekdays and ranger-guided tours are offered on weekends.

In addition, various special events are scheduled throughout the year. Each May 10, there's a reenactment of the original Golden Spike Ceremony, with food, souvenirs, and handicrafts. An 1880s-style baseball tournament is held in late July. On the second Saturday in August, the Annual Railroader's Festival features reenactments of the ceremony, a spike-driving contest, and handcar races and rides. The Annual Railroader's Film Festival and Winter Steam Demonstration, held during the Christmas season, includes classic Hollywood railroad films and a special appearance by one of the resident steam locomotives.

The historic site also has a Junior Engineer program, similar to Junior Ranger programs at other National Park Service properties, for children 8 to 12 years old, who complete projects in a Junior Engineer workbook.

Summers here are usually hot and dry, with highs often in the 90s. Winter days can be sunny and cool and see highs in the 40s and nighttime temperatures well below freezing.

Railroad buffs can drive the self-guided Promontory Trail Auto Tour along 7 miles of the historic railroad grades. You'll see the two parallel grades laid by the competing companies, clearings for sidings, original rock culverts, and many cuts and fills. The free park newspaper contains some descriptive information about the auto tour, and a more in-depth booklet is available for purchase at the visitor center.

The Big Fill Trail is a 1.5-mile loop hike along part of the original rail beds to the Big Trestle site and the Big Fill. The hike can be done on either the Central or Union Pacific rail bed (the Central rail bed is slightly easier) or by going out on one and returning on the other. There are markers along both grades pointing out cuts and fills, quarries, vistas, and caves, as well as the Big Fill and the abutments for the Big Trestle. A trail guide is available at the trailhead.

The Big Fill was created when some 250 dump-cart teams and over 500 workers—mostly Chinese immigrants—dumped load after load of rock and dirt into a ravine to create the 70-foot-deep, 400-foot span required to lay the Central Pacific's track. The Union Pacific put up their trestle just 150 feet away. The trestle was never intended to be a permanent structure; speed was the goal, rather than strength, and by all accounts it was probably one of the flimsiest railroad trestles ever built. The trestle was constructed by hand by Irish and Mormon crews in

1869, and the last spike went into the 85-foot-high, 400-foot-long structure on May 5, just thirty-six days after it was begun.

The easy to moderate trail is rocky, with little shade, so wear good hiking boots, take water, and wear a hat. Be prepared for mosquitoes and ticks, and watch for rattlesnakes. And be glad that you weren't one of the workers in that back-breaking effort of 1869.

GRAND STAIRCASE–ESCALANTE NATIONAL MONUMENT

HOURS/SEASONS:	Overnight; year-round
BEST TIME TO VISIT:	Fall
AREA:	1.9 million acres
ELEVATION:	5,812 feet (town of Escalante)
FACILITIES:	Visitor centers, interpretive exhibits, nature trail, picnic tables, group shelter, restrooms, 17 campsites (no showers or hookups), public telephone
ATTRACTIONS:	Scenic drives, hiking, mountain biking, horseback riding, four-wheeling, bird-watching, wildlife viewing
NEARBY:	Bryce Canyon and Capitol Reef National Parks, Glen Canyon National Recreation Area; Escalante and Kodachrome Basin State Parks
ACCESS:	Via UT 12 from the town of Escalante or US 89 east of the town of Kanab

Covering an area almost as big as the states of Delaware and Rhode Island combined, this vast chunk of southern Utah, which boasts red-orange canyons, mesas, plateaus, and river valleys, became a national monument by presidential proclamation on September 18, 1996.

Known for its stark, rugged beauty, this is one of the last places in the continental United States to be mapped. And, unlike most other national monuments, virtually all of the Grand Staircase–Escalante is undeveloped. It has few all-weather roads, only one maintained hiking trail, and two small campgrounds.

But for the adventurous there are miles upon miles of dirt roads and practically unlimited opportunities for hiking, horseback riding, mountain biking, four-wheeling, camping, and simply gazing out across the vastness at the stunning scenery. In addition, there are numerous archeological sites scattered throughout the monument, ranging from the remains of Ancestral Puebloan dwellings to a variety of rock art sites.

Under the jurisdiction of the Bureau of Land Management, the monument

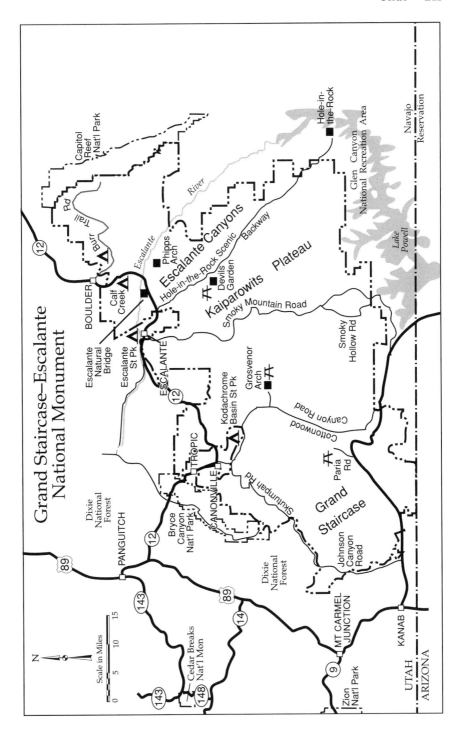

Grand Staircase–Escalante
National Monument

is comprised of three distinct sections: The western part is the Grand Staircase, and contains sandstone cliffs and terraces that include five life zones from the Sonoran Desert to coniferous forests; the center section is the Kaiparowits Plateau, a vast, wild region of rugged mesas and steep canyons; and along the north and east is the Escalante Canyons section, a delightfully scenic area of interconnecting river canyons.

The monument's one maintained hiking trail is located about 15 miles northeast of Escalante via UT 12 in the Calf Creek Recreation Area, which also has a campground, a picnic area, drinking water, and flush toilets. The moderately strenuous 6-mile round-trip hike follows a sandy trail along Calf Creek, past beaver ponds and wetlands, to a beautiful waterfall cascading 126 feet down a rock wall into a tree-shaded pool. An interpretive brochure is available at the trailhead.

Even though the Calf Creek Trail is the monument's only officially marked and maintained trail, there are numerous unmarked cross-country routes that are ideal for hiking and backpacking. It is strongly recommended that hikers stop at the Interagency Office in Escalante or the Bureau of Land Management office in Kanab to get route recommendations, backcountry permits, and to purchase topographic maps. Hikers need to remember that this is wild country and can be hazardous. Rangers recommend carrying at least 1 gallon of water per person per day, and warn that all water from streams should be treated before drinking. The potential for flash flooding is high, especially from July through September, and hikers should check with the Bureau of Land Management before attempting to hike through the monument's narrow slot canyons, which offer no escape during a flash flood. Other hazards include poison ivy in the wetter areas, and poisonous snakes and scorpions in the drier areas. Slickrock, as the name suggests, is slippery, so hikers should wear sturdy hiking boots with good traction.

Popular and relatively easy to follow hiking routes include the path to Escalante Natural Bridge. This hike repeatedly crosses the river, so be prepared to get wet up to your knees occasionally. The easy 2-mile (one-way) hike begins at a parking area at the bridge that crosses the Escalante River near Calf Creek Recreation Area, 15 miles northeast of the town of Escalante. From the parking area, hike upstream to Escalante Natural Bridge, on the south side of the river. The bridge is 130 feet high and spans 100 feet. From here you can continue upstream and explore side canyons or turn around and head back to the parking lot.

Another good route that starts at the UT 12 bridge parking area is a hike downstream to Phipps Wash. This mostly moderate hike goes about 1.5 miles to the mouth of the wash, which enters the river from the west. You'll find Maverick Natural Bridge in a north side-drainage of Phipps Wash. Climb up the drainage on the south side to Phipps Arch.

Although the monument's slot canyons are also popular hiking destinations, it can't be stressed too strongly that you need to check on flood potentials before starting out. Two challenging and very strenuous slot canyon hikes are through Peek-a-boo and Spooky Canyons, which are accessed from the Hole-in-the-Rock Scenic Backway. Check with the Bureau of Land Management for precise directions.

In addition to hiking, there are numerous opportunities for horseback riding, mountain biking, and four-wheeling on numerous designated but rugged dirt roads. Be aware, though, that these dirt roads become deep, sticky goo when it rains. Check with Bureau of Land Management officials for suggestions and current conditions.

The Hole-in-the-Rock Scenic Backway, partly in the monument and partly in the adjacent Glen Canyon National Recreation Area, is a good day trip. Like most roads in the monument, it should be attempted in dry weather only. Starting about 5 miles northeast of Escalante off UT 12, the clearly marked dirt road travels 57 miles (one-way) to the Hole-in-the-Rock, where Mormon settlers in

Rock formations in shades of red and brown dominate the landscape along scenic Utah Highway 12 as it passes through Grand Staircase–Escalante National Monument.

Grosvenor Arch, with an opening 99 feet wide, at Grand Staircase–Escalante National Monument

1880 cut a passage through solid rock to get their wagons down a 1,200-foot drop to the canyon floor and Colorado River below. About 13 miles in, the road passes a marked turnoff to Devils Rock Garden, an area of picturesque red rock formations and arches. A picnic area is located about 0.25 mile off the main road. Beyond the turnoff the byway continues across a desert plateau, ending at a spectacular scenic overlook of Lake Powell. The first 40 miles of the scenic byway are relatively easy (in dry weather) in a standard passenger car. It then gets a bit steeper and sandier, and the last 7 miles require a high-clearance four-wheel-drive vehicle. Allow 7 to 8 hours round trip.

Another scenic route is the Cottonwood Canyon Road, which runs from Kodachrome Basin State Park south some 46 miles to US 89, along the monument's southern edge. The sandy and narrow road is washboard in places, but usually passable for passenger cars in dry weather. It mostly follows Cottonwood Wash, and offers good views of red rock formations plus distant panoramas. About 10 miles east of Kodachrome Basin State Park is a short side road to Grosvenor Arch, a handsome tall stone arch with an opening 99 feet wide that was named for National Geographic Society founder and editor Gilbert H. Grosvenor.

Because of its isolation and rugged terrain, Grand Staircase–Escalante National Monument is a good place to see wildlife, such as mule deer, desert bighorn sheep, foxes, coyotes, and even mountain lions. More than 200 species of birds have been observed, including bald eagles, golden eagles, Swainson's hawks, and peregrine falcons. The best viewing areas are along the Escalante and Paria Rivers and Johnson Creek.

At Calf Creek Recreation Area a tree-shaded picnic and camping area lies along the creek at the bottom of a high-walled, narrow rock canyon. It has thirteen sites, flush toilets, and drinking water, but no garbage removal or other facilities. Although open year-round, from November through March water is turned off and only vault toilets are available. Vehicles must ford a shallow creek, and the campground is not recommended for vehicles more than 25 feet long.

Deer Creek Campground is located 7 miles east of the town of Boulder along the scenic Burr Trail Road. It offers four primitive sites with pit toilets but no drinking water or other facilities. In addition, backcountry camping is allowed in most areas of the monument with a permit, available at monument offices.

Summers here can be hot—sometimes over 100 degrees— with little shade, while winters are relatively cold, with nighttime temperatures usually falling below freezing. Fall is often pleasant, and while late spring temperatures are usually agreeable, spring winds can be bothersome and there is often an abundance of gnats and deerflies in May and June.

Water is the main safety concern here—either too little or too much. This is an arid land, and those going into the monument should carry plenty of drinking water. However, summer thunderstorms can turn the monument's dirt roads into impassable mud bogs in minutes, stranding motorists, and potentially fatal flash floods through narrow canyons can catch hikers by surprise. Those planning trips into the monument should check with Bureau of Land Management officials first on current and anticipated weather and travel conditions.

Several offices/visitor centers serve the monument. These include the Escalante Interagency Office on the west side of Escalante, at 755 West Main Street, and the Bureau of Land Management/Monument Office at 318 North 100 East Street in Kanab. Both offer maps, handouts, and current information on a variety of activities.

Nearby attractions include Bryce Canyon and Capitol Reef National Parks and Glen Canyon National Recreation Area, which are discussed elsewhere in this book. Also worth a visit is Escalante State Park, in the town of Escalante, where hikers and campers discover colorful petrified wood and panoramic vistas, and a 30-acre reservoir provides opportunities for boating, fishing, and swimming. Kodachrome Basin State Park, located on the western edge of the monument, offers hiking and camping in a setting of tall stone towers and pink-and-white sandstone cliffs set among the contrasting greens of piñon and juniper trees.

HOVENWEEP NATIONAL MONUMENT

HOURS/SEASONS: Campground and trails overnight, year-round; ranger station daily 8 A.M. to 4:30 P.M. year-round, but may be closed for short periods while the ranger is on patrol

BEST TIME TO VISIT: Fall

AREA: 785 acres

ELEVATION: 5,220 feet

FACILITIES: Ranger station, interpretive exhibits and trails, picnic tables, restrooms, 30 campsites (no showers or hookups), amphitheater

ATTRACTIONS: Archeological sites, hiking, wildlife viewing

NEARBY: Mesa Verde National Park, Natural Bridges National Monument, Four Corners Monument

ACCESS: 35 miles northeast of Bluff, UT, via US 191, UT 262 (follow signs on US 262); or 47 miles west of Cortez, CO, via US 666 north to Pleasant View (follow signs on US 666 to the monument). Note: Some of these roads are graded dirt and become muddy—sometimes impassably so—during and immediately after rain.

Known for its mysterious and impressive stone towers, Hovenweep National Monument contains some of the most striking archaeological sites in the American Southwest. Operated by the National Park Service, the monument includes six separate groupings of archeological sites, each with short trails to the remains of the stone structures. Trail guides are available at each site.

The people who built these handsome villages, and also constructed the magnificent cliff dwellings at Mesa Verde National Park to the east, were part of the Ancestral Puebloan culture (also called Anasazi), who farmed and hunted in the Four Corners region from about 500 B.C. until about A.D. 1300. At first they lived in simple pit houses, but by about A.D. 700 they began building above ground, multiple-room dwellings.

Then, about 1100, they began constructing sturdy, multistoried stone structures such as those at Hovenweep. They also built rock dams to channel streams and runoff to their fields, where they grew corn, beans, squash, amaranth, and other crops. In addition, it is believed that they were skilled artisans who made attractive and functional pottery. They also traded with other prehistoric groups for food items, feathers, turquoise, and copper.

Archeologists believe that hundreds—possibly thousands—of people inhabited the various settlements on this plateau in the twelfth and thirteenth centuries. By 1300 they had moved on. It is widely believed that their descendents are today's pueblo people of Arizona and New Mexico.

A number of handsome stone buildings can be seen at Hovenweep National Monument.

Here at Hovenweep, whose name is the Ute word for "deserted valley," there are remarkable sandstone towers, some standing more than 20 feet tall. The towers are built mostly on the edges of canyons near reliable water sources. Some of the towers are square, while others are oval, circular, or D-shaped.

The solid towers, which are constructed of shaped chunks of sandstone, have small windows up and down their sides, and even after some 700 years of weathering, many of the walls remain standing. Archaeologists have suggested a variety of possible uses for the towers, such as lookouts, ceremonial structures, residences, or astronomical observatories, and have noted that at the winter solstice the setting sun is aligned through small windows in one of the towers.

In addition to the towers, Hovenweep has the remains of a variety of rooms, walls, cliff dwellings, and a kiva, plus petroglyphs and a reconstructed dam. Round-trip distances on trails range from 0.5 mile to 8 miles, and hiking is limited to established trails.

The best preserved structures are at the Square Tower site, which is the most accessible site and also the location of the ranger station and campground. The 2-mile Square Tower self-guided trail includes two loops that can be hiked individually or together. They wind past the remains of more than a dozen Ancestral Puebloan buildings, including both square and round towers. A trail guide, available at the ranger station, discusses the ruins and identifies desert plants used for food, clothing, and medicine.

One of the first buildings on this trail is stately Hovenweep Castle, probably constructed around A.D. 1200, about the same time many European castles were being built. Once home to several families, this thick-walled stone building contains two D-shaped towers, several kivas (circular ceremonial rooms), and a number of living and storage rooms. The trail then meanders among additional 700-year-old buildings, including Hovenweep House (which was once one of the largest structures here), and a reconstructed dam. It also provides a good look at Rimrock House, a two-story rectangular structure with numerous small peepholes.

Also along the trail is desert vegetation such as yucca, cactus, saltbush, juniper, and even a few cottonwood trees. Watch for lizards and snakes, rabbits, hawks and ravens, and an occasional deer or fox. The Square Tower loops are generally easy, but the trails are rocky and have a few slick and/or steep sections. Those hiking the entire 2 miles will have an elevation change of about 150 feet.

At the Square Tower Site is the ranger station, which includes exhibits on the buildings and Ancestral Puebloans, plus wildlife photos to help with identification. There are also restrooms and a small bookstore. During the summer, rangers periodically give guided walks and other programs; check at the ranger station for the current schedule.

The other five sites are difficult to find, and may be inaccessible in wet weather. Detailed driving directions are available at the ranger station. Be sure to check on current road conditions before setting out.

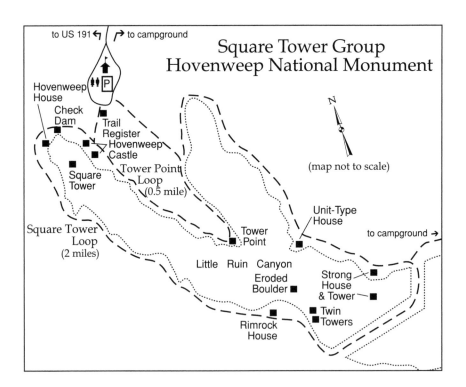

The Hovenweep Campground, set among Utah junipers, is open year-round and has restrooms, drinking water, picnic tables, and fire pits. Although originally designed for tenters, most sites accommodate short trailers and motor homes under 25 feet in length. Reservations are not accepted, but the campground rarely fills, even during the peak summer season.

Hovenweep National Monument is remote, and services at the monument and in the area are limited, to say the least. The monument has no public telephone, and visitors must haul out their own trash. Square Tower is the only section of the monument in which you can obtain drinking water.

Summer temperatures can top 100 degrees, and the monument's water supplies are limited. Visitors are asked to bring water, carry it even on short walks, and drink frequently. Summer nighttime temperatures often drop into the 60s. During winter, daytime temperatures are usually in the 40s and 50s, with nighttime temperatures dropping well below freezing; light snow should be expected. Spring and fall temperatures are best, with highs often in the 70s and 80s and lows in the 30s and 40s. However, in late May and June nasty little gnats invade the area. Fall is the best time to visit.

Nearby are Mesa Verde National Park and Natural Bridges National Monument, which are discussed elsewhere in this book. Four Corners Monument, which is operated as a Navajo Tribal Park, is the only place in the United States

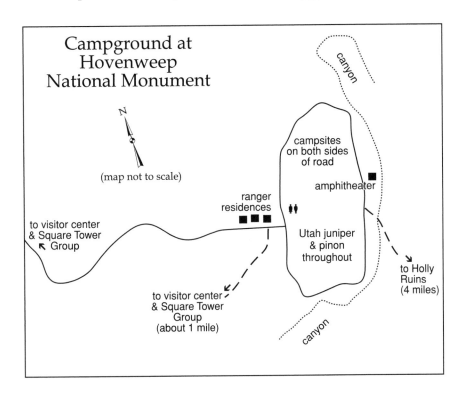

Campground at
Hovenweep
National Monument

N

(map not to scale)

campsites
on both sides
of road

amphitheater

ranger
residences

to visitor center
& Square Tower
Group

Utah juniper
& pinon
throughout

to Holly
Ruins
(4 miles)

to visitor center
& Square Tower
Group
(about 1 mile)

canyon

canyon

where four states meet. It has a flat monument marking the spot where Utah, Colorado, New Mexico, and Arizona come together, on which visitors perch for photos.

NATURAL BRIDGES NATIONAL MONUMENT

HOURS/SEASONS: Scenic drive open daily from early morning until about 30 minutes past sunset; campground open overnight, year-round
BEST TIME TO VISIT: May, September, and October
AREA: 7,636 acres
ELEVATION: 6,505 feet
FACILITIES: Visitor center, interpretive exhibits, nature trail, scenic drive, picnic tables, restrooms, 13 campsites plus overflow camping area (no showers or hookups), amphitheater, public telephone
ATTRACTIONS: Hiking, wildlife viewing, bird-watching, interpretive programs, fishing, archeological sites
NEARBY: Glen Canyon National Recreation Area
ACCESS: 39 miles west of Blanding via UT 95 and 275

The centerpieces of Natural Bridges National Monument are, not surprisingly, its outstanding natural bridges. Carved through solid rock by the power of water over 10,000 to 15,000 years, these three stone bridges can be seen from roadside viewpoints or close up via a series of hiking trails. In addition, this monument, Utah's first National Park Service area, has well-preserved prehistoric cliff dwellings, some delightful prehistoric rock art, a wide variety of wildlife, and a demonstration of the power of the sun to produce electricity.

All three bridges at the monument have been given Hopi names. *Sipapu* means the "gateway to the spirit world" in Hopi legend; *Owachomo* is Hopi for "rock mound," named for a rounded sandstone formation atop one side of the bridge; and *Kachina* received its name because rock art on the bridge resembles decorations found on traditional Hopi Kachina dolls.

Throughout the Southwest are a number of stunning stone arches and bridges, and to most of us they look pretty much the same. However, to geologists there are big differences. Arches result from the erosive forces of rain and snow plus the freezing and thawing that dissolves the cement that holds sand grains together. Bridges, on the other hand, are created when running water, usually a river or stream, slowly bores through solid rock. Usually natural bridges are formed at the bottom of canyons, while arches more often form on mesa tops and other less protected areas.

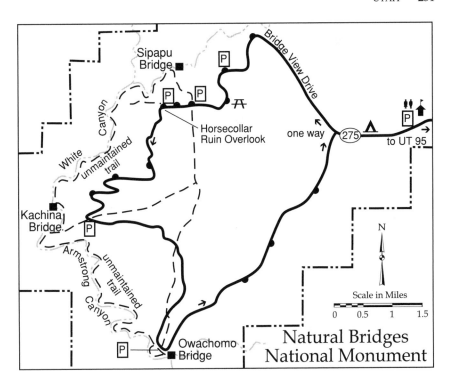

The paved 9-mile Bridge View Drive provides a pleasant drive through the piñon-juniper forest that covers much of this mesa. Short walks from the road's parking areas provide easy access to viewpoints for the natural bridges and the prehistoric cliff dwelling. A road guide, available at the visitor center, discusses the plants and animals of the mesa, the formation of natural bridges, and the people who have lived and worked here.

From the trailheads, you can hike separately to each of the bridges, or start at one and do a loop hike to all three. Those planning to hike the loop can begin at any of the trailheads, although rangers recommend starting at Owachomo. The loop hike, including the walk back across the mesa, is 8.6 miles. Although the trails from the rim to the canyon bottom can be steep, the walk along the bottom is easy.

The easiest hike is the 0.4-mile round-trip trail to Owachomo Bridge, the oldest and most fragile of the three, which is also the smallest at 106 feet high and a span of 180 feet. This trail also offers a view of the twin buttes known as the "Bears Ears" along the eastern horizon.

Giant Sipapu Bridge, at 220 feet high with a span of 268 feet, is the second largest natural bridge in the world, after Rainbow Bridge in nearby Glen Canyon National Recreation Area. The moderate hike to Sipapu Bridge has a 500-foot elevation change, climbing two flights of stairs and three ladders on a 1.2-mile

Owachomo Bridge at Natural Bridges National Monument

round-trip trail. This is the steepest trail in the park, but you'll have a splendid view of the bridge about halfway down.

Kachina Bridge, the monument's youngest bridge, is 210 feet high and has a span of 204 feet. At 93 feet wide, it's also the thickest of the monument's bridges. The moderately strenuous 1.5-mile round-trip hike to the massive bridge has a 400-foot elevation change as it descends steep slickrock with handrails. Under the bridge you'll notice a pile of rocks, the remains of the 4,000 tons of rock that came crashing down in June 1992, enlarging the bridge opening.

In addition to the three natural rock bridges, the monument has one of the best preserved Ancestral Puebloan kivas in the Southwest. Complete with its original 700-year-old roof, the kiva is part of Horsecollar Ruin, a prehistoric cliff dwelling that also includes several groups of living quarters, storage rooms, and probably another kiva. It was named Horsecollar because it has two rooms, believed to be granaries, with doorways shaped like the collar of a horse's harness. The site can be seen from the Horsecollar Ruin Overlook Trail, off Bridge View Drive. The easy trail, with almost no elevation change, is 0.6 mile round trip.

While hiking or driving through the monument, watch for deer, coyotes, several species of squirrels, desert cottontails, numerous lizards, and a variety of songbirds. Swifts and swallows are abundant in spring and summer, and you're also likely to see canyon wrens. Bears, mountain lions, and bobcats live in the area, and although it is unlikely you'll see them, you may see their footprints

The flowers of prickly pear cactus add color to the trails of Natural Bridges National Monument.

along the bank of a water source. The park is also home to the midget faded rattlesnake, which you'll want to avoid.

The monument's primitive campground has pit toilets, tables, tent pads, and grills, but no drinking water, showers, or other facilities. It is limited to camping units (meaning tow vehicle and a trailer) of no more than 26 feet long. Sites are allotted on a first-come, first-served basis, and from spring through fall they are often claimed by early afternoon. An overflow campground, essentially a parking lot, is available about 6 miles east of the visitor center.

The visitor center offers a 10-minute video program on bridge formation, the human history of the area, and the monument's plants and wildlife. It has exhibits on the natural bridge formation and other aspects of the monument, including a large relief map and a "Please Touch" section. There is also a bookstore, and the visitor center is the only place in the monument where you can get drinking water. Just outside the visitor center, the short, easy Native Plants walk has identifying signs on cacti, shrubs, and trees that you'll likely see elsewhere in the monument.

Ranger-led activities, usually presented only from May through October, often include evening campground programs, talks at the visitor center patio, and guided hikes and walks. Schedules are posted at the visitor center. The monument's Junior Ranger program offers a children's newspaper containing puzzles, games, and stories, and badges are awarded to those who complete the necessary number of activities for their age group.

Because of its isolated location, Natural Bridges National Monument has been forced to become self-sufficient, and uses the energy of the sun to provide power for the visitor center, offices, and employee housing. Photovoltaic cells convert sunlight to electricity, and even though only about 10 percent of the sun's energy striking the cells is converted, about 50 kilowatts of power are produced. That is sufficient for the daily needs of the monument and enough extra to store in batteries for use at night and during cloudy periods. The photovoltaic cells and signs describing how they work are located across the road from the visitor center.

Summers are warm at Natural Bridges' 6,500-foot elevation, with high temperatures usually between 85 and 95 degrees and lows dipping into the 50s. Hikers should be prepared for summer afternoon thunderstorms that can cause flash flooding. During winter, days are usually in the 40s and low 50s, while nighttime temperatures are well below freezing and snow is likely. Temperatures are quite pleasant in late spring and fall, with highs often in the 60s and low 70s and nighttime temperatures in the 30s and 40s.

Climbing on the natural bridges is prohibited. Overnight backpacking is not permitted within the monument, and vehicles may not be left unattended overnight. Parking at the overlooks and trailheads is limited, especially in summer, and those towing trailers or extra vehicles are asked to leave them at the visitor center parking lot.

Nearby attractions include the boater's paradise of Glen Canyon National Recreation Area, which is discussed in its own section of this book.

TIMPANOGOS CAVE NATIONAL MONUMENT

HOURS/SEASONS:	Cave and cave trail are open early May through late October only, during which time the visitor center is open daily 7 A.M. to 5:30 P.M.; at other times the visitor center is open daily 8:30 A.M. to 5 P.M.
BEST TIME TO VISIT:	Summer
AREA:	250 acres
ELEVATION:	5,600 feet (at visitor center)
FACILITIES:	Visitor center, interpretive exhibits, nature trail, picnic tables, restrooms, public telephone
ATTRACTIONS:	Guided cave tours, hiking, interpretive programs, wildlife viewing, bird-watching
NEARBY:	Uinta National Forest, Alpine Scenic Drive
ACCESS:	10 miles east of I-15 (exit 287) via UT 92

A steep hike up a mountainside leads to a delightful underworld experience, where mineral-laden water has created three beautifully decorated caves that

are adorned with dozens of formations from stalactites and stalagmites to draperies and helictites. The caves—Hansen, Middle, and Timpanogos—are linked
by manmade tunnels, and can be seen only on guided tours, and only from late
spring through early fall.

Nature began work on these caves some 30 million years ago, when forces
deep underground lifted and then fractured the earth's surface to produce the
Wasatch Mountains. Rising hot water from within the earth, cold water seep-
ing down from above, and naturally occurring carbonic acid worked together
to dissolve beds of limestone, producing the caverns. Then water that had partially filled the caves drained away.

As ground water continued to seep through the remaining limestone that
served as the cave ceilings and walls, it carried calcite and other minerals, de-
positing the minerals on the caves' interior surfaces. This process, continuing
over millions of years, produced the bizarre and fascinating shapes we see today. In fact, it's still going on, and likely will as long as water continues to seep
into the caves from above.

The three caves at Timpanogos have a varied selection of fascinating cave
formations, including stalagmites, stalactites, draperies, flowstone, and popcorn,
in shades of green, red, yellow, and white. In some areas, reflections in mirror-
like pools of water add to the view. Among the many splendid formations, watch
for the Great Heart of Timpanogos, a grouping of several large stalactites cemented together by thin draperies, that is estimated to weigh about 2 tons.

In addition to stalactites and other well-known types of cave formations,
Timpanogos boasts a large number of the lesser-known helictites. These are
small, extremely delicate formations that appear twisted and have tiny tentacles
pointing in all directions.

Cave specialists say that, like stalactites, helictites are formed from dripping
water that creates a type of canal which channels the water to the surface of the
formation. Because the water travels very slowly and in tiny amounts, capil-
lary action seems to defy gravity, and the water deposits its mineral crystals in
what appear to be haphazard and often delightfully fanciful designs. Especially
impressive is the profusion of bizarre, brilliant white helictites in the Chimes
Chamber of Timpanogos Cave.

The actual cave tour is an easy walk, but getting to the cave entrance is another matter. Although paved, the 1.5 mile-long trail to the cave entrance is steep
and physically demanding, with an elevation gain of 1,065 feet from the visitor
center to the cave entrance. The trail is not open to wheelchairs or strollers, and
should not be attempted by those with breathing, heart, or walking difficulties.
Good walking shoes are necessary, and it's wise to carry water and possibly a
snack.

This hike to the caves climbs the northern slope of Mount Timpanogos. There
are strategically placed benches along the way at which you can rest and enjoy

A variety of cave formations are seen on a tour of Timpanogos Cave National Monument, including these stalactites that seem to be reaching for a drink from the pool below.

the views of the American Fork Canyon, the Wasatch Range, and Utah Valley. The trail is partly shaded by Douglas fir, white fir, maple, and oak trees, and alumroot, penstemon, and other wildflowers are often seen blooming among the rocks on the hillside. Hikers should watch for golden-mantled ground squirrels, chipmunks, lizards, and a myriad of birds along the way. A trail guide is available at the visitor center.

Cave tours are limited to twenty persons and each day's tours are often booked early in the day, so it's best to call ahead for reservations. Rangers escort all cave visitors along a paved, lighted, and fairly level route, which begins at the natural entrance to Hansen Cave and continues through Hansen, Middle, and Timpanogos Caves. Most tours also include a period of total darkness, to provide a true sense of the natural state of these caves.

The temperature inside the caves is about 45 degrees (about the same as a refrigerator), so a jacket or sweater is useful. Photographers will want high-speed film or a flash, as tripods are not permitted. Rangers emphasize that the formations are fragile and easily damaged by even the touch of a hand; skin oils change their chemical makeup. Restrooms are available when you reach the cave entrance, but not inside the caves or along the trail.

The visitor center offers a 20-minute film about the caves as well as exhibits and a small bookstore. A snack bar and gift shop are located next to the visitor center, and there are two picnic areas located along the shady banks of the American Fork River. The easy 0.25-mile Canyon Nature Trail, in the canyon bottom across the road from the visitor center, provides views of the canyon as well as a painless geology and biology lesson. A trail guide is available at the trailhead.

During the summer, interpretive programs are usually presented on Friday, Saturday, and Monday evenings, and the Junior Ranger program offers special kids' activities each Saturday morning. Special cave tours, including flashlight, nature, and historic tours, are scheduled periodically during the warmer months, and there are also guided nature walks along the trail to the caves. Talks and other programs are often scheduled in winter. Call for the current schedule.

Summer weather is usually hot, with highs in the upper 90s and lows often dropping into the 50s. In spring and fall, daytime temperatures regularly climb into the 60s and low 70s, while nighttime temperatures are in the 40s. Winters are cold and snowy, with daytime temperatures ranging from the 20s to the 40s and nighttime temperatures dropping well below freezing.

A visit to the monument will take 3 to 4 hours. It is about a 1.5-hour hike up to the cave, cave tours take about an hour, and it's a 30- to 45-minute hike back down.

Although there is no camping at the monument, there are campgrounds as well as practically unlimited hiking and fishing opportunities in the almost 1-million-acre Uinta National Forest that surrounds the monument.

The 20-mile Alpine Scenic Drive, which heads east and then south from the monument along UT 92 and then southwest on US 189 toward Provo, winds through the rugged Wasatch Mountains, offering dramatic views of Mount Timpanogos. The road is completely paved, but winding, mountainous, and narrow, and one section is usually closed by snow from November through late May.

APPENDIX

Sources for Additional Information

ARIZONA

Agua Fria National Monument, Phoenix Field Office, 2015 West Deer Valley Road, Phoenix, AZ 85027-2099; (623) 580-5500; fax (623) 580-5580; *www.az.blm.gov*

Canyon de Chelly National Monument, P.O. Box 588, Chinle, AZ 86503; (520) 674-5500; fax (520) 674-5507; *www.nps.gov/cach*

Casa Grande Ruins National Monument, 1100 Ruins Drive, Coolidge, AZ 85228; (520) 723-3172; fax (520) 723-7209; *www.nps.gov/cagr*

Chiricahua National Monument, Dos Cabezas Route, Box 6500, Willcox, AZ 85643-9737; (520) 824-3560; fax (520) 824-3421; *www.nps.gov/chir*

Coronado National Forest, Federal Building, 300 West Congress Street, Tucson, AZ 85701; (520) 670-4552; *www.fs.fed.us/r3/coronado*

Coronado National Monument, 4101 East Montezuma Canyon Road, Hereford, AZ 85615; (520) 366-5515; fax (520) 366-5705; *www.nps.gov/coro*

Dead Horse Ranch State Park, 675 Dead Horse Ranch Road, Cottonwood, AZ 86326; (520) 634-5283; fax (520) 639-0417; *www. pr.state.az.us*

Fort Bowie National Historic Site, c/o Chiricahua National Monument, 4101 East Montezuma Canyon Road, Hereford, AZ 85615; (520) 847-2500; fax (520) 824-3421; *www.nps.gov/fobo*

Fort Verde State Historic Park, P.O. Box 397, Camp Verde, AZ 86322; (520) 567-3275; fax (520) 567-4036; *www.pr.state.az.us*

Left: *Natural rock formations are one of the trademarks of Zion National Park.*

Glen Canyon National Recreation Area, P.O. Box 1507, Page, AZ 86040; (520) 608-6404; *www.nps.gov/glca*

Grand Canyon National Park, P.O. Box 129, Grand Canyon, AZ 86023; (520) 638-7888; fax (520) 638-7815; *www.nps.gov/grca*

Grand Canyon–Parashant National Monument, Arizona Strip Field Office, 345 East Riverside Drive, St. George, UT 84790-9000; (435) 688-3200; fax (435) 688-3258; *www.az.blm.gov*

Hubbell Trading Post National Historic Site, P.O. Box 150, Ganado, AZ 86505; (520) 755-3475; fax (520) 755-3405; *www.nps.gov/hutr*

Jerome State Historic Park, P.O. Box D, Jerome, AZ 86331; (520) 634-5381; fax (520) 639-3132; *www.pr.state.az.us*

Kaibab-Paiute Indian Reservation, The Kaibab Band of Paiute Indians, HC 65 Box 2, Fredonia, AZ 86022; (520) 643-7245; fax (520) 643-7260

Lake Mead National Recreation Area, 601 Nevada Highway, Boulder City, NV 89005; (702) 293-8907; *www.nps.gov/lame*

McFarland State Historic Park, P.O. Box 109, Florence, AZ 85232; (520) 868-5216; *www.pr.state.az.us*

Montezuma Castle National Monument, P.O. Box 219, Camp Verde, AZ 86322; (520) 567-3322; fax (520) 567-3597; *www.nps.gov/moca*

Monument Valley Navajo Tribal Park, Navajo Nation Parks and Recreation Department, P.O. Box 9000, Window Rock, AZ 86515; (520) 871-6647; or P.O. Box 360289, Monument Valley, UT 84536; (435) 727-3287 or (435) 727-3353; *www. navajonationparks.org*

Navajo National Monument, HC 71, Box 3, Tonalea, AZ 86044; (520) 672-2366; fax (520) 672-2345; *www.nps.gov/nava*

Organ Pipe Cactus National Monument, Route 1, Box 100, Ajo, AZ 85321; (520) 387-6849; fax (520) 387-7144; *www.nps.gov/orpi*

Petrified Forest National Park, P.O. Box 2217, Petrified Forest, AZ 86028; (520) 524-6228; fax (520) 524-3567; *www.nps.gov/pefo*

Pipe Spring National Monument, HC 65, Box 5, Fredonia, AZ 86022; (520) 643-7105; fax (520) 643-7583; *www.nps.gov/pisp*

Saguaro National Park, 3693 South Old Spanish Trail, Tucson, AZ 85730-5699; (520) 733-5100; fax; (520) 733-5183; *www.nps.gov/sagu*

Sunset Crater Volcano National Monument, 6400 North US 89, Flagstaff, AZ 86004; (520) 526-0502; fax (520) 714-0565; *www.nps.gov/sucr*

Tonto National Forest, 2324 East McDowell Road, Phoenix, AZ 85006; (602) 225-5200; *www.fs.fed.us/r3/tonto*

Tonto National Monument, HCO2, Box 4602, Roosevelt, AZ 85545; (520) 467-2241; fax (520) 467-2225; *www.nps.gov/tont*

Tubac Presidio State Historic Park, P.O. Box 1296, Tubac, AZ 85646; (520) 398-2252; *www.pr.state.az.us*

Tumacácori National Historical Park, P.O. Box 67, Tumacacori, AZ 85640; (520) 398-2341; fax (520) 398-9271; *www.nps.gov/tuma*

Tuzigoot National Monument, c/o Montezuma Castle National Monument, P.O. Box 219, Camp Verde, AZ 86322; (520) 634-5564; *www.nps.gov/tuzi*

Walnut Canyon National Monument, 6400 North U.S. 89, Flagstaff, AZ 86004; (520) 526-3367; fax (520) 527-0246; *www.nps.gov/waca*

Wupatki National Monument, 6400 North U.S. 89, Flagstaff, AZ 86004; (520) 679-2365; fax (520) 679-2349; *www.nps.gov/wupa*

Arizona Office of Tourism, 2702 North Third Street, Suite 4015, Phoenix, AZ 85004; (602) 230-7733 or (888) 520-3434; fax (602) 240-5475; *www.arizonaguide.com*

Arizona Public Lands Information Center, 222 Central Avenue, Phoenix, AZ 85004; (602) 417-9300; fax (602) 417-9556

Road Conditions (602) 241-3100 ext. 7623

COLORADO

Bent's Old Fort National Historic Site, 35110 CO 194 East, La Junta, CO 81050-9523; (719) 383-5010; fax (719) 383-5031; *www.nps.gov/beol*

Black Canyon of the Gunnison National Park, 102 Elk Creek, Gunnison, CO 81230; (970) 641-2337 ext. 205; *www.nps.gov/blca*

Colorado National Monument, Fruita, CO 81521-0001; (970) 858-3617; fax (520) 858-0372; *www.nps.gov/colm*

Curecanti National Recreation Area, 102 Elk Creek, Gunnison, CO 81230; (970) 641-2337; fax (970) 641-3127; *www.nps.gov/cure*

Dinosaur National Monument, 4545 East US 40, Dinosaur, CO 81610-9724; (970) 374-3000; fax (970) 374-3003; *www.nps.gov/dino*

Florissant Fossil Beds National Monument, P.O. Box 185, Florissant, CO 80816-0185; (719) 748-3253; fax (719) 748-3164; *www.nps.gov/flfo*

Great Sand Dunes National Monument, 11500 CO 150, Mosca, CO 81146-9798; (719) 378-2312; fax (719) 378-2594; *www.nps.gov/grsa*

Koshare Indian Museum and Kiva, Otero Junior College, 115 West 18th Street, La Junta, CO 81050; (800) 693-5482 or (719) 384-4411; *www.ruralnet.net/koshare*

Mesa Verde National Park, P.O. Box 8, Mesa Verde National Park, CO 81330; (970) 529-4461; *www.nps.gov/meve*

Mueller State Park, P.O. Box 49, Divide, CO 80814; (719) 687-2366; *www.coloradoparks.org/mueller*

Pike National Forest, 1920 Valley Drive, Pueblo, CO 81008; (719) 545-8737; *www.fs.fed.us/r2/psicc*

Rio Grande National Forest, 1803 West US 160, Monte Vista, CO 81144; (970) 852-5941; fax (970) 852-6250; *www.fs.fed.us/r2/riogrande*

Rocky Mountain National Park, Estes Park, CO 80517-8397; (970) 586-1206; *www.nps.gov/romo*

Colorado Travel and Tourism Authority, P.O. Box 3524, Englewood, CO 80155; (800) 265-6723 or (303) 296-3384; *www.colorado.com*

Road Conditions (303) 639-1111

NEW MEXICO

Aztec Ruins National Monument, P.O. Box 640, Aztec, NM 87410; (505) 334-6174; fax (505) 334-6372; *www.nps.gov/azru*

Bandelier National Monument, HCR 1, Box 1, Suite 15, Los Alamos, NM 87544; (505) 672-0343; fax (505) 672-9607; *www.nps.gov/band*

Capulin Volcano National Monument, P.O. Box 40, Capulin, NM 88414; (505) 278-2201; fax (505) 278-2211; *www.nps.gov/cavo*

Carlsbad Caverns National Park, 3225 National Parks Highway, Carlsbad, NM 88220; (505) 785-2232; fax (505) 785-2133; *www.nps.gov/cave*

Chaco Culture National Historical Park, P.O. Box 220, Nageezi, NM 87037; (505) 786-7014; fax (505) 786-7061; *www.nps.gov/chcu*

Cibola National Forest, 2113 Osuna Road NE, Suite A, Albuquerque, NM 87113-1001; (505) 346-2650; *www.fs.fed.us/r3/cibola*

Coronado State Monument, P.O. Box 853, Bernalillo, NM 87004; (505) 867-5589; fax (505) 867-2225

El Malpais National Monument, P.O. Box 939, Grants, NM 87020; (505) 783-4774; fax (505) 285-5661; *www.nps.gov/elma*

El Morro National Monument, Route 2, Box 43, Ramah, NM 87321-9603; (505) 783-4226; fax (505) 783-4689; *www.nps.gov/elmo*

Fort Union National Monument, P.O. Box 127, Watrous, NM 87753; (505) 425-8025; fax (505) 454-1155; *www.nps.gov/foun*

Gila Cliff Dwellings National Monument, Route 11, Box 100, Silver City, NM 88061; (505) 536-9461; fax (505) 536-9461; *www.nps.gov/gicl*

Gila National Forest, 3005 East Camino del Bosque, Silver City, NM 88061; (505) 388-8201; *www.fs.fed.us/r3/gila*

Lincoln National Forest, 1101 New York Avenue, Alamogordo, NM 88310-6992; (505) 434-7200; *www.fs.fed.us/r3/lincoln*

Los Alamos County Chamber of Commerce, 109 Central Park Square, P.O. Box 460, Los Alamos, NM 87544-0460; (800) 444-0707 or (505) 662-8405; fax (505) 662-8399; *www.vla.com/chamber*

Manzano Mountains State Park, Route 2 Box 52, Mountainair, NM 87036; (505) 847-2820; *www.nmparks.com*

Navajo Lake State Park, 1448 NM 511 #1, Navajo Dam, NM 87419; (505) 632-2278; fax (505) 632-8159; *www.nmparks.com*

Oliver Lee Memorial State Park, 409 Dog Canyon Road, Alamogordo, NM 88310; (505) 437-8284; *www.nmparks.com*

Pecos National Historical Park, P.O. Box 418, Pecos, NM 87552-0418; (505) 757-6414; fax (505) 757-8460; *www.nps.gov/peco*

Petroglyph National Monument, 6001 Unser Blvd. NW, Albuquerque, NM 87120; (505) 899-0205, fax (505) 899-0207; *www.nps.gov/petr*

Rio Grande Nature Center State Park, 2901 Candelaria Road NW, Albuquerque, NM 87107; (505) 344-7240; fax (505) 344-4505; *www.nmparks.com*

Salinas Pueblo Missions National Monument, P.O. Box 517, Mountainair, NM 87036; (505) 847-2585; fax (505) 847-2441; *www.nps.gov/sapu*

Salmon Ruin, San Juan Archaeological Research Center and Library, 6131 US 64, P.O. Box 125, Bloomfield, NM 87413; (505) 632-2013; *www.more2it.com/salmon*

Santa Fe National Forest, 1474 Rodeo Road, P.O. Box 1689, Santa Fe, NM 87504; (505) 438-7840; *www.fs.fed.us/r3/sfe*

Sugarite Canyon State Park, HCR 63, Box 386, Raton, NM 87740; (505) 445-5607; fax (505) 445-8828; *www.nmparks.com*

Three Rivers Petroglyph Site, Bureau of Land Management, Caballo Field Office, 1800 Marquess Street, Las Cruces, NM 88005; (505) 525-4300; *www.vivanewmexico.com/se.3rivers.html*

Valle Vidal Unit of the Carson National Forest, Questa Ranger District, P.O. Box 110, Questa, NM 87556; (505) 586-0520; *www.fs.fed.us/r3/carson*

White Sands National Monument, P.O. Box 1086, Holloman AFB, NM 88330-1086; (505) 679-2599; fax (505) 479-4333; *www.nps.gov/whsa*

Wild Rivers Recreation Area, Bureau of Land Management, Taos Resource Area Office, P.O. Box 1045, Taos, NM 87571; (505) 758-8851; *www.nm.blm.gov*

New Mexico Department of Tourism, Room 751, Lamy Building, 491 Old Santa Fe Trail, Santa Fe, NM 87503; (800) 545-2040; fax (505) 827-7402; *www.new mexico.org*

New Mexico Public Lands Information Center, 1474 Rodeo Road, Santa Fe, NM 87505; (505) 438-7542; fax (505) 438-7582; *www.publiclands.org*

Road Conditions (800) 432-4269

UTAH

Arches National Park, 2282 South West Resource Boulevard, Moab, UT 84532; (435) 259-8161; fax (435) 259-8341; *www.nps.bov/arch*

Bryce Canyon National Park, P.O. Box 170001, Bryce Canyon, UT 84717; (435) 834-5322; *www.nps.gov/brca*

Canyonlands National Park, 2282 South West Resource Boulevard, Moab, UT 84532; (435) 259-3911; fax (435) 259-8628; *www.nps.gov/cany*

Capitol Reef National Park, HCR 70 Box 15, Torrey, UT 84775; (435) 425-3791; *www.nps.gov/care*

Cedar Breaks National Monument, 2390 West Utah 56, #11, Cedar City, UT 84720; (435) 586-9451; fax (435) 586-3813; *www.nps.gov/cebr*

Escalante State Park, P.O. Box 350, Escalante, UT 84726-0350; (435) 826-4466; *www.nr.state.ut.us/parks/utahstpk.htm*

Four Corners Monument, Navajo Nation Parks and Recreation Department, P.O. Box 9000, Window Rock, AZ 86515; (520) 871-6647; *www.navajonationparks.org*

Golden Spike National Historic Site, P.O. Box 897, Brigham City, UT 84302; (435) 471-2209; fax (435) 471-2341; *www.nps.gov/gosp*

Grand Staircase–Escalante National Monument, Bureau of Land Management/ Monument Office, 318 North 100 East Street, Kanab, UT 84741; (435) 644-2672; *www.ut.blm.gov/monument*

Hovenweep National Monument, McElmo Route, Cortez, CO 81321; (970) 562-4282; fax (970) 562-4284; *www.nps.gov/hove*

Kodachrome Basin State Park, P.O. Box 238, Cannonville, UT 84718; (435) 679-8562; *www.nr.state.ut.us/parks/utahstpk.htm*

Monument Valley Navajo Tribal Park, P.O. Box 360289, Monument Valley, UT 84536; (435) 727-3287 or 727-3353; or c/o Navajo Nation Parks and Recreation Department, P.O. Box 9000, Window Rock, AZ 86515; (520) 871-6647; *www.navajo nationparks.org*

Natural Bridges National Monument, Box 1, Lake Powell, UT 84533-0101; (435) 692-1234; fax (435) 692-1111; *www.nps.gov/nabr*

Timpanogos Cave National Monument, RR3, Box 200, American Fork, UT 84003-9803; (801) 756-5238; fax (801) 756-5661; *www.nps.gov/tica*

Uinta National Forest, Supervisor's Office, 88 West 100 North, Provo, UT 84601; (801) 377-5780; *www.fs.fed.us/r4/uinta*

Zion National Park, Springdale, UT 84767-1099; (435) 772-3256; *www.nps.gov /zion*

Utah Travel Council, Council Hall/Capitol Hill, Salt Lake City, UT 84114; (800) 200-1160 or (801) 538-1030; fax (801) 538-1399; *www.utah.com*

Road Conditions (800) 492-2400

CAMPGROUND RESERVATIONS

National Parks: (800) 365-2267; *www.reservations.nps.gov*

National Forests: (877) 444-6777; *www.reserveusa.com*

INDEX

ABOUT THE AUTHORS

Residents of northern New Mexico since 1970, Don and Barbara Laine have spent countless hours exploring the Southwest's mountains, deserts, lakes, rivers, and plains. Their interests include hiking, rafting, photography, and wildlife viewing, as well as loafing in shady campgrounds. Don spent more than twenty years in radio and newspaper journalism before becoming a fulltime travel writer and photographer in the early 1990s. His articles and photographs have been published in regional and national newspapers and magazines.

Before turning to travel writing and freelance cartography, Barb worked as a draftsman in a land surveying office, and in administration at a nonprofit arts organization and a small private school. Together Don and Barb have authored several travel guides, including Frommer's Guides to Colorado and Utah. Their selfish goal in researching and writing *Little-Known Southwest* was to spend time in the lesser-known monuments, wildlife refuges, and historic and recreational sites that are dotted across the Southwest. Their more altruistic motivation was to share their knowledge and appreciation of these sites so that more people can discover the wonders of these very special places.